Seafood

Seafood

A Connoisseur's Guide and Cookbook

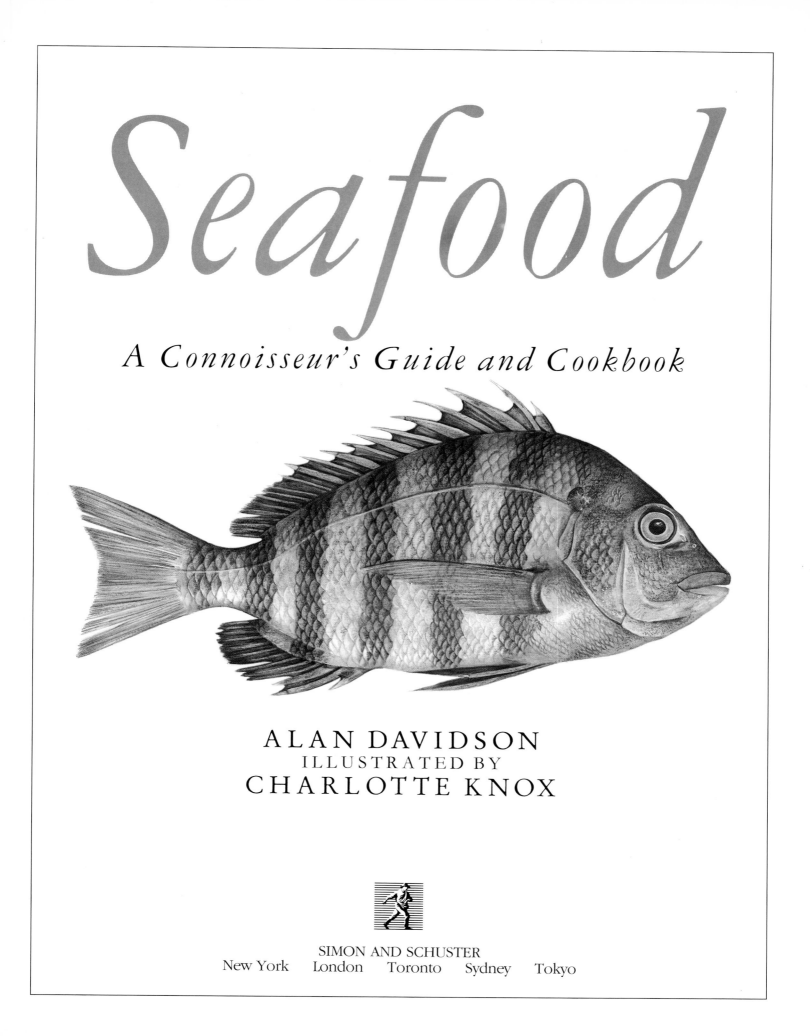

ALAN DAVIDSON
ILLUSTRATED BY
CHARLOTTE KNOX

SIMON AND SCHUSTER
New York   London   Toronto   Sydney   Tokyo

Simon and Schuster
Simon & Schuster Building
Rockefeller Center
1230 Avenue of the Americas
New York, New York 10020

Edited and designed by Mitchell Beazley International Ltd., Artists House,
14–15 Manette Street, London W1V 5LB. Simultaneously published in
Great Britain by Mitchell Beazley Publishers, London.
The author and publishers will be grateful for any information which
will assist them in keeping future editions up to date. Although all
reasonable care has been taken in the preparation of this book, neither
the publishers nor the author can accept any responsibility for any
consequences arising from the use thereof or from the information
contained therein.

Editor   Diane Pengelly
Designer   Mike Brown
Production   Ted Timberlake
Senior Executive Editor   Chris Foulkes
Typeset by Servis Filmsetting Ltd, Manchester, England
Color reproduction by Scantrans Pte Ltd, Singapore
Printed in West Germany by Mohndruck GumbH, Gütersloh.

10 9 8 7 6 5 4 3 2 1

Library of Congress Cataloging in Publication Data

Davidson, Alan, 1924–
    Seafood : a connoisseur's guide and cookbook / Alan Davidson :
illustrations by Charlotte Knox : [edited and designed by Mitchell
Beazley International Ltd.].
        p.   cm.
    Bibliography: p.
    Includes index.
    ISBN 0-671-67011-5
    1. Cookery (Seafood)   I. Knox, Charlotte.   II. Mitchell Beazley
Ltd.   III. Title.
TX747.D2769   1989
641.6'92—dc20   89-6138
                                            CIP

ISBN: 0-671-67011-5

Acknowledgments

from Charlotte Knox
All the illustrations in this book were painted from fresh specimens,
most of which would have been impossible to obtain without the
involvement of two vital sources of supply, whose patience must have
been severely tried by my incessant requests, but whose enthusiasm
and assistance never flagged.
    At new Billingsgate Market in London, Jack Shiells, Dr Robin Bruce,
Chris and Simon Newnes and Michael Sanders-Hewett of C J Newnes &
Partners all helped with my enquiries and supplied many fish from
Europe and the Seychelles, while in New York Richard Lord of Fulton
Fish Market Information Services Inc collected and packed most of the
American fish.
    The American fish were brought to London by Captain James
Nightingale of Virgin Airlines, Dr Dilwyn Knox and Chris Quinn. Some
of the European fish were collected for me in Paris by Philip and Mary
Hyman and brought to London by Dick Turpin. Fish from Malta were
supplied by Jackson and Dr Peter Earle.
    Jim Moran of R W Larkins & Co Ltd, and John Shelton and Steven
Clements of J Bennett Ltd went out of their way to supply specimens of
fish from Asia, Australia and America, as did Joe Camilleri of H J
Brunnings.
    Finally, I would like to thank my long-suffering family for eating a lot
of strange fish, putting up with a freezer full of fish for more than a
year, and occasionally finding sea-slugs in the refrigerator.

from Alan Davidson
I am deeply grateful to the following friends and colleagues for kindly
agreeing to the use or adaptation of recipes from their excellent books
(see Bibliography); Lynda Brown, John Doerper, Tom Jaine, George
Lassalle, Cristine MacKie, Elisabeth Lambert Ortiz, Claudia Roden, Dr
Yan-Kit So, Professor Shizuo Tsuji – and indeed to everyone whose
material or help is acknowledged in the text.
    For help over taxonomy and identification I express my warm thanks
to Dr Walter Fischer of the Fisheries Division of the Food and
Agriculture Organization of the United Nations; and to all the kind
experts in the British Museum (Natural History) who have helped over
the year to guide my amateur steps in marine biology.
    Katsue Aizawa, Dr Pamela Davidson, and Dr Yan-Kit So generously
devoted time to helping me over the common names in Japanese,
Russian, and Chinese; and Abu TM Siddique kindly made available to
me his uniquely comprehensive list of Bengali and Urdu names.
    Vital help in testing recipes was provided by Sibella Baker
Wilbraham, Diane Pengelly, Margaret Ralph, and Kate Scarborough, to
all of whom I am most grateful.

Contents

Introduction

This book provides a visual and literary exploration and interpretation of the world's seafood. It came into being because of Charlotte Knox's wish to paint fish and other seafoods, and a corresponding urge which I felt to write about the subject on a global, not just a European or North Atlantic, basis.

Having written books about seafood in both the western and eastern hemispheres, I had noticed how few works pull the subject together on a worldwide basis. Yet this is desirable, especially now that the world is "shrinking" and it has become commonplace for fish to be flown from New Zealand to California or London, from South America to France, indeed from almost anywhere to almost anywhere.

People tend to think that the seafood of one sea or ocean is different from that of others. The truth is that quite a few species occur right around the world, for example *Xiphias gladius*, the swordfish, and *Mugil cephalus*, one of the gray mullets. Nearly all the families of fish have representatives in both the great ocean areas, and these representatives differ little from the cook's point of view (although the scientists properly distinguish between them by counting their fin-rays or examining their air-bladders). Thus the famous red mullet of the Mediterranean have close relations in the Indo-Pacific; but the latter are known as goatfish, and treated by Asian cooks in a different way, and for this reason people often fail to see the connection.

When it came to choosing the species to be treated in this book, Charlotte and I blended our different but overlapping interests into what we hope will be seen as a harmonious and satisfying result. Charlotte made her selection with a painter's eye, and according to what she could summon up from the fish markets of the world. I had my amateur painter's eye open; but I kept eating quality at the front of my mind, and also sought to ensure that all the major regions of the world would be represented, and all the most important families of fish.

The combination of these points of view has yielded a collection which is not "the hundred best seafoods in the world", nor "the hundred most beautiful", nor "the hundred most commonly met"; but it goes some way towards meeting each of these attractive concepts.

It is also a collection that permits giving a very wide range of seafood recipes. The reader will find that the pages of text opposite the pages of painting almost all include a relevant recipe; or, at the least, guidance on how to cook or prepare whatever it is. But there is also, at the back of the book, a general essay on seafood cookery which is followed by a substantial number of additional recipes.

In choosing recipes, I have generally avoided "haute cuisine" and passing fashions (no octagonal black plates and gossamer-thin pools of sauce for me). I prefer the established traditions in the various parts of the world – for all of which I have tried to ensure representation – and in general I like to keep things simple, not straying far from the mainstream of life and food as most people know them.

Besides, if you have a good fresh fish, there is really no need to festoon it with other ingredients or toil over making a laborious sauce. Nor is there any point in fussing over exact measurements. To be sure, I give them – it would be tedious to over-pepper the recipes with words like "about" or "approximately." But what matters is to keep to the proportions indicated. Even there discretion should be used; some like more seasoning, for example, and others less.

There is one very general point to be made about the recipes. In Britain, the tradition is that fish is either what you have with french fries or something to be served with "two veg", much as meat is usually served here; or, in posh restaurants, by itself as a course which comes before the meat. But these traditions, although spread around the world to some extent by the British Empire, are not widely shared. In most parts of the world seafood is more likely to be one constituent of a spread of different foods, or an element in a one-pot dish, or something which accompanies pasta, or goes into fish balls, fish puddings or pies, or is part of a soup-plus-fish-stew dish. Many such modes of presentation produce delicious results, and make a relatively small quantity of fish "go further". I recommend them.

Opposite each painting in the book, underneath the list of foreign names in the left-hand margin, I have introduced two further lists which I hope will be helpful to the cook. Under the heading *Alternative fish*, I have listed other fish which could happily be substituted for the fish in the recipe. Following that, under *Alternative recipes*, I give the names of other recipes that appear elsewhere in the book. The fish described on the page in question would be an appropriate choice for any of the recipes listed under *Alternative recipes*.

A Note About Names
Scientific names of fish are precise, and established (although they do change as progress is made in taxonomy), and I have given these throughout, so that there will be no doubt about what I am describing or discussing. These names consist of two latinized words, of which the second is the specific or species name, while the first, which has an initial capital, is the

generic name, showing to what genus the species belongs.

It is usual to find several species in a genus; and the genera in turn are grouped in families. Thus in the family Gadidae you have, among others, the genus *Merluccius*. And in this you find *Merluccius merluccius*, which is the European hake, and *Merluccius bilinearis*, which is the silver hake of North America.

The scientific names, indispensable for certain purposes, are obviously unsuitable for everyday use, and were never intended to supplant the "common names" which are what we all use in daily life. I have given the common names of the fish in what seem to me, in each instance, the relevant languages. The Chinese names, by the way, are given in their Cantonese/Hong Kong form, which seems likely to be the most useful.

However, these common names often present puzzles, and can obscure rather than illuminate identities and relationships. There are two sorts of confusion. One is the proliferation of different local names in small coastal communities, often isolated from each other in the past by poor communications. The common gray mullet has over 40 names in Italy. Confusing, yes, but regrettable, no; the names are all real, and their profusion is, as I see it, life-enriching.

The other sort of confusion is definitely regrettable. It afflicts the English language particularly and is a by-product of the era of colonization. Early English colonists applied familiar but inappropriate names to the fish they met in the New World, Australasia and elsewhere. Consider, for example, what fish have been called "salmon" in Australia and New Zealand. None is a salmon, and some of them are not even related to each other. The "Murray cod" of Australia is not even a sea fish, let alone a member of the cod family. I suppose that it would be unfair to reproach these early colonists, especially the convicts who were sent to Australia, for not being ichthyologists. Even so, the heart sinks on contemplation of some of the misnomers for which they were responsible.

One further comment about the common names. Languages vary considerably in richness of vocabulary. Thus in one language there may be a single word which stands for all the gray mullets, while in another there may be a separate name for each species, and even separate names for fish of different size within the species. This book is not the place for going into that sort of thing; but it does mean that the lists of names should be used as a general guide and not treated as though they constituted a dictionary.

Since it has fallen to me to write this introduction, I can exercise the privilege of saying how much I admire and enjoy the paintings. They are marvellously good, and brilliantly varied. One could not hope, with mere words, to evoke with such immediacy the beauty and richness of the world's seafoods.

Alan Davidson

Alan Davidson
February, 1989

Atlantic Salmon

As written communications and records began so much earlier in Europe than in North America, it is a natural accident of history that the fish of the illustrious salmon family were first described in Europe and that *Salmo salar*, the salmon familiar to Europeans, should be regarded by them as **the** salmon. They formerly knew no other; and they knew *Salmo salar* well, because it was abundant. Many tales are told of apprentices or other lowly paid people who struggled hard in medieval times to ensure that their employers were not allowed to feed them salmon more than (say) three times a week.

In fact, this famous species is the Atlantic, not the European salmon. In historic times its range has extended from Portugal up to Norway, across through Greenland and down the eastern seaboard of North America as far, probably, as the Hudson River. But the extraordinary life cycle of the species has brought it up sharply against man-made obstacles in the last two centuries, and in many places where it formerly abounded it is now not found at all.

Every salmon starts life as a tiny blob in the deep gravel of a cold stream where the parent fish deposit their eggs. Out of the eggs come minuscule alevins, and when these emerge from the gravel they are called fry. As they gain in size they become parr, until they make their way out to sea. They then become smolts and have undergone various changes to prepare them for life in salt water.

Salmon which come back to spawn after only one year at sea are called grilse. Those which spend two to four years at sea become adult salmon and are likely to

8

be from 32 inches to 40 inches long. It is on this journey back to spawn, after they have fed well at sea, that salmon have traditionally been caught; in nets, as they approach river mouths, or by anglers as they make their way upstream. Until quite recent times no one knew where they were during the sea phase of their lives. Now that the areas where they congregate, for example off Greenland, have been located, they can be caught there; and this has caused controversy. However, the depredations caused by sea fishing are of little consequence beside the harm done to salmon by the pollution or blockage of rivers. Many rivers which once had salmon in abundance now have none.

Baltic salmon belong to the same species, but form a distinct "race" within it. Their flesh is of a paler pink, presumably because their diet includes a smaller proportion of the crustaceans from which salmon draw the caryatid pigment that makes them pink; and they have a higher fat content.

A close relation of the salmon is the sea or salmon trout, *Salmo trutta*, a species which embraces not only the sea trout (which behave like salmon) but also the brown trout of rivers which differs from it in both behaviour and flavor.

Salmon may be poached whole in a *court bouillon* (see page 177), allowed to cool and then decorated to create a really sumptuous cold dish for a buffet table; or steaks can be broiled. The same applies to salmon trout.

Gravlax

Take 3 pounds of middle cut of salmon, cleaned, scaled, bisected lengthways and deboned. Place one of the two pieces skin side down in a large glass dish, chop a large bunch of fresh dill over it, then sprinkle on a mixture of four tablespoons of sea salt, two of crushed white peppercorns and one and a half of superfine sugar. Cap the preparation with the other piece of salmon, this time skin side up, place a weighted wooden board (larger than the fish) on top and leave the whole in a refrigerator for 36 to 72 hours, turning the fish over completely every 12 hours and basting it (the inside surfaces too) with the juices.

Alternative Fish
Pacific salmon (p 10)
swordfish (p 88)
mahi-mahi (p 66)

Alternative Recipes
Sooke Harbor House Salmon
(p 10)
Steamed Salmon and Roe (p 185)
Fish en Papillote (p 187)

9

Atlantic salmon, *Salmo salar* (center) and sea trout, *S trutta* (top and bottom)

Pacific Salmon

Pacific Salmon
ENGLISH-SPEAKING COUNTRIES

nerka
RUSSIAN

sake, masu
JAPANESE

10

T rue salmon all belong to the temperate or cold waters of the northern hemisphere; so-called "Australian salmon" and fish known as "salmon" in South Africa are not salmon at all.

The salmon of the North Pacific are all members of the genus *Oncorhynchus* (meaning "hook-nose"). There are five of them:

- Sockeye salmon, *O nerka*, length to 34 inches, the most valuable commercial species. At spawning time the male is bright red and has developed a hooked lower jaw (a characteristic of salmon in this genus) and a somewhat humped back; the female is also red. The name "sockeye" has nothing to do with the fish's eyes; it is a corruption of an American Indian name.
- Chinook, king or spring salmon, *Oncorhynchus tschawytscha*, may be up to 51 inches long, has dark spots on its dorsal and tail fins and on its back, and is second in importance commercially.
- Chum salmon, *O keta*, up to almost 38 inches long, no dark spots on back or fins, particularly important in Canada; also called "dog" salmon, because males have greatly enlarged canine-like teeth at spawning time.
- Coho or silver salmon, *O kisutch*, up to 35 inches long, a deep-bodied fish with some black spots on its dorsal fin and the upper part of the tail fin; the flesh cans well, but this species is of secondary importance.
- Humpback or pink salmon, *O gorbuscha*, up to 30 inches long, so the smallest of the group, of considerable value on the Asian side of the North Pacific.

There is, naturally, debate about which of the five species, eaten fresh (canned salmon has different characteristics and is another matter) are best. John Doerper, in his guide to foods of the Northwest Pacific coast (see bibliography), gives a thoughtful assessment, pointing out that some of the salmon spawn not far upstream from tidewater areas, whereas others make enormous journeys up great rivers to the spawning grounds of their choice. The latter, notably the chinook and the sockeye, need to have greater reserves of fat when they arrive at river mouths, and therefore make better eating. Doerper's own preference, with which Japanese connoisseurs agree, is for the sockeye; and in particular those caught in Georgia Strait, ready to tackle the difficult rapids of British Columbia's Fraser and Thompson Rivers. Although their fat content is slightly lower than that of the chinook, their diet (mostly minuscule planktonic crustaceans) may give them the superior flavor which Doerper detects. The recipe is adapted from one recommended by Doerper.

Sooke Harbor House Salmon

4 fillets from a small sockeye salmon	I tablespoon sweet butter
I clove garlic, halved	I tablespoon white wine vinegar
$\frac{1}{2}$ cup dry white wine	2 tablespoons fresh *Alaria* seaweed
salt and pepper to taste	4 tablespoons heavy cream
I small shallot, chopped	I stalk rhubarb
I cup fish *fumet* (page 177)	blue borage flowers (optional garnish)

Alternative Fish
Atlantic salmon (p 8)
swordfish (p 88)
mahi-mahi (p 66)

Alternative Recipes
*Mérou Blanc with Rosemary
Sauce (p 36)*
Bonito à la Asturiana (p 84)
*Fish Steaks in Cream and Lime
Juice (p 106)*

Rub the poaching pan with the garlic, put in the wine, seasoning, shallot, *fumet*, butter and vinegar. Boil gently for five minutes, then add the fish and poach for three minutes. Remove the fish and keep it warm. Strain the poaching liquid into an enamel pan, add the seaweed and the cream and reduce. Meanwhile, peel the rhubarb stalk, cut it into sections, and then blanch them and purée them. Add the purée to the sauce to thicken it, pour it over a serving dish, set the fish on it and (if you wish) decorate with borage flowers. Serves four.

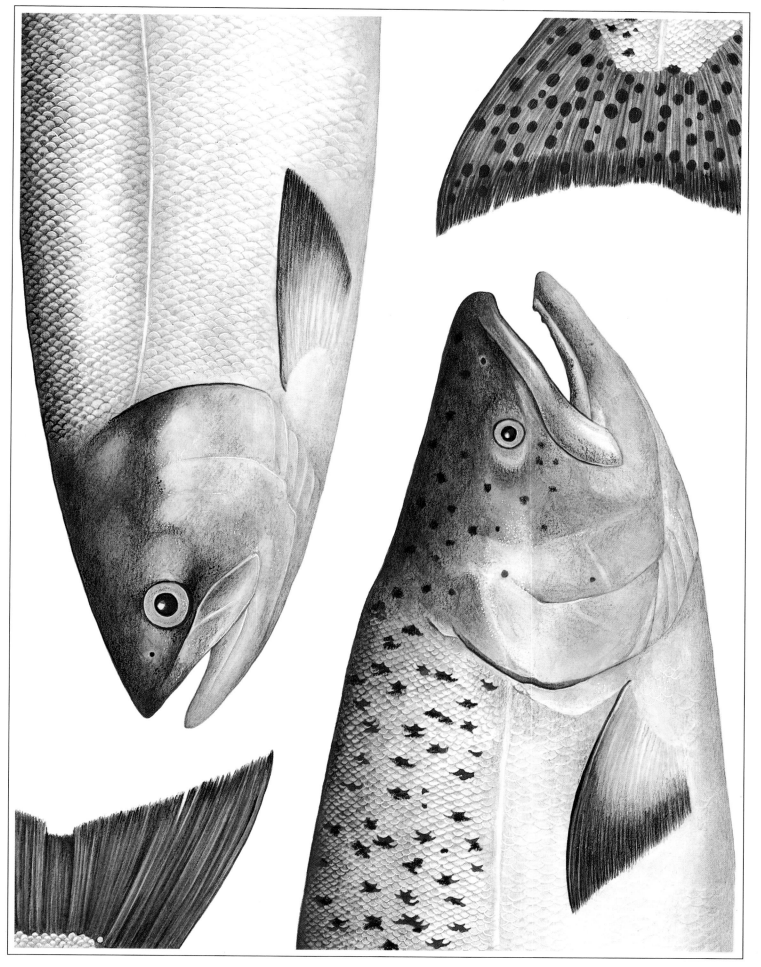

Chinook salmon, *Oncorhynchus tshawytscha* (right) and sockeye salmon, *O nerka* (left)

Smelts

12

S melts come in two main versions, those of the northern hemisphere (family Osmeridae) and those of the southern hemisphere (family Retropinnidae). Since fish studies began in the northern hemisphere it is customary to refer to the former as the "true" smelts; and they are certainly of much greater importance than their antipodean counterparts.

No smelts are large. The maximum length of the main species of the North Atlantic (plus the Baltic and many lakes in northern Europe), *Osmerus eperlanus*, is only 12 inches and, as usual, normal market length is less than that. The Asiatic or rainbow smelt, *O dentex* or *O mordax*, which has a wide distribution in the North Pacific and the Arctic regions, is larger, but still a small fish. There are many land-locked populations, although smelt are basically marine fish which go up rivers to spawn and then return to the sea.

Smelts are well known in parts of France. In Normandy for example, three of them appear on the coat of arms of Caudebec on the Seine.

On the American side of the Atlantic smelts are still the object of an important commercial fishery, although the enthusiasm shown by New Yorkers for them in the nineteenth century has dwindled. It appears that when these fish really engaged the attention of connoisseurs it was the "green" smelts of Raritan Bay which commanded the highest price. These were caught swimming, whereas many of the smelts brought to market had been naturally frozen in the winter ice.

The capelin, *Mallotus villosus*, is a member of the same family. It is not often used as food for humans, except in Greenland; but it is important as food for cod. Among the many fine passages of nineteenth-century American writing on fish is this, a contribution by Charles Lanham to a report published in the 1870s: "The male fishes are somewhat larger than the female, and are provided with a sort of ridge projecting on each side of their backbones, similar to the eaves of a house, in which the female Capelin is deficient. The latter, on approaching the beach to deposit its spawn, is attended by two male fishes, who huddle the female between them, until the whole body is concealed under the projecting ridges, and her head only is visible. In this position all three run together, with great swiftness, upon the sands, when the males, by some inherent imperceptible power, compress the body of the female between their own, so as to expel the spawn from the orifice and the tail. Having thus accomplished its delivery, the three Capelins separate, and, paddling with their whole force through the shallow water of the beach, generally succeed in regaining once more the bosom of the deep."

Smelts, when fresh, have a smell like that of cucumbers. There are not many recipes specifically for them, but I do like this one, which comes from a Dutch marine biologist who is passionately interested in cookery.

Gebakken Spiering met Selderij
(Fried Smelts with Celery)

nearly 2 pounds fresh smelts	1 pound potatoes
1 pound celery	2 tablespoons vegetable oil for frying

Cut the celery stalks into short sections and simmer them in lightly salted water until they are tender. Drain and keep warm. Prepare the potatoes in Dutch fashion, which means boiling them until they are just cooked but still firm, then cutting them into slices and pan-frying them. Meanwhile remove the heads of the smelts and gut them; then pan-fry them too, over a high heat, so that they emerge brown and crisp. Serve them with the celery and potatoes, garnished if you wish with a few celery leaves. Serves four.

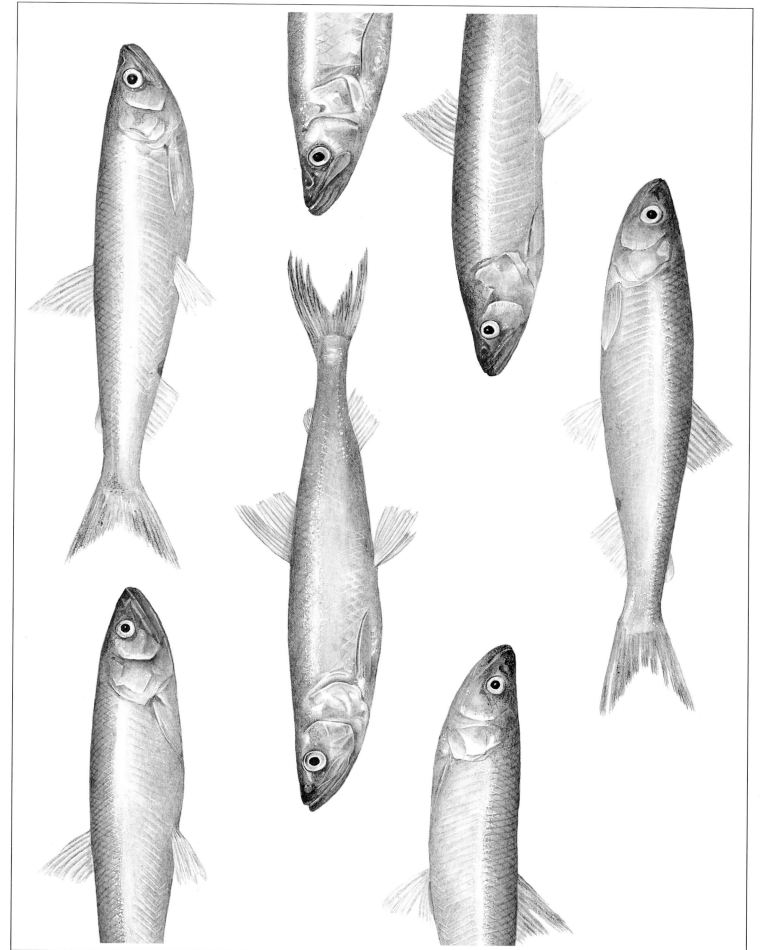

13

North Atlantic smelts, *Osmerus eperlanus*

Sardines

14

When I was a boy growing up in Britain, sardines on toast were an integral part of my family's diet, appearing once a week for dinner. Nothing in my experience then could have led me to think that these fish enjoyed any existence outside the hard-to-open cans in which they came, and indeed still come. But in most parts of the world – and sardines are found all around the world – they are familiar as fresh fish.

All sardines belong to one sub-family in the highly complex group of clupeoid fish (in which there are over 300 species altogether). As so often happens, the common name does not exactly match scientific classifications; but in this instance it is not far out. Most fish in the genera *Amblygaster, Sardina, Sardinops* and *Sardinella* are called sardine (that is, if they are given any English name); and the name is rarely used of any other fish.

There is sometimes confusion between sardines and pilchard. The short answer is that a sardine is a young pilchard and a pilchard a grown-up sardine. However, for Europeans, pilchard refers to a fully-grown specimen of only one species, *Sardina pilchardus*, which has a range extending from the Mediterranean into the East Atlantic and as far north as the south of England (where the pilchard fishery is important, and the name has its origin), and even to Norway.

The other notable sardines of the Mediterranean and Atlantic are:
● *Sardinella maderensis*, the "Madeiran sardinella", French *grande allache*; its maximum length is 12 inches; its range throughout the South Mediterranean and down the African coast to Angola.
● *Sardinella aurita*, the "round sardinella", French *allache*; its maximum length is also 12 inches; its range from the Black Sea (occasionally) throughout the Mediterranean and, in the East Atlantic, from Cadiz down to South Africa. It is also found in a slightly different form (classified by some as *S brasiliensis*) in the West Atlantic from Cape Cod down to Argentina; and also in the West Pacific from Japan to the Philippines.

The sardines of the Indo-Pacific are numerous and some of them have remarkably limited ranges, for example *S neglecta*, which occurs only on the coasts of Kenya and Tanzania. The strangest of all is *S tawilis*, a freshwater species occurring only in Lake Bombon in the Philippines. The commercially important species, apart from *Sardinella aurita* which has already been mentioned, are:
● *S gibbosa*, the goldstripe sardinella. It has a standard length of 6 inches and a thin yellow line along its side separating the blue-green back from the silvery flanks. It ranges all the way round from East Africa to Northwest Australia.
● *S longiceps*, the "Indian oil sardine". Its standard length is 8 inches; it is the most important and abundant clupeoid fish in Indian waters, accounting in some years for 30 per cent of the entire Indian catch of marine fish. Its range is from the Red Sea to the Philippines and Taiwan.
● *Sardinops melanosticus*, the "Japanese pilchard". Its standard length is around $9\frac{1}{2}$ inches and it is one of the most important commercial fishes of Japan. In a recent survey it was ranked as the second most heavily exploited fish in the world. (*S sagax*, a pilchard of Peru and Chile, came third.)

Fresh sardines are excellent when broiled. They may also be fried, but they already contain plenty of oil themselves. Pilchards, being larger, lend themselves to other treatments, for example being made into the traditional English Cornish Stargazey Pie (a tradition of which it is difficult to find traces in Cornwall today).

I also recommend making *Beignets de Sardines* in the Algerian manner. Small sardines are beheaded, gutted, opened out butterfly-fashion and rid of their backbones. They are then placed together in pairs, skin side out, clothed in batter and deep-fried. As the Karsentys explain in *Le Livre de la Cuisine Pied-noir*, they can be used for *kmia* (the Algerian equivalent of the Spanish *tapas*), but they also make a good first course.

15

Small sardines and fully-grown sardine (pilchard), all *Sardinus pilchardus* (top two rows); round sardinella, *Sardinella aurita* (third row); Japanese pilchards, *Sardinops melanosticus*

Anchovies

16

The two salient characteristics of anchovies are their pungent, salty flavor, much sought after as a flavoring agent, and their abundance. Species are found in all the warm oceans, but the uses made of them in different regions vary considerably.

The anchovy of most culinary renown is *Engraulis encrasicolus* of the Mediterranean, the Black Sea and the warmer waters of the East Atlantic. In earlier centuries it was mainly eaten as salted anchovies, which were sold from barrels. It is now more familiar in the form of canned anchovy fillets, which are used to impart a distinctive and salty flavor to many dishes. The preserved anchovies of Collioure, in the south of France, are among the best.

However, the practice of eating fresh or frozen anchovies, unsalted and not canned, is spreading to other European countries from Portugal, Spain and Turkey, where the abundance of the catch had already made it a familiar delicacy. The Turks are beyond doubt the greatest enthusiasts for anchovies, which they call *hamsi*. The intense and proprietorial feelings inspired by *hamsi* in Turkish hearts have found expression in some remarkable poems recited by itinerant troubadours on the Black Sea coast. I quote one in my book, *Mediterranean Seafood*, along with an impressive list of the culinary uses to which *hamsi* are put in Turkey, including their incorporation in a kind of bread.

In the Indo-Pacific region anchovies present a different picture. *E ringens* occurs off the coast of Peru and adjacent countries in shoals so enormous that the catch of the *anchoveta* (its Peruvian name) has often been the heaviest in the world. The cold Humboldt current, which flows northwards in those parts and is very rich in zooplankton, accounts for its abundance. It is made into fish meal.

Although the *anchoveta* is numerically the dominant species, there are many other species in the region. *E australis*, the Australian anchovy, has so far been only lightly exploited, whereas the northern anchovy, *E mordax*, found from British Columbia to California, is the object of an important commercial fishery. In Asian waters there are anchovies of the genera *Stolephorus*, (long-jawed anchovy); *Coilia* and *Setipinna* (hairfin anchovies, with sharply tapering rear ends). There is also *Thryssa*, the moustached anchovy, which has rearward extensions to its upper jaw which are thought to resemble a moustache or the whiskers of a cat, and whose Thai name means cat fish. These are all good food fish, but do not have the special importance in Asian cuisine that the European anchovy enjoys in Europe. The explanation may be that, in Southeast Asia, a special taste which is similar to that of the European anchovy is already present in the daily diet in the fish sauces of the region (which may, incidentally, be made from anchovies).

Those who relish the flavor of anchovy will enjoy an invention of Francatelli, a Victorian royal chef. The Badminton Sandwich is a thick piece of freshly toasted bread split open and filled with anchovy butter and anchovy fillets.

The recipe which I propose, from the vicinity of Genoa, is simplicity itself: no cooking is needed.

Acciughe al Limone
(Anchovies Marinated in Lemon Juice)

12 small anchovies
1-2 lemons

Clean and behead a dozen small (or six larger) fresh anchovies. Split them open on the underside as far as the tail and leave them to marinate in lemon juice for 24 hours. Serve as an antipasto. Serves four.

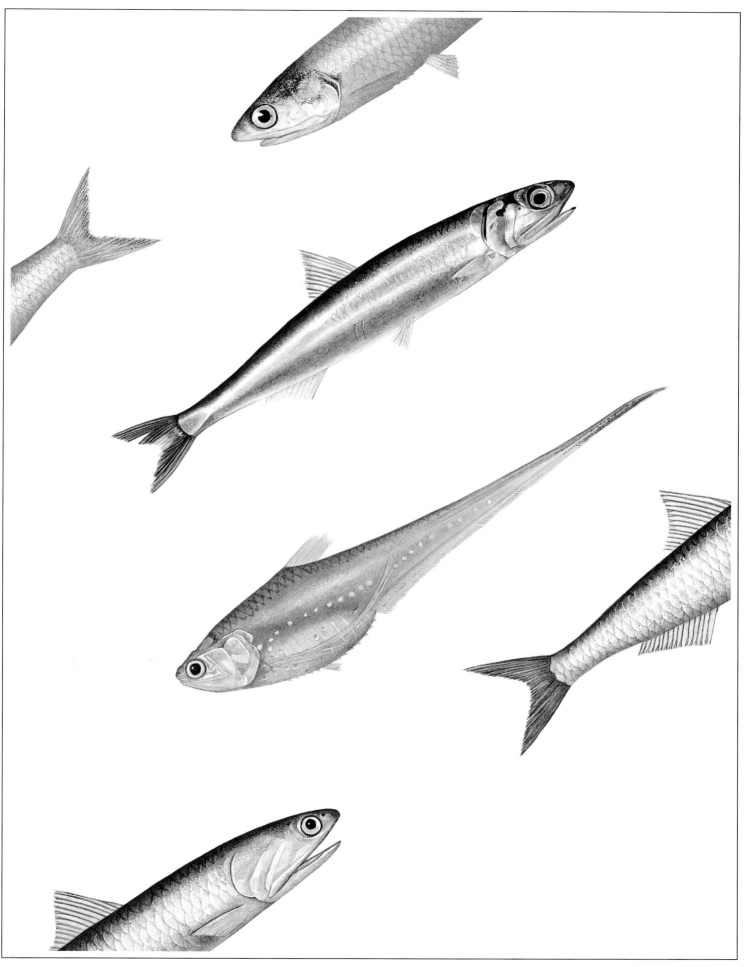

From top to bottom: long-jawed anchovy, *Stolephorus indicus*; European anchovy, *Engraulis encrasicolus*; hairtail anchovy, *Coilia dussumieri*; and northern anchovy, *E mordax*

Herring

18

The unpredictable and mysterious herring, *Clupea harengus*, is the fish which has had most influence on the economic and political history of Europe, outdoing even the cod in this respect. The species is distributed right across the North Atlantic, down to the north of France on one side and Chesapeake Bay on the other. It includes certain "races" which have their own characteristics; thus the Baltic herring is smaller than the Atlantic and has a lower fat content. The common adult length of Atlantic specimens is 5-7 inches.

The name herring is applied also to other fish, of which some (*C pallasi*, the Pacific herring, for example) are true herring, whereas others are more distant relations. None is as important as the Atlantic herring.

Herring typically swim in enormous shoals, but the size and abundance of these shoals have been difficult to predict for as far back as records go. Fluctuations which were attributable to biological causes have been confused in recent times by the effects of over-fishing. The North Sea stock, for example, declined by half between the 1950s and the 1960s.

Much ingenuity has been devoted to finding ways of preserving herring once it has been caught, and a full description of herring "cures" would fill a book. There is one learned work in German devoted entirely to the subject. The cures fall into several categories: hot-smoking (like the English bloater); cold-smoking (notably the kipper); and pickling of various kinds (preferred in continental Europe, where such products as rollmops are in heavy demand). Hot-smoking results in a fish which is both smoked and cooked, so ready to eat, and will keep for only a limited period. Cold-smoked products, which still have to be cooked, keep for longer, and pickled ones for the longest. These traditional products are still popular because of their distinctive flavors, even though the rationale for them has been weakened by the development of freezing and refrigeration techniques.

Fresh herring can best be cooked, say the Scots, by rolling them in oatmeal and frying them. That is a good method, if you can get the right grade of oatmeal (coarse-cut). Alternatively, buy split fresh herring, lay them skin side down, and sprinkle medium-cut oatmeal over the top side. Put the fish under the broiler, dotted with butter, and cook under a high heat to begin with, then a lower one.

However, there are lots of other ways. As the Dutch make more of the *nieuwe haring* (first herring of the season) than any other people, despatching a load of them at once to their Queen, I suggest a Dutch recipe below.

Dutch Baked Herring

4 fresh young herring	4 eggs, separated
$\frac{3}{4}$ stick butter	4 large potatoes, boiled and mashed
4 shallots, chopped	$\frac{1}{2}$ teaspoon sugar
I cup yogurt (or sour cream)	2 pinches salt

Have the herring filleted, steep the fillets in cold water for an hour then drain them and cut into small chunks. Melt a quarter of the butter in a pan and gently fry the shallots in this until they are translucent. Remove them and then mix them with a third of the yogurt (or sour cream) and all the fish.

Meanwhile, melt the rest of the butter in the pan and stir in the rest of the yogurt, the egg yolks and the mashed potato. Beat the egg whites and fold them into the mixture, adding the sugar and salt last.

Butter an ovenproof dish and place half the egg and potato mixture on the bottom, on top of this the herring mixture, then the rest of the egg and potato. Bake for 45 minutes in the oven at 350°. Serves four.

Herring, *Clupea harengus*

Shad

20

Shad, fish of the genus *Alosa* in the herring family, normally live in the sea but ascend rivers in the spring to spawn, and that is when they are caught and are at their best for eating.

The most famous species is the American shad, *A sapidissima*, which was a popular peasant dish on the eastern seaboard of the USA but later graduated to the status of a delicacy (as did its roe). During the 1870s it was introduced to the Pacific coast, where it has flourished and multiplied, with a range extending from the northern part of lower California to Alaska and on to Kamchatka in the Soviet Union. Close relations in America include *Pomolobus mediocris*, the hickory shad.

In Europe, the principal species are *Alosa alosa*, the allis (or allice) shad, and *A fallax*, the twaite shad. The former may reach a length of 24 inches and has a range from the Mediterranean (where it is rare) to southern Ireland; the latter is slightly smaller and is more common in the Mediterranean, besides being found as far north as the Baltic.

Various fish in Indo-Pacific waters are referred to as shad, including the famous Indian hilsa, *Hilsa ilisha*, and a couple of species called "gizzard shad" because they have thick, muscular stomachs like the gizzard of a fowl.

Caught in their prime, shad are good to eat, but there is a notorious difficulty over their numerous small bones. A legend of the Micmac Indians explains that the shad was originally a discontented porcupine which asked the Great Spirit Manitou to change it into something else. In response, the spirit turned the creature inside out and tossed it into the river to begin a new existence as a shad.

There are various theories about how to "melt" the bones before eating the fish. One is that very long cooking achieves this. Another is that the oxalic acid in sorrel will do the trick, and there are numerous traditional recipes which call for cooking shad with sorrel. Experiments carried out a few years ago by Dr George Tee show that there is some validity in the idea. He has still to do the more expensive experiments which would reveal whether cognac is equally efficacious, as asserted by Francis Marre, a "chimiste-expert" at the Court of Appeals in Paris who came from Tressan, where shad fished in the Hérault are given this *de luxe* treatment.

Well known American recipes include Planked Shad, and also a whole range of good recipes for Baked Stuffed Shad. An interesting one from Morocco calls for stuffing the shad with dates which have themselves been stuffed with a mixture including almonds and semolina. The recipe given below is perhaps the most popular in France.

Alose à l'Oseille

a shad weighing (uncleaned) 2 pounds	1-2 teaspoons tarragon mustard
court bouillon (see page 177)	pinch of nutmeg
1 pound sorrel	fresh tarragon leaves (optional)
2 egg yolks	sorrel leaf, chopped (optional)

Clean the shad and cook it gently in the *court bouillon* for about 40 minutes until done.

Meanwhile, boil the sorrel as though it were spinach (with hardly any water) then use whatever device you favor to turn it into a purée. Combine it with the egg yolks, mustard and nutmeg. If you wish, chop into it a few fresh tarragon leaves, possibly supplemented by a little chopped raw sorrel leaf. Make a bed of the sorrel on a warmed platter, lay the shad on it and serve. Serves four.

Alternative Fish
large herrings (p 18)

Alternative Recipes
Planked Fish (p 186)

An Indian shad, *Hilsa toli* (above) and an American shad, *Alosa sapidissima* (below)

Eels & Elvers

22

Eels & Elvers
ENGLISH-SPEAKING COUNTRIES

anguille
FRENCH

Aal, Flussaal
GERMAN

aal, paling
DUTCH

anguilla
ITALIAN

anguila
SPANISH

anguila
CATALAN

eiró
PORTUGUESE

jegulja
SERBO-CROAT

chéli
GREEK

ylan balığı
TURKISH

zmiorka
BULGARIAN

ugor'
RUSSIAN

ankerias
FINNISH

ål
SWEDISH, NORWEGIAN &
DANISH

abir (Mar), vellangoo (Ta)
INDIAN LANGUAGES

sin
CHINESE

unagi
JAPANESE

No fish has a life cycle more peculiar than the common eel, *Anguilla anguilla*, of the Mediterranean and East Atlantic. It begins in the Sargasso Sea, where the eggs hatch out into tiny larvae, which then drift across the Atlantic to Europe in the warm waters of the Gulf Stream, slowly growing in size as they do so. When they arrive at the mouths of European rivers, they are small, transparent and pencil-shaped. It is at this stage, or when they are swimming up the rivers, that they may be caught as elvers, which are regarded as a delicacy.

Those not so caught proceed up-river and establish themselves in fresh water for most of their lives – usually anything from six to 12 years, but the time varies according to conditions. Some eels live to a very great age in fresh water – 30, 40 or even 50 years. During this period they are generally gray in color, but when they reach sexual maturity they turn dark yellow. Every autumn a host of yellow eels undergo a further change, becoming silver, and proceed downstream towards the sea on their last journey. This takes them out into the Atlantic and back to the Sargasso Sea, where they spawn and perish.

A closely related species, *A rostrata*, also spawns in the Sargasso Sea, but moves westwards and is found from the West Indies to Newfoundland. *A japonica* occurs in the temperate regions of East Asia; and there are also, in Australian waters, *A australis*, the short-finned eel, and *A reinhardti*, the long-finned eel.

Unlike most other fish, eels take their rest in burrows; and they are of nocturnal habits, which helps to make them mysterious. There are some remarkable tales told of them, for example that they come up on to land to eat peas (pea pods, to follow the story exactly) or to keep warm in haystacks.

In Japan the farming of eels is a big business; but most elvers acquired by the Japanese come from the Loire or the Severn, so that *A anguilla* is in fact the eel which is most eaten in Japan.

Eels are little appreciated in North America, except where French influence is important. European countries where consumption is high include Britain, Denmark, the Netherlands and Belgium, France, Spain and Italy.

Eel flesh is rich in fat, especially in females who are preparing for their long last journey. They also have a coating of slime on their bodies, hence "slippery as an eel", and there is a tradition of buying them alive . . . But all this can be very off-putting. There are many famous eel dishes, for example Jellied Eel (England), *Anguille au vert* (Belgium), and Eel soup (Hamburg). The Japanese ways with eel are numerous, and they have special eel restaurants, such as one I went to near Tokyo, where nothing but eel is served: Eel Liver soup; Roast Eel, Fried Eel and Steamed Eel. The Japanese seem to be less keen on smoked eel, which is odd. This delicacy is best in Denmark and the Netherlands. Eels for smoking are never skinned. Similarly, if you spit-roast sections of eel, tucking sage leaves and sprigs of rosemary between the sections, leave the skin on.

As a simple recipe, I recommend this one from Venice.

Bisato Sull'ara
(Baked Eel with Bay Leaves)

Take a piece of cleaned and skinned eel weighing $1\frac{1}{2}$ pounds and cut it across into two pieces, to fit an oblong oven dish. Make incisions right round the pieces at intervals 2 inches, as if to cut right through them, but without doing so. Strew fresh bay leaves generously over the bottom of your oven dish, place the fish on top, sprinkle with salt and pepper and a little water, then cover them with more bay leaves. Cook thus in the oven at 290° for 45 minutes or more, until the eel is tender. Serves four.

Alternative Fish
nothing suitable

Alternative Recipe
Thai Grilled Caramelized Fish
(p 54)

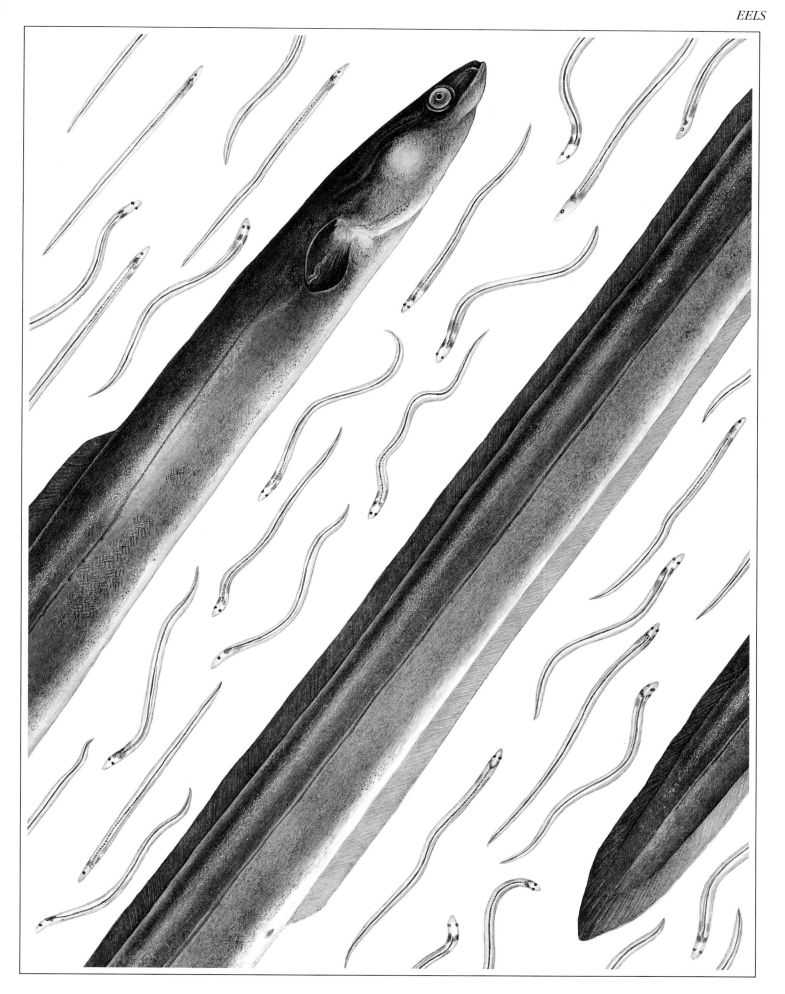

Silver eel and elvers, *Anguilla anguilla*

Conger Eels

24

People in Aberdeen used to call the conger eel, *Conger conger*, "evil-eye", because of its fierce appearance . It is, as its facial expression suggests, a voracious fish, found in the Mediterranean and East Atlantic with a close relation in the West Atlantic, *C oceanicus*. It may be up to $6\frac{1}{2}$ feet in length, though specimens of this huge size are uncommon. It is of variable color, mostly gray or brownish, depending on its habitat.

The conger comes out to feed at night, hiding by day in rocky crevices, under piers, in sunken wrecks or other seabed debris, often close to the shore. It is disconcerting to find such a large and terrifying fish in waters where bathers risk disturbing it if they are probing among inshore rocks, for example. It is fierce enough to do battle with the redoubtable octopus, whose chief enemy it is. Its life-style is such that it has to be caught on lines, with the result that the catch brought to market is limited.

The range of *C conger* in the East Atlantic extends down to southern Africa; but in other parts of the southern hemisphere, notably Australasian waters, it is replaced by other species. In Indo-Pacific waters the principal fish of this group, often called conger-pike, is *Muraenosox cinereus*: the Thai name for this means dragon fish. In Asian cuisines it is often used for making fish balls. The Chinese count it as one of the 1001 aphrodisiacs in their repertoire and recommend boiling it with Chinese "five spices" to produce an efficacious general tonic.

The flesh of the conger seems to be most esteemed in Spain and on the Atlantic coast of France (it is even complimented by the name "*boeuf bellilois*" in Belle-Ile), and in Southwest England and Wales. In Wales there used to be some interesting methods of fishing for it with a long iron rod, equipped with a blunt, hooked end; or even with firearms.

Mr Rogers of Llandulas in Wales, arch-exponent of the iron rod method of fishery, explained to me what to do with a freshly caught conger. Hang it up with a cord by the neck. Make an incision with a razor-blade right around the neck, below the cord, making sure that the skin is cut through but not the flesh. Then use nippers and roll the skin back from the cut towards the tail. "It's hard work until you get half-way down – then it comes off like a glove." The conger, now all pearly white, is then gutted and cut across into steaks, ready for cooking. Mr Rogers steams them for 20 minutes, then removes them and lets them dry out a little, and finally pan-fries them in pure pork dripping.

The bony tail-end of a conger is best reserved for soup, but a middle cut can be poached or braised, or even roasted like meat, with good results.

Conger Cooked in Milk

This recipe is similar to some found in Southwestern France but I have added a Cornish touch with the marigold petals.

about 2 pounds center cut of conger
butter for greasing
1 pound potatoes
1 medium onion

salt and pepper
4 cups milk
marigold petals (optional)

Skin and bone the piece of fish, slice it, and cut the slices into small squares or rounds. Put these in a buttered oven dish.

Peel and thinly slice the potatoes and onion, add them to the fish, season generously, pour over the milk and cook for $1\frac{1}{2}$ hours in the oven at 325°. Garnish the dish with marigold petals. Serves four.

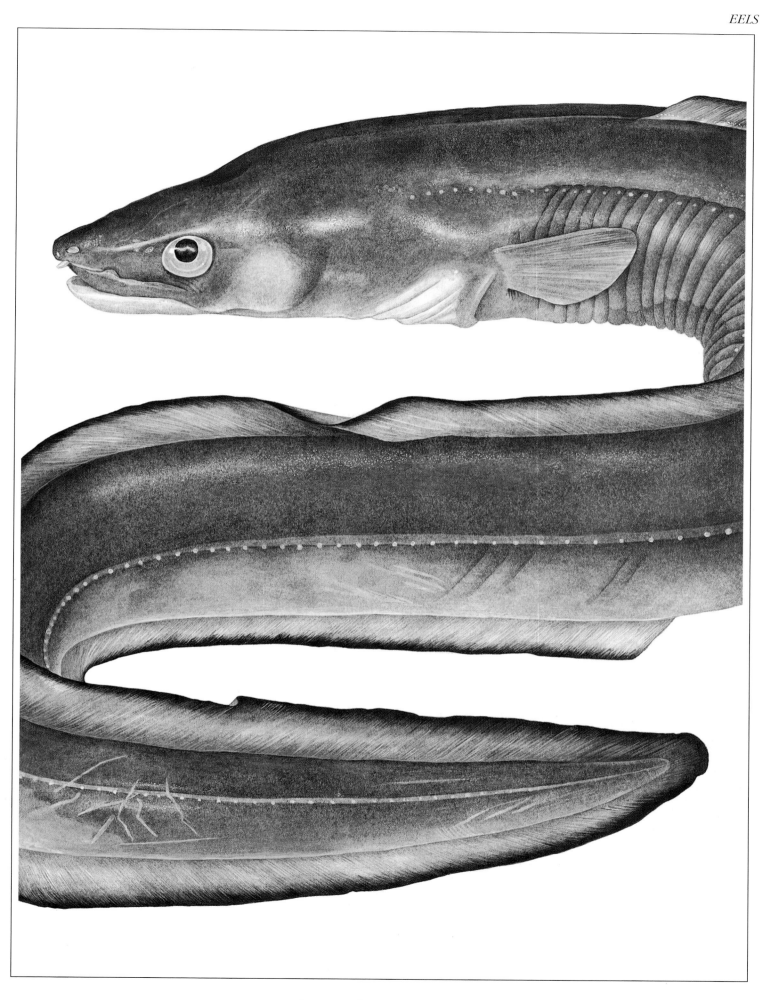

Conger eel, *Conger conger*

Cod

26

od, by any criterion one of the most important fish in the history of mankind, continues to be one of the foremost marine food resources: as fresh or frozen fish, in the form of *bacalao* (dried and salted cod) and stockfish (dried cod), and for its roe. The North Atlantic cod, *Gadus morhua*, is the better known fish, but the smaller North Pacific species, *G macrocephalus*, is also important.

There was a time, before all the fishing grounds had been exploited, when one Atlantic cod was recorded as weighing over 200 pounds and measuring nearly 6 feet. This seems almost incredible nowadays when an average market specimen weighs only 10 pounds.

Exploitation of available fishing grounds was heavy in medieval times, largely because of the demand for salted and dried cod for Lent, but it was nothing compared to the present scouring of the sea with sophisticated equipment. On this, see William Warner's *Distant Water* (1983); and compare him with Kipling in *Captains Courageous* (1922) writing of the days when fishing was done in dories launched from parent schooners. A good survey of the history of cod and its fisheries is given in Albert Jensen's *The Cod* (1972).

The coloration of cod varies. The lateral line is distinctively pale, standing out clearly on a body which is greenish, gray or even of a reddish hue, depending on habitat, and usually dappled with spots or patches. Cod feed mainly on other fish, but also eat crustaceans and have been known to devour inanimate objects such as a "book in three treatises" taken from the stomach of a cod captured in 1626 and presented, fittingly, to the Chancellor of Cambridge University.

As cod has become scarcer and more expensive, its culinary merits have been more widely recognized. Its reputation suffered in the past from its being, in salted and dried form, of unattractive appearance and a prime example of "penitential" food. In more recent times, it continued to suffer from being available cheaply in very large quantities. But its flesh, which separates into large flakes, is excellent, especially if really fresh. This was recognized in the nineteenth century, when floating cod chests were used to keep cod alive for the market at English ports such as Harwich. Even now it is customary to buy cod alive from big tanks in the fish market at Bergen, Norway.

Cod is an adaptable fish from the cook's point of view, and may be prepared in any of the standard ways. Since the Russians are now probably catching more cod than anyone else, I have chosen a nineteenth-century Russian recipe.

Cod with Cherry and Red Wine Sauce

$1\frac{1}{2}$ pounds cod in thick fillets
milk for poaching
1 tablespoon butter
$\frac{1}{2}$ cup unsweetened cherry purée
1 cup fish stock (or water)

1 tablespoon sugar
2 cloves
pinch of cinnamon
2 teaspoons potato flour, dissolved in a little water
1 cup red wine

Poach the fillets in the milk until cooked but still tender. Meanwhile, melt the butter in a large pan and cook the cherry purée in it for a short time. Add the fish stock, sugar, cloves, cinnamon and potato flour and bring to the boil, then turn down the heat and simmer for 15 minutes. Next, pour in the red wine and bring it almost but not quite back to the boil.

Drain the poached fish, pour the sauce over it, and serve with hot buttered boiled potatoes. Serves four.

Cod, *Gadus morhua*

Hake

28

Hake was a name which originally referred only to *Merluccius merluccius*, a member of the cod family which has a distribution from the Mediterranean to Norway. Later, use of the name silver hake was extended to the North American species *M bilinearis*. The name also applies to the Australasian species *M australis* (but is sometimes wrongly used for a quite different Australasian fish which is properly known as gemfish). In addition, there is a South African species, *M capensis*, known as hake or stockfish, which is the most important commercial fish of the region; and a Pacific species, *M productus*, which is of some importance. South America also has a couple of species, one on the Pacific side and the other in the South Atlantic.

In North America, two members of the genus *Urophycis* have inherited the name: *U tenuis*, the white hake (or Boston ling) and *U chuss*, the smaller red hake (or squirrel hake). These resemble the true hakes in having two dorsal fins, one anal fin and no barbel. Other members of the cod family (Gadidae) have either three dorsal fins, like cod and haddock, or only one, like cusk and the bearded rocklings.

The European hake, the female of which is larger than the male and may reach a length of 39 inches, has a mouth which is gray-black inside; that of the silver hake is dark blue. The silver hake, in accordance with its name, has a silvery iridescent sheen when freshly caught.

Hake is most popular in Spain and Portugal, but it is everywhere counted as a fine eating fish and some think it the best of the cod family. However, it must be very fresh, since the flesh becomes insipid after being kept for a while. It can be poached, steamed, or baked. Steaks can be fried, then marinated and eaten cold, as in Italy. The flesh can also be used to make superior fish balls, as in Scandinavia.

The red or squirrel hake is more appreciated now than it used to be. However, it is still the case that only a small proportion of the catch is sold as fresh fish; most is salted.

Merluza en Salsa Verde
(Hake in Green Sauce)

4 thick steaks of hake	3 medium potatoes, thinly sliced
I lemon	I tablespoon flour
olive oil	I bay leaf
4 cloves garlic	4 tablespoons parsley, chopped

Wash the steaks and pat them dry, then squeeze the lemon juice over them.

In an earthenware casserole heat two or three tablespoons of olive oil. Brown the cloves of garlic in the oil, then remove them and keep them ready in a mortar. Next, fry the potato slices a little, then remove the casserole from the heat while you add the flour with about half a cup of water and the bay leaf. Continue cooking for a few minutes until the potato is soft. At this point, season the hake steaks with salt and put them in too, followed by the garlic and parsley which you have pounded together in the mortar with a few drops of water. Resume cooking, shaking the casserole over the heat occasionally.

The dish will be ready in 20-30 minutes and is served in the casserole. The sauce will be light green and may be garnished with a sprinkling of fresh parsley at the last minute. Serves four.

Red Hake, *Urophycis chuss* (left); European hake, *Merluccius merluccius* (right)

Haddock

30

Like the cod, to whose family it belongs, the haddock is of commercial importance on both sides of the North Atlantic. Its range descends as far as the Bay of Biscay in the east and New England in the west but it may venture a little further south in the summer. Specimens over 36 inches long have been recorded, but the normal maximum is 32 inches and the market length is 16-24 inches.

This fish, whose scientific name is *Melanogrammus aeglefinus*, has a dark greenish-brown or purplish-gray back. The painting shows its black lateral line and the "thumb-print" on each side. In this last particular it resembles the John Dory (see page 98); it too has been thought to be the fish which St Peter picked up and on which his thumbs left their imprint. But it could not be as it is not found in the Mediterranean, still less in the Sea of Galilee.

For the cook, the haddock and the cod are close competitors. Some prefer one, some the other. Icelanders, who are in a particularly good position to judge, rate haddock above cod. In the north of England there is an odd dividing line between Lancashire, where people prefer cod for their fish and french fries, and Yorkshire, where they choose haddock (but a few places in Yorkshire, like Huddersfield, are in a gray area where a tendency to favor cod may be noted and the atmosphere is accordingly schizophrenic).

Haddock does not take salt as well as cod, so the traditional ways of curing it are by drying and smoking. "Rizzared" haddock in Scotland were simply sun-dried. "Finnan haddies" (from the fishing village of Finnan, near Aberdeen) used to be smoked over a peat-reek, but achieved such renown that they are now prepared by less traditional methods elsewhere, including the USA (where one eminent ichthyologist, in a moment of aberration, referred to them as "Finland haddocks").

Smoked haddock has become popular in France. When the French refer to "haddock", which has become a French word, they mean smoked haddock.

In practice, smoking is preceded by cleaning, splitting, and brining. What are called "Glasgow pales" are small haddock which have been given this treatment but removed from the smoke when they have acquired no more than a pale straw color.

Although salting is unsuitable as a long-term method of preserving haddock, very light salting is carried out in some places, producing for example the "green-salted haddock" of Denmark (see page 184) and the "night-salted haddock" of Iceland. Both products are intended for early consumption.

Haddock roe is a delicacy, less well-known than cod roe.

Smoked Haddock with Bacon

I used to have this for "high tea" as a boy in Glasgow, Scotland, and my Aunt Norah gave me her recipe.

4 fillets of smoked haddock, skinned
butter for greasing
4 large or 8 small strips of bacon

Alternative Fish
cod (p 26)
hake (p 28)

Alternative Recipes
Green-salted Haddock (p 184)

Rub a shallow oven dish with buttered paper, then put the fillets in it in a single layer. Place the strips of bacon on top, again in a single layer. Cover with the buttered paper, buttery side down, and cook in the oven at 300° for half an hour. Remove the buttered paper from the dish for the last five minutes, so that the bacon will become crisp.

Serve with thin slices of bread and butter. Serves four.

Haddock, *Melanogrammus aeglefinus*

Striped Bass & Sea Bass

32

The striped bass or "striper", *Morone saxatilis*, is not the only American relation to the European sea bass. *M americanus*, usually called the white perch, is another; and *Centropristes striatus*, the black sea-bass, is a third. But the striper is the most highly esteemed. Its range is from the Gulf of St Lawrence down to the Gulf of Mexico; but it was successfully introduced to the Pacific coast in the nineteenth century and now provides sport for anglers there also. The striper is the lower fish in the painting.

A silvery fish, with a maximum length of 40 inches, the sea bass has a range which extends from the Black Sea through the Mediterranean and in the East Atlantic from Senegal up to the south coast of England (*D punctatus*) or as far as Norway (*D labrax*). It is a favorite fish for anglers, especially on the south coast of Ireland.

The flesh of the striped bass is firm and relatively free of small bones, and it holds its shape well after cooking. This makes it an ideal fish to serve at a cold buffet and the consequent demand for it from restaurants is a factor in the high price it fetches. Since the fishery for it is necessarily on an artisanal scale, or conducted for sport, it would anyway be expensive. However, since striped bass can live in saltwater lagoons, they can be "farmed", as is done in France and Italy.

The European sea bass, *Dicentrarchus labrax* (and *D punctatus*), remains one of the most prized fishes of Europe as it was in the times of classical Rome. The Roman author Pliny the Elder stated, surprisingly, that specimens taken in rivers, which these fish penetrate some way upstream, were preferred; but nowadays

those taken from the sea are counted best.

All these fish can be poached, often to be served cold, when they present a handsome appearance. Or they can be broiled (whole, if not too large) and served with some simple accompaniment such as a herb-flavored butter (see page 200). The recipe I give below is more complex.

Loup de Mer Farci, Grillé et Flambé à la Farigoulette

3½-pound striped bass, cleaned and scaled
salt and black pepper
4 tablespoons tarragon mustard
4 tablespoons freshly made tomato sauce
2 tomatoes, thinly sliced

1 onion, thinly sliced
2 large bouquets wild thyme
(*farigoulette*) or garden thyme
4 tablespoons olive oil
2 teaspoons wine vinegar
a little brandy (optional)

Season the fish as usual, then paint its gut cavity with half the tarragon mustard and all the tomato sauce. Insert half the tomato and onion slices and use one bouquet of thyme to fill the cavity.

Make two or three slanting cuts along the sides of the fish, reaching in as far as the backbone. Rub these with the rest of the tarragon mustard and season lightly with salt and pepper. Insert into the cuts alternating slices of tomato and onion. Sprinkle the fish with half the olive oil and vinegar, then grill it over charcoal for four to five minutes on each side, after which it will be half cooked. At this point, transfer it to an oven dish and pour over it the rest of the olive oil and vinegar.

Finish cooking the fish in the oven at 350° for about 20-25 minutes, basting often. For the last few minutes, place the remaining bouquet of thyme in the oven to allow it to dry and to warm up. When the fish is cooked, transfer it to a heated metal platter, pour its juices over it and place on top of it the second bouquet. Set this alight, with flaming brandy if you wish, and serve. The burning thyme imparts its flavor to the fish. Serves six.

Alternative Fish
groupers (pp 36, 38)
snappers (pp 60, 62)

Alternative Recipes
Pargo con Salsa de Aguacate
(p 44)
Ikan Masak Molek (p 62)

Sea bass, *Dicentrarchus labrax* (left) and striped bass or striper, *Morone saxatilis* (right)

Barramundi

The name barramundi, of aboriginal origin, is used in Australia both for a fine sea fish, *Lates calcarifer* (also known as giant sea perch) and for freshwater fish of the family Osteoglossidae (meaning bony-tongued fish). The latter, the bony-tongued fish, live in slow-flowing rivers. Their flesh is good, but they are not the fish with which we are concerned here.

The giant sea perch, the barramundi which is the subject of the painting, is considered by purists to be less deserving of the name barramundi; but this has become so familiar in Northern Queensland that it seems bound to stay. It is a prized game fish, attaining large dimensions (maximum length 5 feet), which is gray, brown or greenish above and silvery below, with brown fins and noticeably small red eyes. It is found all the way from the Persian Gulf to the Philippines, and it is everywhere prized for its excellent flesh. Although a marine species, it does enter fresh waters, presumably to spawn and also perhaps in search of smaller fish to eat.

I have yet to find an explanation for the name given to this fish by the British in India: cock-up. It is probably one of these embarrassing situations where the explanation is so obvious to everyone but myself that no one has bothered to write it down. I draw comfort from the fact that Henry Sullivan Thomas, the learned author of *The Rod in India* (1881), also declared himself baffled by the name.

In Australia, the range of this fish extends from Western Australia round the northern coast and down the east coast as far as the Mary River. It favors river mouths, where it thrives in salt, brackish or even fresh water, and is plentiful in waters flowing into the Gulf of Carpentaria. Roughley, the author of *Fish and Fisheries of Australia*, wrote that "it has earned the reputation of being one of the finest food-fishes of Australian waters. Its flesh is white, tender but firm, and of extremely good flavor. It was also a favorite food of the aborigines, who wrapped it in the leaves of the wild ginger plant and baked it in hot ashes. This method of cooking is sometimes adopted by white people in North Queensland and it is considered to be unsurpassed by any other method or treatment."

While recommending the aboriginal method to readers who have wild ginger plants, and also wondering whether some of the wild fruits of the Australian bush, such as the *quandong*, would not make good companions for barramundi, I have chosen a more conventional recipe. Grant Blackman, whose comprehensive book on Australian fish cookery largely reflects European culinary traditions, puts this recipe as number one in his list of proposals for doing honor to the delicate flavor of barramundi.

Broiled Barramundi Steaks

4 barramundi steaks, each of about 7 ounces	3 tablespoons almonds, blanched and chopped
juice of I lemon	2 tablespoons shallots, chopped
4 tablespoons clarified butter	ground black pepper
	sprigs of parsley

Squeeze the juice of the lemon over the barramundi steaks and let them stand for a quarter of an hour.

Use a little of the butter to brush the steaks, then broil them for five to eight minutes on each side, depending on their thickness and the heat of the broiler. Put the remaining butter in a pan, add the almonds and shallots, and sauté them until the almonds are golden-brown, then pour them over the fish, add a sprinkling of black pepper and a garnish of parsley, and serve. Serves four.

Barramundi, *Lates calcarifer*

Groupers

Groupers
ENGLISH-SPEAKING COUNTRIES

mérou
FRENCH

Sägebarsch, Zackenbarsch
GERMAN

garoupa
PORTUGUESE

mero
SPANISH

anfós
CATALAN

cernia
ITALIAN

rophós
GREEK

orfoz, roufo
TURKISH

mennani
ARABIC (MEDITERRANEAN)

mierou
RUSSIAN

36

Grouper, the common name usually applied to fish of the genus *Epinephelus* and some close relations, is of uncertain derivation. The explanation that these fish, although normally solitary, sometimes congregate in large groups does not seem plausible, especially when one notes the prevalence of names like *kerapu* in South East Asia. It seems much more likely that *kerapu* was turned into *garoupa* by the Portuguese, and then passed into English as "grouper".

Whatever the origin of the name, these fish occur in warm and tropical waters worldwide. They are heavy-bodied and some species grow to a great size. Coloration varies, being generally such as to camouflage the fish and therefore depends on its habitat. The life-style is generally solitary, and a given fish will probably stay in its own territory throughout its life. There are records of groupers being regularly visited in the same spot by divers, and even of their making friends with these divers and learning to perform tricks for them. Many divers, however, seek them out to kill them, since they make impressive trophies; and most groupers are excellent to eat, with firm, flaky meat of a good flavor.

The very numerous species include five in the Mediterranean (not counting a couple of Indo-Pacific species which have penetrated the East Mediterranean via the Suez Canal). All five, which have maximum lengths of 40 inches or more, are also found in the East Atlantic. Within the Mediterranean most species are more common in the southern and central waters, but the most common and best known species, *Epinephelus guaza*, is present throughout.

Groupers are more numerous in the Caribbean region. *E striatus*, the Nassau grouper, is marked by distinctive bands. It was a fish of this species which was recorded as picking the pockets (full of crayfish tails) of a Nassau underwater photographer (Böhlke and Chaplin, 1968, a work in which the various Caribbean groupers are well catalogued). A smaller grouper, the so-called rock hind, is *E adscensionis*, common on the reefs and covered all over with spots. The giant of the family, *E itajara*, has been known to reach a length of 8 feet. It is known as giant sea bass or jewfish.

The painting shows a Mediterranean grouper, an American one and one of the Indo-Pacific species treated on the following page.

Mérou Blanc with Rosemary Sauce

This recipe is from Cyprus. The woman who gave it to me lives in Bellapais, familiar to readers of Lawrence Durrell's *Bitter Lemons* as the village of "breathtaking congruence", with its tree of idleness and ruined monastery.

2 pounds grouper, cut into slices	4 cloves garlic, peeled and crushed
flour to coat	2 tablespoons flour
olive oil for deep-frying	4 tablespoons wine vinegar
for the sauce	generous $\frac{1}{2}$ cup water
1 cup olive oil	sprigs of rosemary

First make the sauce by heating the olive oil in a pan, adding the crushed garlic, followed by the flour. Stir and allow to cook for two or three minutes. Then add the wine vinegar, water and salt, keeping the pan on a low heat and stirring all the time. When the sauce is nearly thick enough add the sprigs of rosemary.

Next, flour the pieces of fish, and deep fry in oil until cooked. Remove the sprigs of rosemary from the sauce and serve with the cooked fish. Serves four.

Alternative Fish
bass (p 32)
barramundi (p 34)

Alternative Recipes
Aurado i Poumo d'Amour (p 42)
Parrotfish Steamed with Julienne
Vegetables (p 70)

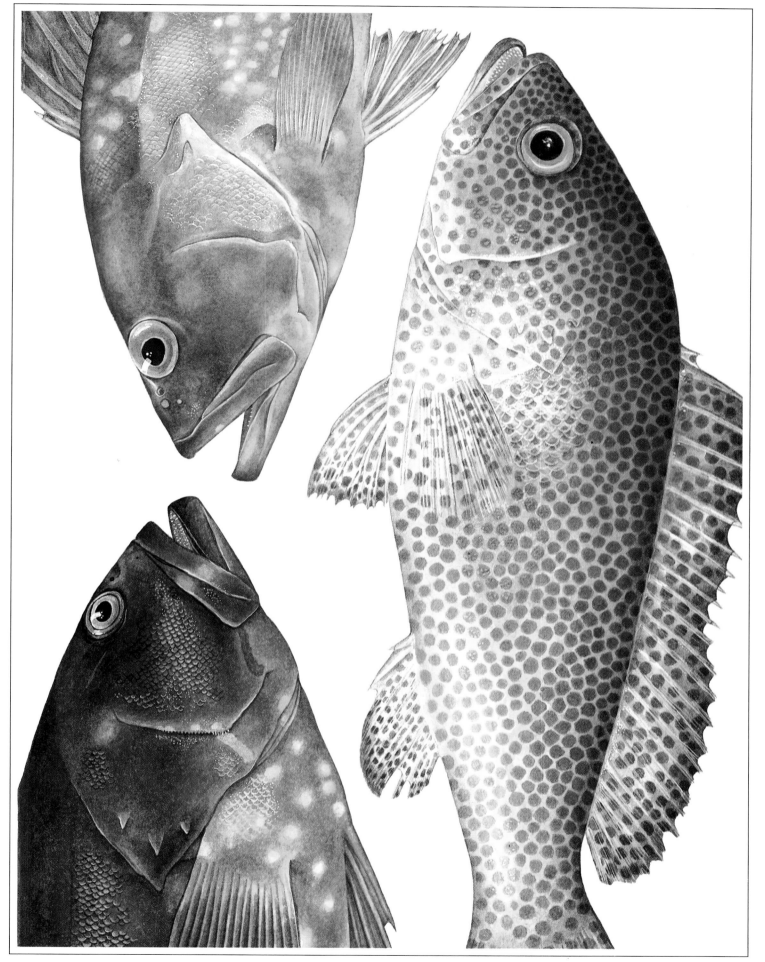

The red grouper from the USA, *Epinephelus morio* (top left); the dusky grouper or mérou from the Mediterranean, *E guaza* (bottom left), and the vieille maconde from the Seychelles, *E chlorostigma* (right)

More
Groupers

38

The groupers which are found in Indo-Pacific waters number several dozen and in many instances each species has its own name in many languages. The names given in the left-hand column are general names, corresponding to "grouper". However, there is one source of confusion among the English-language names. Australians often use the name "groper" for certain wrasses and parrotfish (see pages 68 and 70) and apply the inappropriate names "rock cod" or "coral cod" to what ought to be called groupers. For some species the name "coral trout" is more widely in use.

The polka-dot grouper, *Cromileptes altivelis*, is one of the most expensive of all fish in Hong Kong, although it has an unattractive Chinese name meaning "rat grouper". This is a grouper of medium size, with a maximum length of 24 inches, and the superb quality of its flesh bears out the general principle that in this family it is the medium-size fish which offer the best eating.

Despite this principle, it is of interest to read about the largest grouper of all, *Promicrops lanceolatus*. The maximum length of this huge fish is said to be about 12 feet, and weights up to 1,100 pounds have been reported. Adult specimens are dark brown, almost black, and must make a terrifying spectacle when they rush out of their hiding places to attack fishermen, as they reputedly do. An author who combined scientific knowledge of fish with practical fishing experience records that he and a Malay fisherman caught one grouper whose weight was estimated at 880 pounds and that they had to sink their boat in order to get it "aboard" (which sounds a rather self-defeating procedure).

Reverting to the groupers which are best to eat, I mention *Epinephelus akaara*, which is the most expensive of all in Hong Kong, where it is known as *hung-paan*. When visiting the Pescadores Islands (west of Taiwan), I found that special measures are taken there to capture this species alive and to keep it alive until it is sold thus in the Hong Kong market. It is referred to as the "red grouper", but is really a brownish fish with red spots. It is indeed delicious, but I have never discovered what accounts for its outstanding quality; perhaps a superior diet, although all groupers tend to eat similarly, feeding on small fish and crustaceans.

Among the so-called "coral trout", *Plectropomus leopardus*, the leopard coral trout is outstanding. It is relatively large (maximum length 7 feet) and has a variable but always striking coloration; the body is pink, or even orange, and largely covered with dark-edged blue spots. *Variola louti*, sometimes called the "croissant trout", is also in the painting.

There are lots of things you can do with a grouper, and choice will depend partly on size and quality, both of which can vary considerably. Assuming that you have a good smallish grouper, this recipe will serve very well.

Steamed Grouper with Crab and Egg-white Sauce

1 grouper weighing about 2 pounds, cleaned	whites of 3 eggs
1 cup thick mushroom soup	1 tablespoon lard, melted
¼ cup crab meat	1 tablespoon cornstarch
	salt to taste

Steam the cleaned and scaled fish until it is just cooked through (10-15 minutes). Meanwhile, bring the soup to a boil and cook the crab meat in it for a few minutes. Mix the egg-white, lard, cornstarch and salt with a little water, add the mixture to the soup and bring to a boil again. Pour it over the steamed fish when you serve it.

This is my version of a recipe which originally came from Hong Kong. You can use various thick soups; tomato does well. Serves four.

Leopard coral-trout, *Plectropomus leopardus* (left); croissant trout, *Variola louti* (right)

Sea bream, large and small, provide a glistening array of tempting fare in Mediterranean markets. Mostly members of the large family Sparidae, they are particularly abundant in that sea. A fishmonger's display may range from the little annular bream and the two-banded bream through medium-sized fish such as the bogue and the pandora, the striped bream and the saddled bream, to larger fish such as the gilt-head bream (see page 42), perhaps the best of all.

Sea bream generally have oval, narrow bodies and are well suited to being broiled or baked whole but the quality of the flesh varies. Of the two fish shown whole in the painting, the upper is a dentex, one of the best. There are several species of dentex, and the names given (the A names) are the general ones; our specimen is *Dentex maroccanus*, not the biggest (its maximum length is 12 inches, whereas *D dentex* can be three times larger) but of excellent quality.

The lower of the two whole fish, the one with gold stripes, is the one to which the B names apply. It is the salema, *Sarpa salpa*, a herbivorous fish which is therefore called *chèvre* (goat) in Algeria. There is a saying in Tunisia, where the islanders of Kerkenna eat a lot of this fish, broiled, that it is at its best – most succulent – during the grape harvest. At other times it will benefit from steeping in a herby marinade before being cooked.

At the top of the painting we glimpse the black sea bream, *Spondyliosoma cantharus*. It is *griset* in French and *tanuta* in Italian. Classical authors found its lifestyle rich in lessons for humanity: Oppian declared that it was strictly monogamous, and Aelian commented that a black bream would fight for its mate with the same bravery that Menelaus showed in his combat with Paris over Helen.

The red bream, *Pagellus bogaraveo*, is the fish at the bottom. Like the black bream, it is of medium size (with a maximum length of 21 inches) and of good, but not outstanding, quality. Its big eye (not shown) accounts for the Italian name *occhialone*; while the French know it as *dorade commune* (note the spelling – *dorade* is not the same as *daurade*, which is the gilt-head bream).

Sea Bream with Fresh Fennel and White Wine

This is a favorite recipe, demonstrated to me in Marseilles by Mme Totte Feissel. She used an oven tray which held the juices and had a grid fitted over it to hold the fish just above them. If lacking this piece of equipment, use a shallow oven dish with a grid of some kind fitted into it.

1 or 2 fish of the sea bream family, weighing 2 pounds	salt and pepper to taste
sprigs of fresh fennel	1 cup dry white wine
sprigs of fresh thyme	1 tablespoon olive oil
1 tablespoon butter	several slices of tomato
	$\frac{1}{2}$ lemon, sliced thinly

Clean the fish and make incisions almost through to the backbone in its upper sides. Insert into these the feathery sprigs of fennel. Place the sprigs of thyme in the fish's belly cavity with the butter and salt and pepper. Now put the fish on its side on the grid (see above) and pour over it the white wine and olive oil, most of which will collect in the pan below. Add the slices of tomato to the liquid and place the lemon slices on top of the fish. Cook in the oven at 350° for 15-25 minutes, until the fish is cooked through (Mme Feissel emphasized that some members of the bream family cook faster than others). Baste from time to time if you can, but this is not essential. Strain off the cooking juices and serve them as a sauce with the fish. Serves four.

Alternative Fish
porgies (p 44)
small snappers (pp 60, 62)
ocean perch (p 94)

Alternative Recipes
Aurado i Poumo d'Amour (p 42)
Pargo con Salsa de Aguacate
(p 44)
Thai Grilled Caramelized Fish
(p 54)

From top to bottom: black sea bream, *Spondyliosoma cantharus*; dentex, *Dentex maroccanus*; salema, *Salpa salpa*, and red bream, *Pagellus bogaraveo*

Mediterranean Sea Breams

Gilt-head Bream
ENGLISH-SPEAKING COUNTRIES

daurade
FRENCH

Goldbrasse
GERMAN

doirada
PORTUGUESE

dorada
SPANISH

orada
CATALAN

orata
ITALIAN

tsipoŭra
GREEK

çipura
TURKISH

jerraf
ARABIC

The finest of the Mediterranean sea breams is *Sparus aurata*, the gilt-head bream, best known by its French name *daurade*. It is as well to know that there is a less good bream called *dorade* (see page 40), and to avoid any confusion. Both species occur also in the Atlantic, as far north as the English Channel.

The gilt-head has a maximum length of 28 inches, but it is unusual to find any in the markets which measure more than 18 inches. The crescent-shaped golden band which runs across the head between the eyes (a golden eyebrow, as one French author puts it) is a good recognition point and accounts for the "gold" motif which occurs in almost all the vernacular names. In classical times this fish was regarded as sacred to Aphrodite, the goddess of love.

There is increasing activity in the Mediterranean in the aquaculture of fish which have a high market value; the gilt-head, which is quite happy in brackish waters, is therefore farmed at various places in France, Italy (including Sicily) and Spain. Efforts are being made to do the same in Cyprus, Greece and Israel. In Tunisia, fishermen have long taken advantage of the willingness of the gilt-head to enter the huge Lake of Tunis and grow to a good size therein. (The only problem is that in a long spell of calm weather the level of oxygen in the waters of this lake sinks too low for the health of the fish. This is remedied by having speedboats zoom to and fro in the lake, oxygenating the water and providing a remarkably pleasant occupation for the speedboat-drivers.)

One reason for the esteem which the gilt-head enjoys is its convenient size. People sometimes overlook the existence of related species which have just as good a flavor but are too small to serve more than one person. These are often consigned to fish soups, but may deserve being broiled or fried. One of the best is *Diplodus vulgaris*, the two-banded bream (*sar doré* in French, because it has thin yellow bands running along its body, besides the two dark vertical bands). The *sar commun* (this is the French name – there is no real English name), *D sargus*, is larger (up to 18 inches) and also a good buy. So is the annular bream, *D annularis*.

However, my recipe is for the gilt-head bream. It is a simple Provençal affair, but has an additional paragraph which will refine it for those so inclined.

Aurado i Poumo d'Amour
(Gilt-head Bream with Tomato)

I gilt-head bream of 2¾ pounds, or 2 smaller ones	4 tomatoes, peeled, de-seeded and roughly chopped
½ stick butter	2 tablespoons parsley, chopped
I onion, peeled and finely chopped	salt and pepper to taste
	generous ½ cup white wine

Gut, scale, rinse and pat dry the fish, and cut it into four pieces. In an oven dish of suitable size, put the butter, onion, tomato, parsley and seasoning. On this bed place the pieces of fish, pour the wine over all, and cook, covered loosely with foil, in the oven at 355° for about 20 minutes, until the fish is done. Turn the fish over at the halfway point.

To refine the dish, make about 1 cup of *Sauce velouté* (see page 202), using really good chicken stock. Remove the fish from its dish and keep it hot. Pour the *Sauce velouté*, hot, into the juices in the dish, and reduce this mixture, stirring, for about ten minutes. Then strain the sauce.

You have now jumped from Provence to Paris and have made *Daurade à la Dugléré*. Serves four.

Alternative Fish
porgies (p 44)
snappers (pp 60, 62)
pomfret (p 96)

Alternative Recipes
Rougets à la Niçoise (p 48)
Red Snapper "Maraval" (p 60)

Annular bream, *Diplodus annularis* (top left); gilt-head bream, *Sparus aurita* (center);
two-banded bream, *Diplodus vulgaris* (bottom right)

Porgies

Porgies
ENGLISH-SPEAKING COUNTRIES

daubenet, sar, pagre
FRENCH (WEST INDIES)

pluma, sargo
SPANISH (WEST INDIES)

Moving from Europe to the other side of the Atlantic we encounter a change of name; most of the sea breams on the American side are called porgies.

Indeed there is one striking illustration of this. The species *Sparus pagrus,* which belongs to the Mediterranean and East Atlantic and is the French *pagre* (English, sea bream), occurs in the Caribbean too, as the European or red porgy. The reason why it, alone of the Mediterranean sea breams, is found in the West Indies is interesting. Westerly currents flow from the vicinity of the Strait of Gibraltar to the Caribbean and, naturally, carry with them among many other things the eggs of various kinds of fish. Any such eggs which hatch in mid-Atlantic are doomed; there is no continental shelf, equipped with nutrients for tiny fish, poised underneath. However, there happens to be a coincidence between the hatching time of the eggs of *Sparus pagrus* and the time which the currents take to bring them to the haven of Caribbean waters. There the tiny fish, unaware of the perilous journey they have made, hatch and thrive.

One of the two most important porgies on the eastern seaboard is the northern porgy or scup, *Stenotomus chrysops,* a fish whose alternative names perpetuate two parts of the Narragansett Indian name *mishcuppauog,* which early settlers abbreviated to "scuppaug" and which then split into two. The scup, which is brownish above and silvery below, has a maximum length of 18 inches and is a good fish, with firm and flaky flesh.

The sheepshead, *Archosargus probatocephalus,* enjoys even greater esteem. The natural historian Mitchill, who published a survey of the fishes of New York waters in 1815, declared that: "The outfitting of a Sheepshead party is always an occasion of considerable excitement and high expectation, as I have often experienced. Whenever a Sheepshead is brought on board the boat more joy is manifested than by the possession of any other kind of fish."

Further south, the number of species increases. The knobbed or Key West porgy, *Calamus nodosus,* is among the best and the most beautiful of those which frequent the shores of the southern United States and the Caribbean. It has knobbly protrusions in front of its eyes, above bright blue and yellow speckled cheeks.

Porgies may be steamed, broiled, fried; or, as below, poached. The recipe is adapted from Elisabeth Lambert Ortiz's *The Complete Book of Caribbean Cooking.*

Pargo con Salsa de Aguacate
(Porgy Cuban Style with Avocado Sauce)

In this recipe the *court bouillon* (see page 177) could include ½ teaspoon each of thyme and oregano, and the juice of 2 limes.

1 porgy of nearly 2 pounds (cleaned weight)	1 tablespoon lime juice
court bouillon	2 tablespoons vegetable oil
for the sauce	½ teaspoon salt
2 medium avocados	ground black pepper to taste

Alternative Fish
Mediterranean sea breams
(pp 40, 42)
snappers (pp 60, 62)
pompano (p 54)

Alternative Recipes
Aurado i Poumo d'Amour (p 42)
Ikan Masak Molek (p 62)

Poach the fish in the *court bouillon* for 20 minutes or until done. Lift it out carefully onto a wooden board and peel off the skin on both sides. Then transfer it to a heated platter (if serving hot) or leave to cool (if serving cold). Meanwhile, peel and seed the avocados, then mash them with a fork. Add the other ingredients and beat to the consistency of a mayonnaise. Pour over the fish. Serves four.

Three porgies: sheepshead, *Archosargus probatocephalus* (left); northern porgy or scup, *Stenotomus chrysops* (head and tail only); knobbed or Key West porgy, *Calamus nodosus* (right)

Asian Breams & Threadfins

46

The sea bream (also called porgy in the US) and related families are represented in the Indo-Pacific, and especially in Asian waters, by lots of species, many of which are of little gastronomic interest, but some of which certainly deserve attention. They are carnivorous fish, abounding among coastal reefs. Like the snappers (page 60), they have strong teeth and are often red in color; or, as with the threadfin breams, pink and yellow.

The best Asian member of the family Sparidae (that of the true sea breams or porgies) is *Mylio berda*, the black sea bream. It is not black, but dark gray/silver, or olive/brown with a black spot at the base of most scales and silvery or brassy reflections. Its range extends right down to South Africa, where it is called picnic bream. A close relation is *Argyrops spinifer*, which is smaller and red, and with its dorsal fin prolonged into filaments (although it is not classified as a "threadfin").

Another good fish, belonging to the family Pentapodidae, and possessing the attractive name "ginkgo fish", is *Gymnocranius griseus*. Its larger relation, *G rivulatus*, shown at the top of the painting, reaches a length of 24 inches, and is the capitaine blanc of the Seychelles. The name "capitaine", the origin of which has eluded my enquiries so far, crops up again in the Seychelles names for a couple of fish in the family Lethrinidae, the pigface breams; *Lethrinus nebulosus*, for example, is the capitaine rouge. Pigface is perhaps not quite right for the shape of the face seen at the foot of the painting; this face belongs to the "red emperor", *L lentjan*.

Midway between breams and true threadfins come the "threadfin breams" such as the pink and yellow *Nemipterus japonicus*, which has a filament extending from its tail fin as well as its ventral fin. This is a smallish fish, as can be seen from the pair in the center of the painting, but of commercial importance. However, the threadfin bream which is best known in Hong Kong, and indeed reputedly the most abundant seafood there, is *N virgatus* – locally called *hung sam* or golden thread.

It is not difficult to see why the real threadfins, tropical fish of the family Polynemidae, are so called. The lower part of their pectoral fins consists of very long rays, sometimes longer than the body of the fish. These serve as organs of touch, helping them to detect their prey.

Eleutheronema tetradactylon, a species which has a range from India through Southeast Asia, may reach a length of over 5 feet, but is usually much smaller. It is silvery green above and creamy below. It is a fish of commercial importance in India, and is highly esteemed in Thailand – to be fried, boiled, steamed, roasted, pickled, or dried. The specific name means "four-fingered", referring to its four long rays. Some related species have six or seven, but the one which costs most in Thailand, where it is in demand for some special fish soups, is *E tridactylon*, which has three.

Polynemus indicus, a rather small species with a similar range (but not in Australian waters), is a golden fish which enters estuaries. It is common on the west coast of Malaya. *P paradisius*, the *tupsi* fish of India and the mango fish (*nga-pon-na*) of Burma, is quite small (just over 8 inches) but is regarded as a delicacy in both countries. In Thailand it is *pla nuat phram*, meaning the fish with a Brahmin moustache.

The genus *Polydactylus* ("many-fingered" – they gave up counting) is represented in the East Pacific (Peru to California) by *P approximans*; and in the West Atlantic by *P virginius*, which is common in the West Indies. Both of these are small fish.

All these fish may be treated in the same ways as the other sea breams described on the two preceding pages. For those who would like to match their Asian origin with an Asian recipe, I particularly recommend a "curry" fish dish such as that given on page 110.

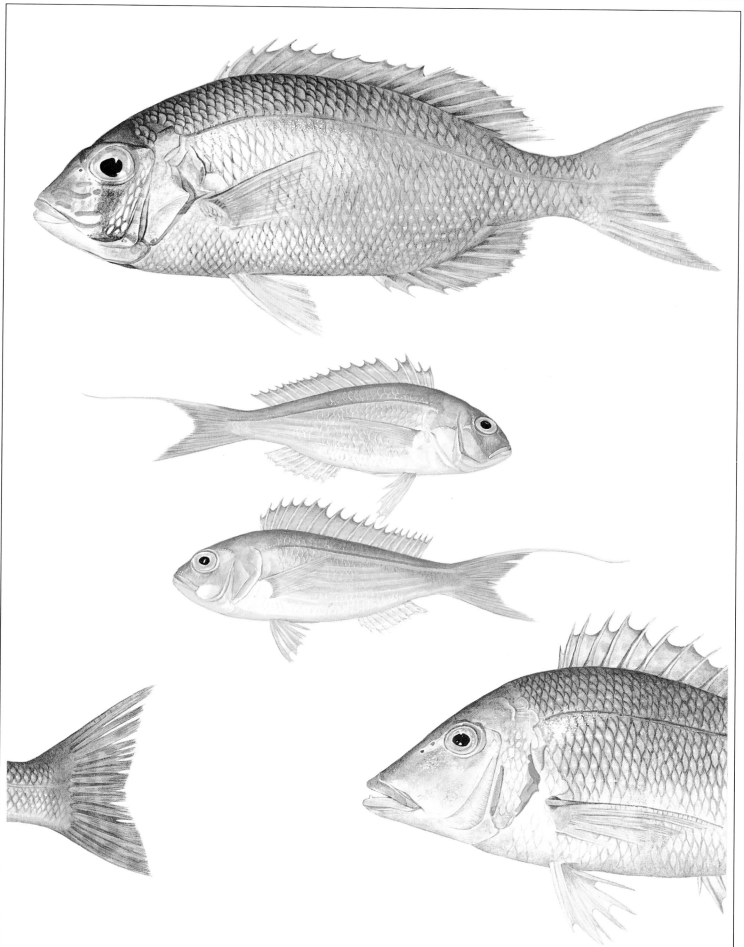

From top to bottom: capitaine blanc, *Gymnocranius rivulatus*; threadfin breams, *Nemipterus japonicus*, and red emperor, *Lethrinus lentjan*

Red Mullet

Red mullet are among the most prized fish of the Mediterranean, distinguished by their crimson color and delicate flesh, and by the twin barbels with which they "frisk" the sea bottom for their food. The two most common species, *Mullus barbatus* and *M surmuletus*, are also found in the Atlantic as far north as the south coast of Britain.

M barbatus is smaller, with a maximum length of 10 inches, and paler than *M surmuletus* whose maximum length is 16 inches. The latter usually bears horizontal yellow stripes on its sides, and many of its common names mean "of the rocks" (thus, French: *rouget de roche*, Italian: *triglia di scoglio*).

In classical antiquity there was a craze for large red mullet. Wealthy Romans would pay the equivalent of, say, $2,000 for a really outsize specimen. This was foolish, because they do not improve as they grow larger; if there is a difference, it is the small and medium-size fish which have the finest texture and flavor.

Other species of red mullet are now found in the Mediterranean. When de Lesseps built the Suez Canal, he was creating a passage for ships, not fish; and at first fish could not get through because the water in the two Bitter Lakes through which the Canal passes was too salty for them. But in recent decades the salt level in these lakes has declined to a level which fish can tolerate, and a couple of Indo-Pacific species of red mullet (or "goatfish" as they are known in Asian waters because of their barbels) have taken advantage of this and established themselves as breeding populations in the eastern Mediterranean.

Meanwhile at the western end, the species *Pseudupeneus prayensis*, the West African goatfish (or *rouget-barbet du Sénégal*) has also penetrated Mediterranean waters. It is this species which is illustrated.

There are over a dozen species of goatfish in Indo-Pacific waters, some with a very wide range, from East Africa and the Persian Gulf through Southeast Asia, up to China and Japan and down to parts of Australia and even New Zealand. Among the best known are *Parupeneus indicus*, the Indian goatfish; *Upeneus moluccensis*, the goldband goatfish (one of the immigrants to the Mediterranean); and *U vittatus*, with a bronze head and back and dark bronze longitudinal bands.

In Mediterranean countries it is usual to broil or fry red mullet, or to bake them. In Asian countries they are often boiled or steamed. Either way, the liver is a delicacy which should not be overlooked. (Indeed many people advocate cooking red mullet whole and uncleaned.)

Rougets à la Niçoise

4 medium-size red or 8 small mullet	4 tomatoes, peeled and chopped
generous ½ cup olive oil and a little more	½ teaspoon tomato paste
for frying	1 *bouquet garni*
1 onion, chopped	6 tablespoons white wine
1 clove garlic, finely chopped	8 black olives
2 tablespoons parsley, chopped	slices of lemon

Heat the olive oil and lightly brown the onion in it, with the garlic and parsley. Add the tomatoes, tomato paste (which is not to be omitted, though the quantity is small) and *bouquet garni*; season and cook for 15 minutes.

Meanwhile clean and scale the red mullet and fry them lightly in the rest of the olive oil, just enough to stiffen them.

When the sauce has cooked for 15 minutes, add the white wine, the red mullet and the olives. Cook for ten minutes more, covered, over a low heat. Serve with slices of lemon. Serves four.

Red mullet (goatfish) of the western Mediterranean and West Africa, *Pseudupeneus prayensis*

Croakers

50

Croakers are fish of tropical and warm temperate waters, found worldwide. Most are edible, but not especially good. A few croakers are excellent fare. But they are all good at croaking, loudly, like frogs. They make this noise when they are pulled out of the water but also, and primarily, when they are in the water. In Malaysia, fishermen employ one of their number, who is known as *Jeru selam*, to lower himself under water and listen for the noise. From what he hears he can infer the size of the shoal, the species, and its approximate position, so that he can tell the fishermen how to set their nets.

The question poses itself: why do they croak? One suggested explanation is that many of these fish, all of which belong to the family Sciaenidae, live at least part of the time in turbid estuarine waters where additional navigational equipment, such as a sonar system provides, is desirable. This theory is buttressed by the observation that they are in other respects better equipped than most fish to find their way around in murky waters, having remarkably well developed otoliths (ear stones, another piece of sonar equipment).

It is in the West Atlantic, where they are more likely to be called drums, or by names which have nothing to do with noise (some sciaenid fish, oddly, cannot croak), that the family seems to be at its best. The northern kingfish, *Menticirrhus saxatilis*, common from Chesapeake Bay to New York, is perhaps the best of all. The southern kingfish, *M americanus*, has a more southerly range, as does the Gulf kingfish, *M littoralis*, (often called "mullet" in the Gulf of Texas). All these species lack croaking equipment; it is said that to make up for this they grind their teeth, thus making at least some noise.

The red drum, *Sciaenops ocellata*, well known southwards from Chesapeake Bay, is also good; and the weakfish (so called because its tender flesh tears easily), *Cynoscion regalis*, is fine if eaten very fresh. The females of this last species are mute, whereas the males can croak strongly; a fact which leaves one wondering about the finding-their-way-around theory, unless of course one supposes that the males gallantly guide the females. The weakfish also goes under the name *squeteague*; but it and its close relation the spotted weakfish are also called "sea trout", which is confusing since they are not trout at all.

Most Australian croakers are known by the mysterious name "jewfish", but one of the best, *Sciaena antarctica*, also bears the name mulloway. The so-called "meagre", *Argyrosomus regius*, which appears in the painting, is a croaker of excellent quality found in the Mediterranean and East Atlantic.

Fried Drum Southern Style with Hush Puppies

4 croaker fillets
4 tablespoons white cornmeal
2 teaspoons paprika (optional)
oil for frying and deep frying
for the hush puppies
8 tablespoons white cornmeal
3 teaspoons baking powder

2 tablespoons vegetable oil
4 tablespoons milk
4 tablespoons flour
$\frac{1}{2}$ teaspoon salt
1 teaspoon sugar
$\frac{1}{4}$ teaspoon black pepper
2 tablespoons minced onion

Coat your fillets of fish in white cornmeal, colored with paprika if you wish, fry them, and keep them warm while you prepare the accompaniment.

Mix the hush puppy ingredients together and drop the mixture, a teaspoonful at a time, into hot deep fat, using a wire basket. Turn the puppies at once, using a fork, and lift them out when they are brown, after two or three minutes. Drain, and serve with the fried fillets. Serves four.

From top to bottom: the spot, *Leiostomus xanthurus*; the meagre, *Argyrosomus regius*; and the weakfish, *Cynoscion regalis*

Bluefish

Here is a prime example of a fish which has a very wide distribution, yet is thought of in certain places as being purely local. For anglers on the eastern seaboard of the USA, the "blues" are "theirs". In Turkey, one will find people who suppose that the beloved *lüfer*, as they call it, is not to be found except in the region of the Bosphorus. Yet *Pomatomus saltatrix*, to give it its proper name, is found in many parts of the world, in temperate and semi-tropical seas, though not quite as widely distributed as some books suggest. (Many authors state that the bluefish is ubiquitous in the Indian Ocean and Southeast Asian waters, but I have never found it there, nor any convincing evidence of its presence except in Southeast African and Australian waters.)

Bluefish, which may reach a length of 4 feet, are among the most voracious of fish. Swimming in groups, they ruthlessly attack shoals of smaller fish, often killing far more than they can eat. A graphic description of the carnage they wreak was given by Jordan and Evermann in 1902: ". . . they move along like a pack of hungry wolves, destroying everything before them. Their trail is marked by fragments of fish and by the stain of blood in the sea, as, when the fish is too large to be swallowed entire, the hinder portion will be bitten off and the anterior part allowed to float or sink. It has even been maintained that such is the gluttony of this fish, that when the stomach becomes full the contents are disgorged and then again filled!"

Bluefish are said to be cannibals, and it follows from this that any group of them will consist of fish of the same size; otherwise the bigger ones would be apt to eat

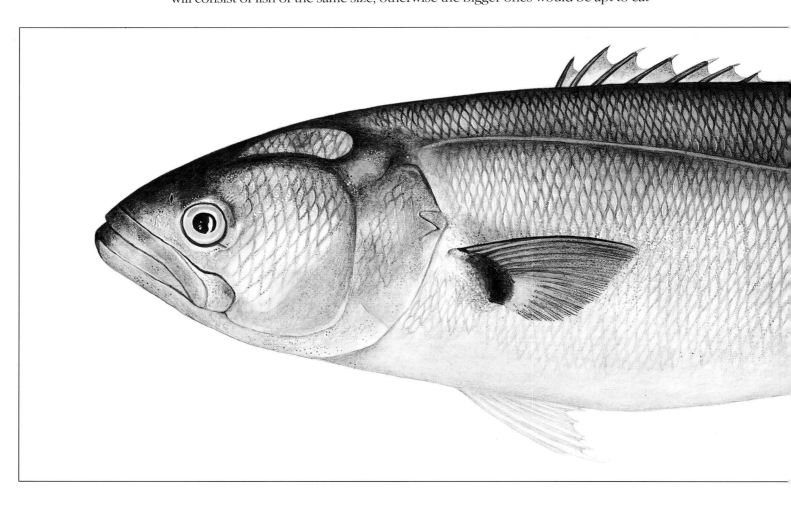

the smaller ones. Movements of the shoals are governed by changes in water temperature, and fishing for them progresses up the eastern seaboard of the USA from spring to summer to fall. Their annual migrations through the Bosphorus give rise to corresponding seasonal fisheries there. The Black Sea and Turkey apart, the region of the Mediterranean where bluefish are most commonly marketed seems to be Tunisia, which is where I got to know it.

In Australia the bluefish is called tailor. What is called bluefish in New Zealand is a quite different fish, *Girella cyanea* of the drummer family.

Bluefish should be eaten very fresh, since their flesh, which is moderately oily, begins to soften quite quickly to an undesirable extent. However, they freeze well. They may be broiled, fried, baked, or poached; smoked bluefish are also fine. The recipe which follows is from the Black Sea coast of Romania.

n'gotte
MAURETANIA

eschtiqué
SENEGAL

elf or elft
SOUTH AFRICA

Lacherdă la Grătar cu Sos de Muştar şi Smântână
(Bluefish with Mustard Sauce)

1½ pounds cleaned and skinned bluefish	2 tablespoons butter
3 tablespoons olive oil	1 tablespoon flour
salt and pepper	1 tablespoon white wine
juice of ½ lemon	1 tablespoon made mustard
3 tablespoons parsley, chopped	2 small canned sardines, finely chopped
and for the sauce	2 tablespoons lemon juice

Rub the fish with the olive oil, lemon juice and seasoning and leave it for at least an hour with the chopped parsley strewn over it. Gently rub the marinade into it every now and then, then broil the fish. To make the sauce, melt the butter, stir in the flour, add ½ cup water and the wine, and stir. Then add the mustard and sardines. Simmer for another three or four minutes, add the lemon juice and simmer for three minutes more. This sauce is served with the fish. Sour cream is served as a separate accompaniment. Serves four.

Alternative Fish
Spanish mackerel (p 82)
scabbard fish (p 74)

Alternative recipes
Pangek Bungkus (p 57)
Pla Tod Laad Prik (p 74)
Bonito à la Asturiana (p 84)

53

Bluefish, *Pomatomus saltator*

Jacks

Pompano, Horse Mackerel & Trevally

54

The Jack family, the subject of this and the following page, is a large one which contains over 200 species, some very good to eat and others less so. The painting opposite shows, from top to bottom: the lowly horse mackerel of the Mediterranean and East Atlantic, the splendid pompano of the Caribbean and West Atlantic and the trevally of Australasia.

Being surface swimmers, and sharing with other fish a general anxiety to escape detection by predators, jacks typically have blue-green backs and silvery undersides. Their length varies. Some are small, whereas *Caranx sexfasciatus*, the great trevally which occurs widely in the Indo-Pacific, may reach a length well over 4 feet. Some are much deeper in the body than others, but they all have relatively narrow bodies.

It would really be better to refer to the group as the carangid family, rather than jacks. To be sure, many of them are called jacks; but the names scad and trevally, and pompano too, are applied in a confusing way to many of them. There is even one species which bears the name "crevalle jack". As is often the case with fish in waters far from England, the English names bestowed by colonists are not a good means of identification.

The horse mackerel, *Trachurus mediterraneus* and *T picturatus*, are not highly esteemed as food, being thin and somewhat dry. Yet people in the Mediterranean, with their long traditions of fish cookery and of exploiting all food resources, know how to make them palatable.

In contrast, the pompano, *Trachinotus carolinus*, which has a maximum length of 18 inches, is excellent fare. "As a food fish there is none better than the pompano, either in the fresh waters or in the seas. This is practically the unanimous verdict of epicures and all others who have had the pleasure of eating the pompano, fresh from the water. The flesh is firm and rich, and possesses a delicacy of flavor peculiarly pleasing to the palate." So said Jordan and Evermann, the great American authorities.

Enthusiasm for *T ovatus*, a species found on both sides of the Atlantic and in the Mediterranean, is less great, perhaps because it is less plentiful. It is a fine fish, which the French call *palomine*, and the Spaniards *palometa blanca*.

The trevally of New Zealand and Australia, *Caranx georgianus*, sometimes called silver or white trevally, has a fine flavor but has to be eaten without delay, since it does not keep well unless it is smoked.

To cater for such a wide variety of fish, a versatile recipe is needed, such as this one from Thailand. There, it would often be used for flatfish, but it is equally suitable for smallish jacks, with their relatively thin bodies.

Thai Grilled Caramelized Fish

4 small, thin-bodied fish or 2 larger ones
1 teaspoon salt
juice of 1 lime
4-6 tablespoons light brown sugar

Rub the fish with the salt and lime juice and leave in a cool place until they are ready to be grilled. The longer you can leave them, the better. Just before grilling, rub the fish all over with the sugar and grill them over charcoal for about three minutes on each side, turning them once. Serve immediately. In Thailand, some sort of chili sauce would accompany the dish. Serves four.

Horse Mackerel
ENGLISH-SPEAKING COUNTRIES

saurel; séveran (Midi)
FRENCH

Stöcker, Bastardmakrele
GERMAN

borsmakreel
DUTCH

carapau, chicharro
PORTUGUESE

jurel
SPANISH

suro
ITALIAN

savridi
GREEK

istavrit
TURKISH

Pompano
ENGLISH-SPEAKING COUNTRIES

palomine
FRENCH

Bläuel
GERMAN

sereia
PORTUGUESE

palometa blanca
SPANISH

leccia stella
ITALIAN

litsa
GREEK

yaladerma
TURKISH

Trevally
ENGLISH-SPEAKING COUNTRIES

cavalla, scad
INDO-PACIFIC

sui chan
CHINESE

Alternative Fish
any fish suitable for being broiled

Alternative Recipes
few recipes suit all the jack family

From top to bottom: the pompano, *Trachinotus carolinus*; a horse mackerel, *Trachurus mediterraneus*;
and a trevally, *Caranx georgianus*

56

The large jack family includes the two fish shown here. The right-hand one is an amberjack of the Mediterranean and Atlantic, *Seriola dumerili*, which is quite a large fish (up to 50 inches). It is appreciated in the Mediterranean, where fishery statistics suggest that it is relatively abundant in the waters round Cyprus, although the largest catches seem to be made in Israel. In the Caribbean, however, it may be a source of cigatuera poisoning (see page 76) and is not popular. The amberjacks also include several smaller species in the Indo-Pacific, where rudderfish and yellowtail are the English names often used; one of these is *S nigrofasciata*, which has a wide distribution.

The other fish shown is one of those which has achieved a circumglobal distribution in tropical waters. It is the rainbow runner, *Elagatis bipinnulatus*, and in life its colors are sufficiently vivid and rainbow-like (a bluish green back with broad blue stripes and yellow lines running along it) to justify the name; but the colors fade after death. The fish in the painting came from the Indian Ocean, but might just as well have come from the Caribbean.

Although the rainbow runner is of good edible quality, it has never been prominent in markets, no doubt because it is a roving fish of the deep seas, rarely found in inshore waters, and there has been little commercial fishing for it. However, its reputation as a game fish is high. It has been recorded as reaching a length of 4 feet and a weight of 31 pounds.

For these and many other fish one could not do better than follow the excellent

recipe by Sri Owen (from her *Indonesian and Thai Cookery*) which I give below.

Pangek Bungkus
(Sumatran Oven-steamed Fish with Spices and Herbs)

I whole fish of 4-5 pounds
juice of I lime or lemon
I teaspoon salt
½ teaspoon chili powder
I stalk lemon grass
2 Kaffir lime leaves or bay leaves
for the spice mixture
4 shallots
2 cloves garlic

3 candlenuts (optional)
2-4 large red chilies, de-seeded and chopped
1¼ cups very thick coconut milk
I teaspoon ground coriander
pinch galingale powder
¼ teaspoon turmeric powder
2 tablespoons mint or basil, chopped
6 scallions, thinly sliced

Gut and scale the fish. Then make three diagonal slashes on each side of it, and rub the fish inside and out with the lime or lemon juice, salt and chili powder. Put the lemon grass and Kaffir lime leaves or bay leaves inside the fish. Leave the fish in a cool place while preparing the rest of the ingredients.

Put the shallots, garlic, candlenuts (if used) and chilies in a blender with 4 tablespoons coconut milk, and blend to a smooth paste. Put the paste in a saucepan, bring to the boil, stir and add the ground coriander, galingale powder, turmeric powder and salt. Adjust the seasoning and leave to cool.

Lay the fish on three layers of wide foil. Pour over it half the thick spiced mixture and spoon a small amount inside the cavity. Turn the fish over and pour the rest of the mixture over the other side. Then spread the chopped herbs and scallions all over the fish. Wrap the foil around it and steam in the oven at 350° for 35 to 40 minutes. Serve hot or cold. Serves four.

pla sam lee
THAI

pisang pisang
MALAY

(names for rainbow runner:)
fogueteiro-arco-iris
PORTUGUESE

tsumuburi
JAPANESE

pla kluay kaw
THAI

pisang pisang
MALAY

sunglir
INDONESIAN

salmon
PHILIPPINES

Alternative Fish
almost any fish of suitable size

Alternative Recipes
Broiled Barramundi Steaks (p 34)
Mérou Blanc with Rosemary Sauce (p 36)
Sri Lankan Fish "Moilee" (p 64)
Soho Fish Pie (p 194)

57

The rainbow runner, *Elagatis bipinnulatus* (left); and an amberjack, *Seriola dumerili* (right)

Tilefish

Tilefish
ENGLISH-SPEAKING COUNTRIES

blankbil
RUSSIAN

ma tau
CHINESE

amadai
JAPANESE

One of the most brilliantly colored of all fish is the tilefish of the Northwest Atlantic, *Lopholatilus chamaeleonticeps*. It may be over 40 inches long, but the usual adult length is 32 inches.

The specific name *chamaeleonticeps* is not quite appropriate. A chamaeleon can change its coloration at will, whereas a tilefish cannot; it merely exhibits a remarkable range of colors. Leim and Scott have described it as "bluish to olive-green on back and upper part of sides, changing to yellow and rose on lower sides and belly, latter with white midline. Head reddish on sides, white below. Back and sides above lateral line thickly dotted with irregular yellow spots. Dorsal fin dusky with larger yellowish spots . . . ; anal fin pinkish with purple to blue iridescence; pectoral pale sooty-brown with purplish reflections." This astonishing coloration fades rapidly after death, so the painting, which is of a tilefish as you would see it in a fishmonger's shop, does not mirror it.

The range of this tilefish extends from Venezuela to Nova Scotia, but its presence in the northern part of the range has fluctuated considerably. An influx of cold water into these haunts can kill it off by the million. Since it is a deep-water offshore species, the tilefish was unknown until some were caught in 1879; but, once "discovered", it became a favorite table fish. Its flesh is fine-grained and has an excellent flavor. The advice usually offered to the cook is to treat it like cod.

The name tilefish has a wider application; it may refer to other species in the family Branchiostegidae, most of them confined to warmer waters such as those of

the Caribbean. The soberly colored gray tilefish, *Caulotilus microps*, is an example. The other members of the family which have some culinary renown are the Japanese tilefish, of which three kinds occur: red, yellow, and white. The white is considered the best.

Since the Japanese have devoted more attention than anyone else to ways of cooking tilefish, I give a Japanese recipe, adapted from a version which Professor Tsuji expounds in his *Japanese Cooking*, which to my mind is the best book on the subject. He explains that the dish has its origins in the time when tilefish had to be salted in order to preserve them on their journey from Wakasa Bay, where they were caught, to Kyoto.

Tilefish Wakasa

I tilefish weighing 2 pounds	*for the garnish*
salt	lettuce
for the basting mixture	2 lemons, quartered
½ cup saké	a few pickled ginger shoots
½ cup light soy sauce	(ask for *hajikaji shoga*)

Cut the fish into two fillets, leaving the skin, scales and pectoral fins in place, but using tweezers to remove any small bones. Salt lightly on both sides and leave for two hours. Wash well, pat dry and thread onto skewers passed crosswise through the front end of each fillet. Hang in a cool, dry place for 24 hours.

Cut each fillet into two or three pieces and re-skewer them in such a way that the pieces will broil evenly. First, grill them skin side down over a hot charcoal fire for five minutes. Then turn the skewers over and grill for another three minutes, but further from the heat (or, as Tsuji suggests, protecting the flesh with a layer of damp paper). As soon as the second side becomes lightly browned, brush both sides with the basting mixture and broil until this dries, then repeat the process. Serve on a bed of lettuce with garnish as indicated. Serves four.

Alternative Fish
mahi-mahi (p 66)
bass (p 32)

Alternative Recipes
Lampuki Pie (p 67)
Steamed Parrotfish and Julienne
Vegetables (p 70)

59

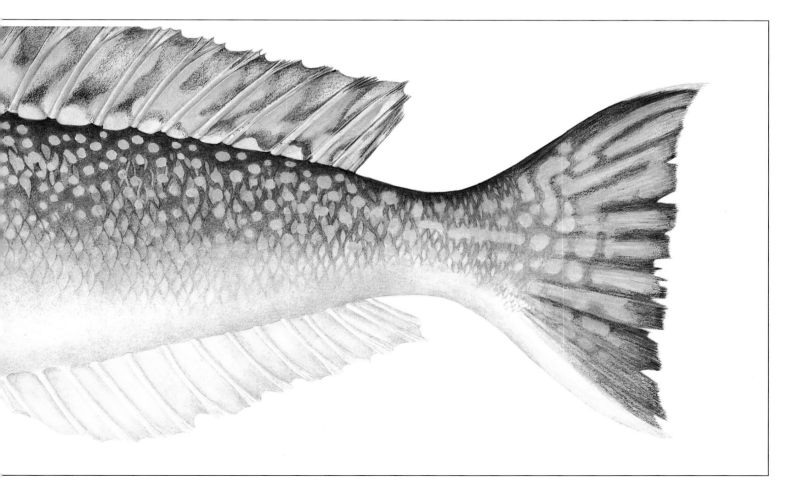

The tilefish of North American waters, *Lopholatilus chamaeleonticeps*

Caribbean Snappers
ENGLISH-SPEAKING COUNTRIES

vivaneau
FRENCH

Schnapper
GERMAN

castanholas
PORTUGUESE

pargo
SPANISH

60

The snappers, of which there are numerous species in the family Lutjanidae (although not all members of that family bear the name), are indigenous to the tropics and of great interest to cooks there. But nowadays cooks elsewhere are taking more of an interest, since the fish are marketed further and further from their waters of origin. The fish are mostly of medium size, typically about 14-25 inches long when adult, and distributed around the world. They are sparsely represented in the East Pacific, and not at all in the Mediterranean, which is not warm enough. Their heads are usually long and pointed, and their jaws, equipped with canine-like teeth, can snap vigorously. Most of them are good edible fish, some outstandingly so.

The painting here shows some snappers from tropical West Atlantic waters.
● *Ocyurus chrysurus*, the yellowtail snapper, whose colorful body is bluish with yellow spots and a horizontal yellow stripe. Its maximum length is 22 inches. Cubans like it fried, but it is also a fine eating fish when broiled or baked.
● *Lutjanus vivanus*, the silk snapper, which has lots of other names, for example "yellow-eye" in the Carolinas and "day red snapper" further south. Its maximum length is 35 inches, but market size is about two-thirds of this.
● *Rhomboplites aurorubens*, the vermilion snapper, which is relatively small (maximum length 24 inches) but very common. It fetches almost as high a price as *L campechanus* (see below), and is perhaps even redder.

But these are not the only snappers in the Caribbean area, which is rich in species. Others of repute include *Lutjanus campechanus*, the red snapper, and the most highly esteemed of all (which accounts in part for the fishmongers' habit of describing any snapper which is even faintly reddish as "red snapper") which can be 40 inches long.

Red Snapper "Maraval"

This recipe is taken from Barrow and Lee (see bibliography) two amateur cooks of the West Indies who wrote in vivid detail of their experiences in the kitchen.

I red snapper, weighing nearly 2 pounds (cleaned weight)	bunch of chives, thyme, celery leaves, parsley, minced
I tablespoon flour	*and for the sauce*
2 tablespoons oil for frying the fish	$\frac{1}{2}$ stick butter
for seasoning	I onion, minced
I clove garlic, minced	$\frac{1}{2}$ cup white wine
I teaspoon salt	I teaspoon sugar
I teaspoon white pepper	$\frac{1}{2}$ tablespoon salt
I tablespoon rum	juice of $\frac{1}{2}$ lime
	$\frac{1}{2}$ teaspoon cornstarch

Alternative Fish
Asian snappers & jobfish
(pp 62, 64)
Mediterranean sea breams,
porgies (pp 40, 42, 44)

Alternative Recipes
Sea Bream with Fresh Fennel and
White Wine (p 40)
Meuilles à la Charentaise (p 78)
Turbot with Lime and Green
Ginger (p 100)

Season the fish with the ingredients indicated, but using only half the minced herbs, and leave to absorb the flavors for at least an hour. Dust the fish in the flour and fry it in the oil for long enough to make the skin really crisp. Remove it and drain. Melt the butter in a large frying pan. Add the onion, with the rest of the minced herbs and fry until tender, but do not allow to brown. Add the wine, sugar, salt, lime juice, and about four tablespoons of water. Put the fish in the pan with this sauce, cover, and cook on a low heat for ten minutes. Turn the fish over and cook for another ten minutes. Then remove the fish to a heated serving platter. Dissolve the cornstarch in a little water and stir into the sauce to thicken. Pour the sauce over the fish and serve. Serves four.

Three Caribbean snappers: yellowtail snapper, *Ocyurus chrysurus* (right); silk snapper, *Lutjanus vivanus* (center); and vermilion snapper, *Rhomboplites aurorubens* (left)

Asian Snappers

Asian Snappers
ENGLISH-SPEAKING COUNTRIES

hamrah
ARABIC (PERSIAN GULF)

ranga (Be), rangu (Te); konde sevalai (Ta: Malabar snapper)
INDIAN LANGUAGES

nga-pahni
BURMESE

hung yu (red snappers)
CHINESE

sennendai, fuedai
JAPANESE

pla kaphong
THAI

ikan merah (red snappers)
MALAY & INDONESIAN

maya-maya
PHILIPPINES

The profusion of snappers in Asian waters, and their importance as seafood, calls for some introductory remarks, well provided by J S Scott: "The family includes some of the best-known of the Malayan fishes, several species being known collectively as *ikan merah*, that highly-esteemed, almost essential part of any important dinner . . . The different species exhibit a wide range of colors . . . but most have a fairly characteristic body-shape in common . . . They are small to medium-size fishes, most of them with a fairly straight ventral profile and an arched dorsal profile with a pointed snout and large, well-toothed mouth, the snapping of which, when they are caught, giving them their common name. They are for the most part brightly colored, the larger specimens in general deep red, the smaller predominantly yellow or silvery, usually with colored lines or spots."

Among the finest of these fish are:

- *L argentimaculatus*, red snapper (or "mangrove jack"), which grows up to 31 inches in length. Its coloration is gray to pink above, shading to pink below, sometimes with a silvery spot on each scale.
- *L sanguineus*, also called the red snapper, which is very similar but has a black saddle just in front of the tail fin. It belongs to the western side of the Indian Ocean.
- *L malabaricus*, the Malabar blood snapper, which is shown on the left of the painting, half the size of the preceding species, and red or orange-red. It is one of the main commercial species in the Persian Gulf: *hamrah* in Kuwait, scarlet sea perch in Australia.
- *L gibbus*, the humpback snapper, shown on the right of the painting, is of similar size. Its distinctive tail fin gives it the name "paddle-tail" in Australia.
- *L sebae*, the emperor or "Government bream", shown in the center of the painting. Its maximum length is about 40 inches. The adults are red but darker above, whereas younger specimens are pale and bear bold stripes resembling the arrow mark which was used to identify government property in Malaya (or, I suppose, because the stripes suggest that the fish is entangled in red tape).
- *L kasmira*, the common bluestripe snapper, which grows up to 14 inches in length. It is yellow with four bright blue stripes along the sides.

Ikan Masak Molek
(Steamed Snapper "Yazmin")

1 whole snapper weighing 2 pounds, cleaned
1 teaspoon powdered turmeric
coconut cream from 1 whole coconut
7 ounces shallots, peeled
6 slices fresh ginger, cut into strips
2 dried slices of "apple tamarind" (or substitute a very little regular tamarind)
salt and pepper to taste
4 fresh red chili peppers, each partly quartered, for garnish

Alternative Fish
Caribbean snappers (p 60)
Mediterranean sea breams, porgies (pp 40, 42, 44)

Alternative Recipes
Loup de Mer Farci (p 33)
Aurado i Poumo d'Amour (p 42)
Pargo con Salsa de Aguacate (p 44)

"*Molek*" is an epithet which, when applied to a young woman, indicates a multiplicity of attractive features of which physical beauty is just one.

On the assumption that the snapper comes ready gutted and scaled, rinse it and set it to steam until cooked through (about 20 minutes). Meanwhile add the turmeric to the coconut cream and heat it gently to simmering point, add the shallots, ginger, apple tamarind and seasoning and simmer until the shallots are tender. Put the fish on a platter. Pour the sauce over it, garnish, and serve with steamed rice. Serves four.

Three Asian snappers from the Seychelles: Malabar snapper or bordemer *Lutjanus malabaricus* (left); emperor, government bream or bourgeois, *L sebae* (center); and humpback snapper or therese, *L gibbus* (right)

Jobfish

64

Job was a prophet, but I don't think that it is he who is being referred to in the name jobfish, which is given to fish of the snapper family in three of its genera: *Aphareus, Aprion* and *Pristipomoides*. These are found in tropical waters around the world, especially the Caribbean and the Indo-Pacific, and are important food fishes in some regions, notably the islands of the Indo-West Pacific. They are all small to medium in size. To give an idea of how many different fish there are in this one branch of the snapper family, I list some of the species:

● *Aphareus rutilans*, the small-toothed (or rusty) jobfish or silvery-gilled snapper, maximum length 32 inches (*A furcatus* is very similar but half the size). It ranges from the Seychelles to the Pacific Islands, regularly marketed in some places, including Hawaii and Hong Kong (where it is known as *ngun soi gor lay*).

● *Aprion virescens*, the green jobfish, maximum length 40 inches, widely distributed from East Africa to the Pacific Islands, a good eating fish which is usually marketed fresh but may also be dried and salted. It is highly rated in Hawaii, where frying (of fillets) is the cooking method recommended by local authors.

● *Pristipomoides auricilla*, the goldflag jobfish, maximum length 18 inches; it is a common foodfish in Samoa and Guam, for example.

● *P filamentosus*, the crimson (or rosy) jobfish, maximum length 32 inches, range from South and East Africa to Hawaii. It is of good quality and important (as *opakapaka*) in Hawaii.

● *P flavipinnis*, the golden eye jobfish, maximum length 24 inches, range from East Indonesia into the Pacific, an important market fish in some areas.

● *P sieboldii*, the lavender jobfish, maximum length 24 inches, ranging from the Seychelles to the Pacific Islands. It is marketed in, for example, Japan (as *himedai*) and Hawaii (as *kalikali*).

● *P typus*, the sharptooth jobfish or big-eyed snapper, maximum length 28 inches, found in the tropical West Pacific and possibly in the Indian Ocean. It has a dorsal fin with gray spots, and is a good fish, usually marketed fresh.

Although the jobfish are classed with the snappers, and some of them may be called snappers, they are generally distinguished by having less deep, leaner bodies. In shape they are not unlike the striped bass (see page 32) and, although their flesh is not quite as good, it may be prepared in similar ways.

My recommended recipe provides four small portions, which would be served with other dishes. "*Moilee*" in Sri Lanka is the same as "*moolee*" in India.

Sri Lankan Fish "Moilee"

1 pound fillets of jobfish	4 small green chili peppers, sliced
3 tablespoons oil for frying	4 slices ginger, chopped
2 sprigs curry leaves	1 cup coconut milk
2 small red onions, sliced	$\frac{1}{2}$ cup coconut cream
$\frac{1}{2}$ pound potatoes, peeled and cubed	2-3 teaspoons fresh lime juice
4 cloves garlic, sliced	2 teaspoons vinegar

Cut the fish fillets into eight portions. Heat the oil in a pan, add the curry leaves and onion, and cook lightly until tender but without letting the onion brown. Then add the fish, potato, garlic, chili pepper, and ginger. Sauté all this for a couple of minutes.

Now add the coconut milk, bring to the boil and simmer until the potato is cooked, by which time the liquid will be somewhat reduced. Finally, add the coconut cream, bring just back to the boil, add the lime juice and vinegar and remove from the heat. Serves four.

Alternative Fish
snappers (pp 60, 62)
sea breams, porgies
(pp 40, 42, 44)

Alternative Recipes
Cod with a Cherry and Red Wine
Sauce (p 26)
Fried Drum Southern Style (p 50)

Green jobfish, *Aprion virescens* (left) and crimson jobfish, *Pristipomoides filamentosus* (right)

Mahi-mahi

Mahi-mahi, Dolphin fish
ENGLISH-SPEAKING COUNTRIES

coriphène
FRENCH

Goldmakrele
GERMAN

lampuga
ITALIAN

lampuga, dorado
SPANISH

llampuga
CATALAN

doirado
PORTUGUESE

lampuka
MALTESE

kynigós
GREEK

zolotistaja makrel
RUSSIAN

boomaachh (Be), badahlan (Ta)
INDIAN LANGUAGES

nga-ba-yin
BURMESE

66

Which is the most beautiful fish in the sea? Many would say the mahi-mahi, *Coryphaena hippurus*. In Britain it is called the dolphin fish (which is not to be confused with the dolphin, which is a marine mammal). But only fishermen see it in all its glory: its iridescent colors of blue-green, silver and gold fade rapidly once it has been taken from the water.

The mahi-mahi is found all around the world in tropical and semi-tropical seas, but nowhere, with the possible exception of the waters round Malta, in the quantities desired. It may attain a length of 5 feet or even more, and it has a remarkably long dorsal fin, extending from just above the eye almost to the tail. As it grows older the male develops a pronounced "forehead", which gives it an increasingly sagacious look.

The mahi-mahi has the habit of swimming in small shoals around patches of flotsam, or floating logs, and is attracted by rafts or drifting boats. This characteristic is exploited by Maltese fishermen in their *kannizzati* fishery. This is a method used to catch both the mahi-mahi and the pilot fish, *Naucrates ductor*, and operates between August and December, when both species appear in Maltese waters. Floats are anchored in the water and, when the fish congregate under them, they are taken with an encircling net. This is so successful that in many years the catch of mahi-mahi at Malta exceeds that of any other species, despite its being seasonal. A similar sort of fishery is practised in the Seychelles, and in some places in Japan.

There is a smaller species, *C. equisetis*, known in Britain as the pompano dolphin fish. This too has a circumglobal distribution and is not easily distinguished.

The mahi-mahi has excellent flesh. Slices or steaks may be broiled, fried or steamed. If broiling is the method chosen, my advice is to take steaks about 1 inch thick and marinate them first in a mixture of olive oil, lemon juice, salt, pepper, and a little crushed garlic.

In Malta the various ways of preparing them include making them into a magnificent pie with vegetables.

ngau tau yu
CHINESE

shiira, kumabiki
JAPANESE

pla na mawn, pla eeto mawn
THAI

belitong, golok
MALAY

lemadang
INDONESIAN

durado
PHILIPPINES

mahi-mahi
HAWAII

Lampuki Pie

about 1½ pounds steaks or slices of mahi-mahi
flour, salt, pepper
olive oil for frying
1 cauliflower, divided into florets
2 medium onions, chopped

2 tablespoons parsley, chopped
8 olives, stoned and chopped
6 Italian canned cooking tomatoes (*pelati*)
2 tablespoons capers
½ teaspoon dried mint
pie-crust (see method)

Dip the pieces of fish in the seasoned flour and fry them lightly in the olive oil in a large pan. Meanwhile steam the cauliflower. Remove the fish when cooked, then fry the onions in the same oil. Add to them the florets of cauliflower with the parsley, olives, tomatoes, capers and mint, simmer for five to ten minutes, then remove from the heat and allow to cool. Make the pastry for the pie crust in your usual way (or better still for this recipe, using ¼ cup red wine as the liquid and 5 tablespoons olive oil as the fat to 2 cups all-purpose flour). Cover the bottom and sides of a pie dish with it, lay the fish on this bed, and pour the sauce over it. Cover the top with pastry and bake in the oven at 350° until golden brown. Allow up to an hour. Serves four.

Alternative Fish
threadfins (p 46)
tilefish (p 58)

Alternative Recipes
Merluza en Salsa Verde (p 28)
Fried Drum, Southern Style (p 50)
Fish en Papillote (p 187)

67

Mahi-mahi, *Coryphaena hippurus*: male (left) and female (right)

Wrasses

68

Wrasse is the usual English name for fish of the family Labridae, of which there are hundreds of species around the world in temperate, sub-tropical and tropical waters. Only a small proportion of them are marketed and eaten. The typical wrasse is a fairly small fish, brightly colored, thick-lipped, and well-toothed. Features of their life-style have been well described by Alwyne Wheeler:

"Many species of wrasse have been found to act as cleaner fishes, picking external parasites off other fishes at recognized stations. This has even been reported in the temperate waters off England and New Zealand, although it is best known among tropical species. Wrasses also show most interesting breeding behavior, the differential coloring of males and females leading to elaborate pre-spawning displays. Some species construct nests out of plant material which are guarded, once the eggs are deposited, by the male. As a group they are well known for their habit of sleeping at night, either buried in the sand on the bottom or wedged between rocks. Observation of sleeping wrasses in the Bermuda Aquarium has shown that they go through a period of rapid eye movement (REM) which, in higher vertebrates, is usually associated with dreaming. It thus suggests that some wrasses dream."

Four of the best known European wrasses are *Labrus bergylta*, the ballan wrasse; *L viridis, labre vert* in French; *L merula*, French *merle*; and *L bimaculatus*, the cuckoo wrasse. The first of these belongs to the East Atlantic and is usually recognizable by its profusion of white spots on a darker background. The second (normally green in color) and the third belong principally to the Mediterranean, while the fourth is found in both the Mediterranean and the East Atlantic. The first three may reach a length of 21 inches or so; the fourth is smaller. All are eaten, and their smaller relations usually finish up in fish soups. In the West Atlantic there are numerous species, mostly small reef fish. The tautog, *Tautoga onitis*, which may reach a length of 36 inches is an excellent food fish.

Californians who fish for sport pursue *Pimelometopon pulchrum*, the California sheephead. A large specimen once taken weighed over 36 pounds. The flesh is fine-grained and mild in flavor.

In Asian waters, there are only a few wrasses which are highly rated as food fish. One is *Choerodon schoonleini*, known as *tsing yi* at Hong Kong, where it is an expensive delicacy if sold alive, and is usually steamed.

Fish Baked as in the Island of Spetsai

2 pounds wrasse
$\frac{3}{4}$ cup olive oil
1 large tomato, peeled and chopped
parsley, chopped

1 clove garlic, crushed
salt and pepper
2 tablespoons breadcrumbs
scant $\frac{1}{2}$ cup white wine (if needed)

Clean the fish. Make the sauce by mixing together the olive oil, tomato, parsley, crushed garlic and salt and pepper.

Oil a baking dish and lay the fish in it, surrounded and covered by the sauce. Put half of the breadcrumbs on top of this, then spoon the sauce on top. Add the remaining breadcrumbs and then more sauce and more parsley.

Cook in the oven at 375° for up to an hour (depending on the size of the fish), basting the fish from time to time with the sauce. Watch carefully to see whether the sauce is reducing too much and the fish becoming dry. Should this happen, add white wine.

Serve, either hot or cold, with lemon wedges. Serves four.

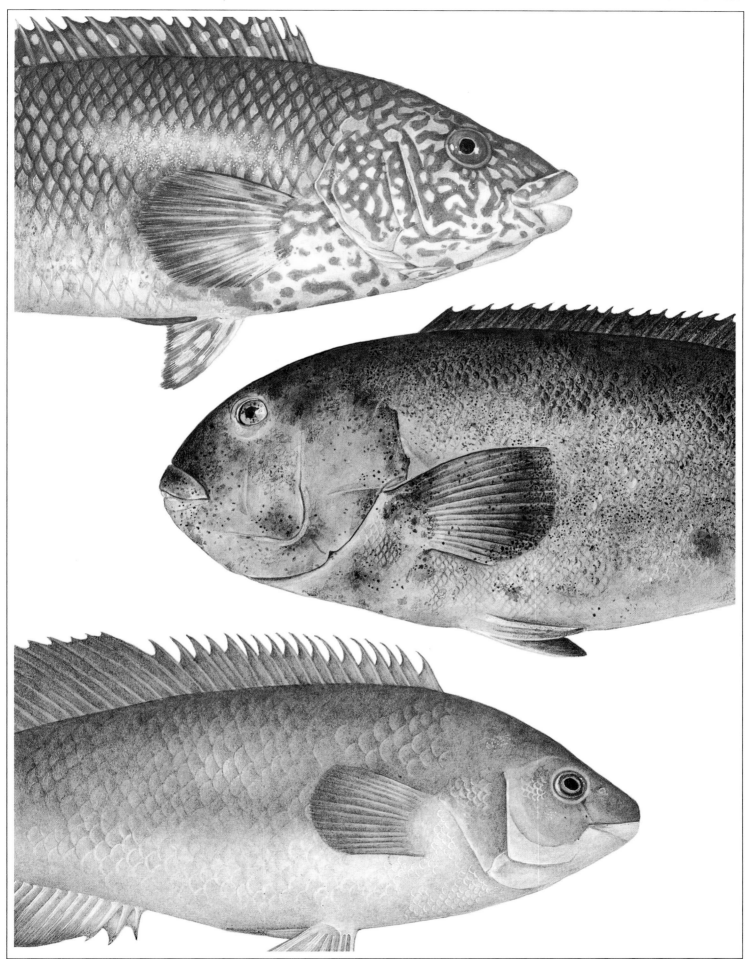

From top to bottom: ballan wrasse, *Labrus bergylta*; tautog, *Tautoga onitis*; and French merle, *L merula*

Parrotfish

Parrotfish
ENGLISH-SPEAKING COUNTRIES
(European names refer mainly to
Sparisoma cretense, Asian names
mainly to S ghobban)

perroquet-vieillard, scare de
Grèce
FRENCH

vieja colorada
SPANISH

papagáio, bodião
PORTUGUESE

scaro, cucca, marzapani
ITALIAN

marzpan
MALTESE

scáros
GREEK

papas balığı
TURKISH

kanaria (in Morocco), jakkbán
(in Algeria), gäzla (in Libya),
zollai' (in Lebanon)
ARABIC

nga-sein
BURMESE

ying gor lee
CHINESE

budai (Leptoscarus japonicus)
JAPANESE

pla nok kaew see plerng
THAI

bayan
MALAY

kakatua biru
INDONESIAN

ogos, mulmul
PHILIPPINES

70

Parrotfish is the appropriate common name of fish of the family Scaridae, which are found in tropical, sub-tropical and warm temperate waters around the world. Their teeth are configured somewhat like a parrot's beak, to facilitate their crunching of coral, from which they filter out the algae which they eat, excreting the sand. Their activity is thought to be a principal factor in the wearing down of coral reefs.

Parrotfish are related to the wrasses (page 68), and resemble them both in their bright coloration, which varies with age and sex, and in their habit of sleeping at night; but some of them grow to a larger size than any wrasse and they can be distinguished by the fusing of their front teeth into a "beak".

The one parrotfish present in the Mediterranean, *Sparisoma cretensis*, occurs throughout the eastern basin and all along the southern parts, but is rarely marketed except in Morocco, Cyprus, Turkey and Greece; its range also includes the East Atlantic from Portugal and the Azores south to Senegal. It is esteemed as a table fish, but not as much as in classical times, when Roman epicures thought so much of it that the Roman admiral Optatus transplanted some to the west Italian coast in the hope of establishing a breeding population there. Roman taste in fish was influenced by color, and it may be that the reddish color of the females was thought to be especially attractive (males are usually gray-brown or purplish).

The largest parrotfish are found in the West Atlantic. Both *S coeruleus*, the blue parrotfish, and *S guacamala*, the rainbow parrotfish, may reach a length of 4 feet. These species apparently wrap themselves in a mucous "envelope", like a sleeping blanket, at night before falling asleep. The same applies to the smaller queen parrotfish of the same region, *S vetula*. It may also be true of the species in the painting, which is the amusingly named stoplight parrotfish, *S viride*. It has a maximum length just over 21 inches.

In Asian waters *S ghobban* is one of the larger species (maximum length 36 inches) and is sought after by restauranteurs in Hong Kong. A species of Japanese waters, *Leptoscarus japonicus*, is good enough to be eaten raw as *sashimi*, although it is often poached and served with a special sauce.

For the cook, frying or steaming is recommended. The recipe proposed is a free adaptation of one which comes from Japan.

Parrotfish Steamed with Julienne Vegetables

I pound fillets of parrotfish	I bunch watercress (stems only)
I carrot	I egg white, lightly beaten
6 ounces green beans	I large piece dried kelp (*konbu*, optional)
I bunch *enokitake* mushrooms, or	silver sauce (see page 203)
I cup field mushrooms	

Salt the fillets lightly and let them rest for an hour, then cut them into thin strips. Make *julienne* (thin strips) of the carrot and green beans. If using field mushrooms, cut them into thin strips too. Put the prepared vegetables into a bowl, add the watercress stems, salt lightly and toss. Five minutes later, when the salt has penetrated, add the egg white and toss again so that everything is coated.

In Japan, it would be usual to compose individual helpings in bowls and steam them thus. It is simpler to steam everything together and then make up the individual helpings. Place the vegetables in a steamer, with the piece of kelp (if used) below them and the fish on top. Steam for ten minutes.

Compose the servings, with the fish on top, and serve with the silver sauce or with a delicate lime sauce (see page 200). Serves four.

Alternative Fish
wrasses (p 68)
mullet (p 78)

Alternative Recipes
Conger Cooked in Milk (p 24)
Cá Sào Mäng Tuoi (p 108)

The American stoplight, *Sparisoma viride* (bottom right) and the head of the Mediterranean *S cretensis* (top right) amongst a selection of parrotfish found in the scores in the Indian Ocean

Weevers

72

Weevers are not generally thought of as fish for epicures. However, as explained below, there is evidence that they enjoyed a vogue in France around 1700, and I have always myself thought them under-rated.

The name weever is applied to any fish of the family Trachinidae, which is represented only in the Northeast Atlantic and the Mediterranean. All weevers have venomous spines on their back and on the gill-covers. Since they have the habit of burying themselves in the sand, they can be a hazard to barefoot bathers. It is usual, and prudent, to have these spines cut off by the fishmonger when the fish are bought.

Trachinus draco, the greater weever, has a maximum length of nearly 16 inches. It is called "greater" in contrast to *Echiichthys vipera*, the lesser weever (which always measures less than 6 inches), with which it shares an extensive range from Norway to the eastern Mediterranean. The other two species, which are found only in the Mediterranean, may also be about 16 inches long; these are *Trachinus araneus*, the spotted weever, and *T radiatus*, the streaked weever.

A closely related Mediterranean fish with similar characteristics and uses is *Uranoscopus scaber*, the stargazer, so called because its eyes look upwards even more markedly than those of the weevers. It is said to be the fish with whose gall Tobias recovered his sight, although it seems improbable that a fish of this species should have leapt out of the River Tigris and appeared large enough to devour him. It has an interesting range of common names, including: *boeuf* or *rat* in French; *miou* or *muou* in Provence; and *kurbağa balığı* ("frog-fish") in Turkish.

The firm flesh of weevers gives them a useful role in *bouillabaisse* and other fish soups and stews. But large specimens can be cooked in various ways, for example broiled or filleted and fried. They are eaten in Belgium, France and most Mediterranean countries, but not in England.

It is interesting that the foremost French cookbook author of the 1690s and early part of the following century, Massialot, thought fit to include eight quite elaborate recipes for cooking weevers in his main work. All of these were purloined and translated and published in England by whoever was responsible for the second edition of Patrick Lamb's *The Complete Court Cook*, no doubt because this person reorganized Lamb's book on A-Z lines and was short of entries under W. Seven of the eight recipes reappeared shortly afterwards in John Nott's *Cook's Dictionary*.

All this has created the erroneous impression, admittedly in rather limited circles, that weevers were frequently cooked at that time in England. Perhaps they were, but all we can infer from the theft of the eight French recipes is that English people would have known what weevers were.

All these recipes are long, so here, in place of a single recipe, I give a summary of most of them, thus offering the ambitious cook more ideas than any modern book would supply for dealing with these fish.

Weevers, cleaned, scored on both sides, and then dredged with flour, were fried in butter; they were then served with a caper or cucumber sauce. Broiled weevers were placed on a bed of stewed lettuce, the liquid bound with a *coulis* of crayfish. Weevers poached in white wine, with numerous added flavors, were laid in a dish and had an oyster sauce poured over them. Pieces of weever were tossed in a pan with butter, mushrooms, truffles and herbs, then moistened with fish stock and white wine and stewed for a while, after which egg yolks beaten up with verjuice were used to thicken the sauce. Stuffed weevers . . . . but no, this one and Roast weevers are just too off-puttingly complicated!

From top to bottom: star-gazer, *Uranoscopus scaber*; greater weever, *Tracinus draco*; and streaked weever, *T radiatus*

Scabbard Fish

74

I f fish were ever called upon to give a theatrical performance, the scabbard fish would undoubtedly have the role of stage villain, "wicked Sir Jasper" or the like, because of its facial appearance.

These long, thin, and usually silvery fish, of the family Trichiuridae, are found in many parts of the world. The English names which have been used for them include hairtail (for those species whose tail ends in a point, rather than being forked), cutlass fish and sabre fish, ribbon fish, and (in the southern hemisphere) frostfish. One interesting variation on these themes is the Filipino name *bolungonas*, meaning "sugarcane leaf".

The maximum length of the various species varies between 3-7 feet. The largest, *Lepidopus caudatus*, occurs on both sides of the Atlantic and in the Mediterranean. Another Atlantic species, *Aphanopus carbo*, is the dominant fish in the catch at Madeira, besides being taken frequently off the Portuguese coast. It likes deep water and is of a blackish color.

There are a number of species in the Indo-Pacific including *Trichiurus haumela*, a common species; *T muticus* (tin-white in color, accounting for the emphatic Malay name *timah-timah*, meaning "tin-tin"); and *T savala*, whose range extends to Australia. The frostfish of New Zealand is *Lepidopus lex*; it bears its common name because it is often found washed ashore on frosty nights. Parrott (1960), states that frostfish have been observed swimming ashore "apparently in a state of temporary insanity, endeavoring as it were to commit suicide".

From the cook's point of view, the rear end of the scabbard fish offers little; but sections cut further forward yield excellent flesh which can be fried, baked, or broiled. In the western hemisphere there are signs of appreciation in Madeira (above all), in Portugal, and in certain Mediterranean countries. Interest in the Indo-Pacific is more widespread; for example, scabbard fish have occupied fourth place in importance in the marine fisheries of India, where they are mostly sun-dried before being marketed.

Pla Tod Laad Prik
(Fried Scabbard Fish with Chili Sauce)

When I found this recipe in Thailand it was recommended for grouper, but it works particularly well with scabbard fish. The "fish sauce" listed as an ingredient is the product found almost everywhere in Southeast Asia and available (usually from Thailand, Hong Kong, or the Philippines, but it might be from Vietnam) in oriental food stores.

4 sections of scabbard fish, weighing 7 ounces each	2-3 small heads of garlic, crushed and chopped
3 tablespoons fish sauce (*nam pla* in Thailand) + 1 more teaspoon	2 large red chili peppers, thinly sliced
2-3 tablespoons oil	2 tablespoons sweet and sour sauce (equal amounts of lime juice and honey)

Put the sections of fish in a dish just big enough to take them side by side. Cover with three tablespoons of the fish sauce and marinate for at least 15 minutes.

Heat the oil in a wok and fry the sections of fish in it until they are brown and crisp on both sides. Towards the end, add a little of the garlic and let that start to turn brown too. Remove fish and garlic to a heated platter.

In the same oil, cook the rest of the garlic with the chili peppers, the rest of fish sauce, and the sweet and sour sauce. Once this second batch of garlic is turning brown, pour the mixture over the fish and serve. Serves four.

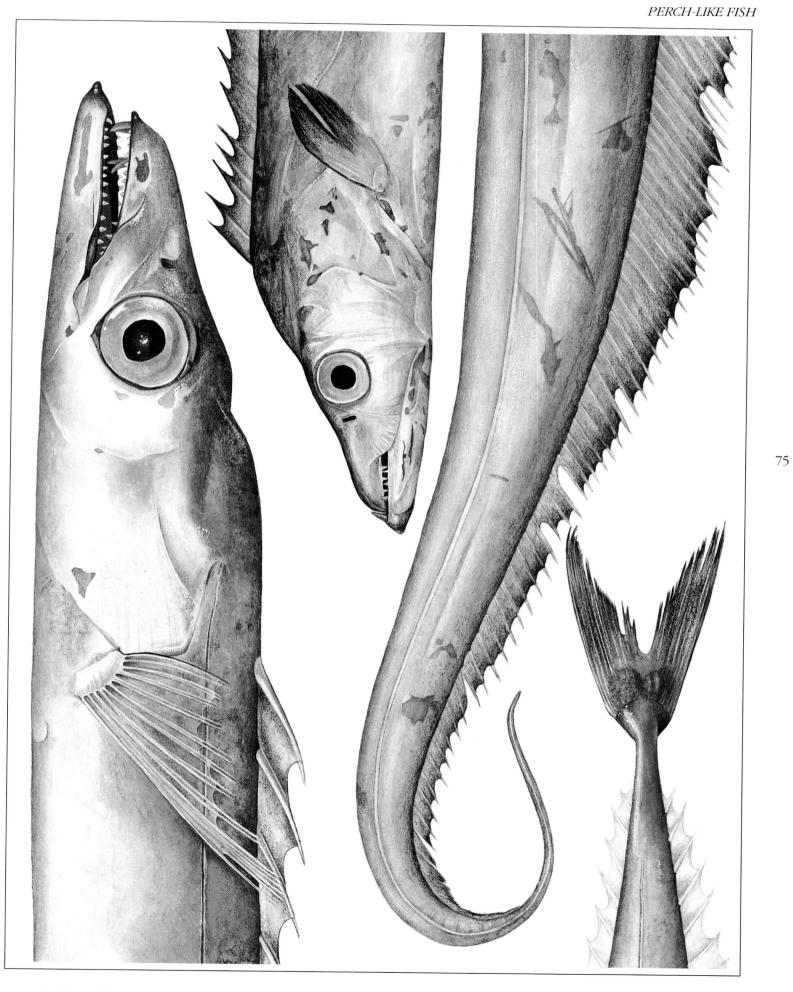

Scabbard fish, *Lepidopus caudatus* (left and right) and ribbon fish or hairtail, *Trichiurus haumela* (center)

Barracuda

Barracuda, fierce fish with large jaws and a devastating array of teeth, belong to the genus *Sphyraena*. The great barracuda, *S barracuda*, is found in tropical waters all round the world, but especially in the Caribbean and adjacent regions.

It is a solitary fish (unlike some small relations, which swim in shoals) and presents a double danger to man. As far as direct attacks are concerned, it is reputedly (although probably not in reality) a greater peril than any shark. It has certainly been responsible for some severe injuries; the two nearly parallel rows of punctures which its teeth produce are distinctive. Also, it is one of those fish which in certain conditions are responsible for what is called "cigatuera" poisoning. There has been much debate among scientists about the precise cause of this. Whatever the cause, it seems to operate only in the more southerly, and therefore warmer, waters of the barracuda's range. The maximum length of this species, and of *S jello*, a species found only in the Indo-Pacific, is around 6 feet. A smaller species of the Caribbean region, *S guachancho*, is known as the guachancho. It seems to be free of the cigatuera danger. The Mediterranean species, *S sphyraena*, may be up to 4 feet long but is usually much smaller.

The name "oceanic barracuda" is sometimes applied to a different fish, the wahoo (or peto) *Acanthocybium solanderi*. It is a short-lived, fast-growing, fast-swimming predator which is popular as a game fish in the Caribbean area and the Indo-Pacific; indeed it has a global distribution in tropical waters, although it is not

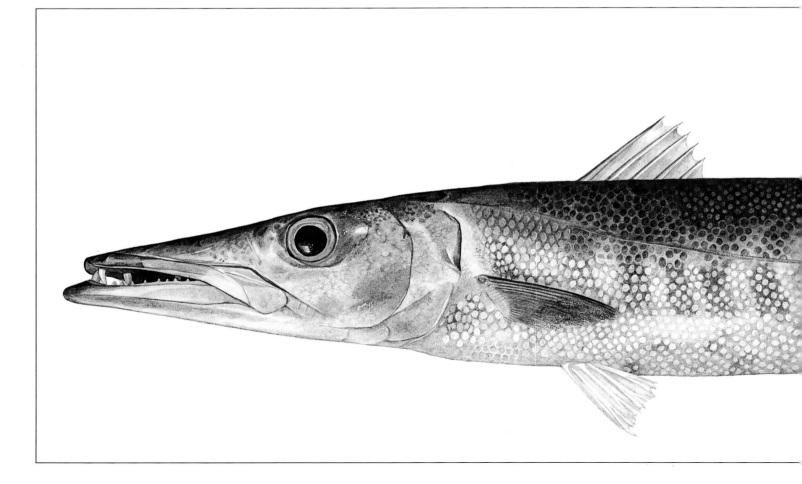

kamasu
JAPANESE

pla nam dok mai
THAI

kachang-kachang (small), alu-alu (medium), tenak (large)
MALAY

alu-alu
INDONESIAN

plentiful anywhere.

Frying steaks of barracuda is recommended, but the fish may also be prepared in other ways. Small ones can be cooked whole (for example in a Creole *court bouillon*).

The Burmese recipe below seems to have a Chinese origin. "*Tauk tauk*" refers to the noise made by the twin chopping movements of a Chinese cook as he minces food with his sharp cleavers. The Burmese friend who gave me the recipe said that it could be used for many fish, but barracuda was the first she mentioned as suitable. The fish sauce listed as an ingredient is *ngan-pya-ye* in Burma, but similar sauces from Thailand (*nam pla*) or Vietnam (*nuoc mam*) or the Philippines (*patis*) are more easily obtainable.

Tauk Tauk Kyaw
(Burmese Fried Barracuda)

2 pounds barracuda, boned and minced
3 cloves garlic, chopped
6 tiny onions, chopped or sliced
¾ cup cooking oil
salt to taste
fish sauce to taste

I teaspoon sugar
½ cup carrot, thinly sliced
½ cup oriental radish (*daikon*), thinly sliced
4 small leeks, cut into short lengths
2 eggs, beaten

The method is simple: fry, fry, fry.

First fry the garlic and the tiny onions in the oil, then add the fish with salt, fish sauce, and sugar. When the fish is cooked, add the thin slices of carrot and radish. When these are half-cooked, which will be almost at once, add the leeks and beaten eggs. Continue to stir-fry for a few minutes, then check the seasoning and serve. Serves four.

Alternative Fish
any fish

Alternative Recipes
Baked Fish Spetsai Style (p 68)
Pla Tod Laad Prik (p 74)

77

A *barracuda*, Sphyraena jello

Mullet

Mullet, so called in the USA and Australia, are known as grey mullet in Britain in order to distinguish them from red mullet (page 48). They are beautifully streamlined fish which exist in a number of genera and species in tropical and warm temperate waters around the world. One species, *Mugil cephalus*, has a worldwide distribution. *M chelo*, the thick-lipped mullet and the most common European species, is found from the Black Sea through the Mediterranean and as far as Scotland, while *M saliens*, the leaping mullet of the Mediterranean, ranges down to southern Africa. This species is liable, because of its leaping habit, to be caught in surface nets. *M capito* (also called *Liza ramada*) shown at the top of the painting, is the thin-lipped mullet, which has names in the south of France meaning "pig".

M curema, the white mullet, occurs on the West Atlantic coast from New England to Brazil and also on the East Pacific coast. *Liza subviridis*, the green-backed mullet, and *L vaigiensis*, the diamond-scaled mullet, are just two of many Asian species.

The vegetarian disposition of these fish excited the admiration of the Greek poet Oppian, who thought them the most gentle of fish, "harming neither themselves nor any other creatures, never staining their lips with blood but in holy fashion feeding always on the green seaweed or mere mud". Oppian was also impressed by the gallantly amorous attitude of male mullet, observing that if a fine plump female was trailed through the water a throng of admiring males would pursue her (and thus be caught). In fact, the food of the mullet includes, besides diatoms and algae, minute animal material which they extract from mud, so they are not really strict vegetarians.

At their best, mullet are fine fish to eat. But Oppian's reference to mud can serve as a warning that those which have been browsing in unattractively muddy water may taste of mud. The eggs of the female, removed in their intact membrane, salted, washed, pressed, dried in the sun and encased in wax, make the delicacy known as *poutargue* or *boutargue* (France), *bottarga* (Italy), *avgotáracho* (Greece), and *putago* (Turkey); it is cut into very thin slices and served with a simple dressing of olive oil, lemon juice and pepper.

Meuilles à la Charentaise
(Mullet, Charentes Style)

4 mullet, ½ pound each, uncleaned	½ cup tomato paste
4 cloves garlic	*for the court bouillon*
2 tablespoons parsley, chopped	2 sprigs of thyme, a bay leaf,
1 stick butter	a few cloves and salt and pepper
salt and pepper	7 tablespoons dry white wine
	3 tablespoons grated cheese

Clean the fish. Bring to the boil 4 cups or more of water (the amount will depend on the shape of your cooking vessel) with the ingredients of the *court bouillon*. Poach the fish in this, covered, for seven to ten minutes, until done. Remove the fish and leave to drain.

Meanwhile, pound the garlic and parsley into the butter, with a little seasoning, then melt it in a pan and mix in the tomato paste.

Lay the drained fish side by side in an oven dish just big enough for them. Pour the garlic and tomato sauce over them, add the wine, sprinkle the cheese on top, and leave in the oven at 350° for 15 minutes. Serves four.

Alternative Fish
cod (p 26)
parrotfish (p 70)

Alternative Recipes
Steamed Parrotfish with Julienne
Vegetables (p 70)
Gurnard with Almond Sauce
(p 90)

From top to bottom: thin-lipped mullet, *Mugil capito*; striped mullet, *M cephalus*; and thick-lipped mullet, *M chelo*

Mackerel

80

With its brilliant greeny-blue back marked with dark curving lines, its metallic sides and white belly, the mackerel is a handsome fish. One might almost describe it as flashy in appearance, noting that the French name *maquereau* also means "pimp" and that in the past "mackerel" was a term for dandy in England.

Mackerel are oceanic fish, which normally swim in very large shoals. The best known mackerel, *Scomber scombrus*, is a common fish of North Atlantic and Mediterranean waters with a range extending from the Black Sea and the Mediterranean to the north of Norway and Iceland; and from Labrador on the American side down to Cape Hatteras. Its maximum length is 12-14 inches. The chub mackerel, *S colias*, is common in the Mediterranean and is also found on the Iberian and French Atlantic coasts, and in New England waters. This species is smaller and has more delicate markings and bigger eyes (hence the Sicilian name *occhi-grossi*). Fishmongers have little reason to distinguish it from its better known relation, but in many Mediterranean languages it has its own names. It is a cosmopolitan species which is found also in the Indo-Pacific, where large catches are taken by the Japanese, and in Chile and Peru.

There is another close relation to the Atlantic mackerel present in the Indo-Pacific. This is *S australasicus*, for which there are important fisheries in Japan and southern Australia (where the unattractive name "slimy mackerel" is sometimes used for it). Besides mackerel of the genus *Scomber*, there are several other Indo-Pacific species, of which *Rastrelliger kanagurta*, the rake-gilled mackerel (which can be up to 18 inches long), and *R brachysoma*, the short-bodied mackerel (up to 26 inches long), are the most common. They are the favorite marine fishes of the Thai people; and the latter is an important food fish in the Philippines.

Mackerel have a relatively high oil content and spoil quickly. This is why, since the end of the seventeenth century, there has been a special dispensation to sell them in England on Sundays. It also explains why a tart, acid sauce is recommended to go with the fish. Gooseberry is the best known, but unsweetened cranberry or rhubarb are also good. The acidity of tomatoes also suits these fish. The flesh of a fresh mackerel has an excellent flavor, and is easily separated from the bones.

Hot-smoked mackerel, which needs no further cooking, is popular in Western countries; and so is mackerel pâté.

In the Orient there is a large range of recipes for mackerel – such as the one I propose (from Perlis in Indonesia) – and the fish are also available dried.

Bapsetek Ikan

8 tiny mackerel or 4 small ones, cleaned	a little flour
8 tablespoons palm (or other) oil	5 fresh red chili peppers, split lengthwise
4 potatoes, peeled and sliced	2 tablespoons tomato sauce
8 small red onions, diced	2 tablespoons superfine sugar
4 cloves garlic, chopped	salt to taste

First, fry the fish in the oil until they are well browned all over and remove from the pan. Next, fry the potato slices until brown, and reserve. Then fry the onions and the garlic cloves, mix the flour with a little water to make a paste and combine this with the onion and garlic. Let it simmer briefly before adding the chili peppers, tomato sauce, sugar and salt. When this mixture has been brought back to simmering point, add the fried fish and potatoes. Let it cook for a couple of minutes longer, add a little water, taste and correct the seasoning and serve. Serves four.

Alternative Fish
Spanish mackerel (p 82)

Alternative Recipes
Gravlax (p 8)
Dutch Baked Herring (p 18)
Fish en Papillote (p 187)

Mackerel, *Scomber scombrus*

Spanish Mackerel

Spanish mackerel, a name which is sometimes applied to the chub mackerel (page 80), is of more importance as the principal English name for fish of the genus *Scomberomorus*. These are large fish, found especially in Southeast Asia and the Caribbean and in the southern hemisphere. Those accustomed to the vagaries of popular nomenclature will not be surprised to hear that none of them is found in Spanish waters.

In the West Atlantic, the species include *S regalis*. The principal species in the Indo-Pacific are:

● *S commersoni*, the largest in Southeast Asian waters, which is known also as the narrow-banded Spanish mackerel in Australia, where it provides great excitement for anglers in the region of the Great Barrier Reef. It is commonly just under 40 inches long but sometimes reaches almost 5 feet. The sides are marked by wavy vertical gray stripes, more noticeable on the lower part of the body. The adjectives in parenthesis among the Southeast Asian names listed apply to this species.

● *S guttatus*, the spotted Spanish mackerel, is smaller and has three rows of roundish spots on its silvery sides. Its range extends from India to Japan. Its Australian counterpart, *S queenslandicus*, the school mackerel, is very similar.

● *S lineolatus*, the streaked Spanish mackerel, is a little bigger than its spotted brother, and has streaks of brownish spots along its sides.

● *S niphonius*, which Australians call the spotted Spanish mackerel, is another species of the southern hemisphere and so is *S semifasciatus*, the broad-banded Spanish mackerel of North and West Australia.

● *S concolor*, the Monterey Spanish mackerel, is found in the Northeast Pacific, while *S sierra* is a more southerly East Pacific species.

These are fine fish to eat, with compact flesh and a really good flavor. Charcoal-grilling produces excellent results, but any of the usual ways of cooking fish can be applied to them.

The recipe below from Negri Sembilan in Malaysia has interesting accompaniments, designed to make a relatively small quantity of fish go a long way.

Ikan Masak Puteh

1 pound Spanish mackerel, cleaned weight
1 piece (1 inch) fresh ginger, pounded
1 teaspoon ground black pepper
a little salt
2 carrots, sliced
2 scallions, sliced
2 sprigs coriander leaves
outer leaves of a lettuce

1 pound potato, sliced and fried
10 small onions, sliced and fried
for the sauce
5 red chili peppers
3 cloves garlic
oil for frying
1 cup thick coconut cream
1-2 teaspoons vinegar
sugar to taste

Mix together the pounded ginger, black pepper and salt, then rub the pieces of fish with the mixture. Place it in a steamer with the carrots, scallions and coriander leaves. Steam until cooked through (around ten minutes). Keep warm.

Meanwhile, make the sauce. Pound together the red chilis and the garlic, fry the mixture very briefly, then add the remaining ingredients plus a little of the liquid (a tablespoon or so) from the steamed fish. Cook this for a couple of minutes. Check for seasoning and if necessary add a very little salt.

Make a bed of lettuce on a platter, and put the steamed fish in the center. Surround it with the fried potato and onion. Either pour the sauce over the fish, or serve it separately. Serves four.

Scomberomorus guttatus, the spotted Spanish mackerel of the Indo-Pacific, (top left and bottom right), and a Spanish mackerel of the West Atlantic, *S maculatus* (center)

Bonito

84

The bonito, *Sarda sarda*, is a fish of the scombrid (mackerel and tuna) family. It is found on both sides of the South and North Atlantic, as far north as Cape Cod in the west and the south coast of Britain in the east; throughout the Mediterranean; and in the Black Sea, whence it migrates south at the end of the year, returning in the spring.

The name bonito is also used in connection with other species, such as the striped or oceanic bonito, more correctly called skipjack; indeed in German this fish is the *Echter* (meaning "true") *Bonito*. *S sarda* is sometimes called the Atlantic bonito to avoid confusion.

There are three similar species, mostly slightly bigger, in the Indo-Pacific region: *S orientalis*, the oriental bonito, which has a wide distribution from the Red Sea to West Australia, Japan, Hawaii and the west coast of Central America; *S australis* which is found off southeastern Australia; and *S chiliensis*, whose range covers much of the western coasts of both North and South America. The first and last of these are of commercial importance.

The back of the bonito is steel-blue with dark blue slanting stripes; its sides and belly are silvery. Its maximum length is three feet, although it is never as big as this in European waters.

These are shoaling fish and vigorous predators, with the habit of leaping out of the water when in pursuit of prey such as herring and squid.

The compact and light-colored flesh of the bonito is excellent, and often canned. In Japan, however, it has a special significance. One of the most prominent ingredients in Japanese cookery is *katsuobushi*, dried fillets of bonito flesh. These are treated by steam and then dried so that they become as hard as wood and indeed resemble wooden boomerangs. The Japanese tradition is to use a special implement to shave off very thin slices, usually destined for the preparation of *dashi*, the basic Japanese soup stock. However, the procedure is laborious, and various time-saving *katsuobushi* products are available, including instant *katsuobushi* granules and *ito-kezuri-katsuobushi*, which are "thread shavings" for use as garnish.

Bonito à la Asturiana

Bonito is a traditional main dish for Christmas dinner in Asturias. But this popular dish can be made any day of the year.

nearly 2 pounds bonito, cleaned weight
coarse salt
flour
7 tablespoons olive oil
1 pound onions, sliced
2 cloves garlic, finely chopped
2 sprigs parsley, chopped

a drizzle of vinegar
$\frac{1}{2}$ teaspoon paprika or cayenne
salt to taste
7 tablespoons chicken broth
strips of mild red pepper (fresh, seared and peeled; or canned)

Cut the bonito into steaks about $\frac{3}{4}$ inch thick. Season these with the salt, coat them with the flour, and fry them in hot oil on both sides until they are golden. Remove them to a shallow heatproof dish and keep them warm.

Strain the oil and use it again to fry the onion, garlic and parsley, without allowing them to become too brown. Then add the vinegar and paprika or cayenne. Add salt to taste and then the chicken broth.

Pour this sauce over the fish and put it in the oven at 350° for 20 minutes. Garnish the dish with the strips of red pepper and serve. Serves four.

Bonito, *Sarda sarda*

Tuna

86

Tuna or tunny? Either name can be used, but tuna has become the more common. This group of large and medium-size oceanic fish are a food resource of primary importance and of great gastronomic interest. They are also unusual fish, being warm-blooded and having an exceptionally great need for oxygen. Their only means of getting enough oxygen to survive is to swim continuously at a speed at least as fast as a fast human swimmer, so that oxygen-rich water is constantly driven over their gills. Since they are thus condemned to swim literally all their lives, they have powerful muscles, need large amounts of food, and are formidable predators capable of bursts of speed well over 40 mph.

Tuna are also great nomads. As a Spanish writer commented in the eighteenth century: "All the sea is their native country. They are wandering fish." This makes conservation measures and management of the fisheries for them very complicated. Over 60 nations make significant catches of tuna but two, Japan and the USA, account for half the total catch. The same two countries together with France, Spain, Italy and West Germany account for 90 per cent of tuna consumption.

The name tuna, like many general fish names, is not applied in a uniform way and does not always correspond to the scientific classification of these fish. With rare exceptions it is used only of fish in the family Scombridae, and within that family is reserved almost exclusively for members of the two genera *Thunnus* (all of whose members except one are always called tuna in English) and *Euthynnus* (where names such as little tunny, *thonine*, and kawakawa prevail). Within the same sub-family as these are two other genera, whose members are likely to be referred to in scientific works as tuna, but which have other common names. These are *Katsuwonus* (one species only, but an important one, often just called skipjack, sometimes skipjack tuna), and *Auxis* (whose members are usually called frigate mackerel). One close relation is the bonito (see page 84).

The principal tuna of the world in the genus *Thunnus* with their common names, maximum lengths, distribution, and special characteristics are listed below. The first three species form a group, dividing the northern, equatorial, and southern oceans between them.

● *T thynnus*, northern bluefin tuna; up to 10 feet long; record angling weight around 2,150 pounds; found in the Atlantic and Pacific, always north of the Equator and as far north as Norway; the largest tuna and the one most familiar to Europeans.

● *T obesus*, big-eye tuna; about 7 feet long; found worldwide in tropical and subtropical waters (but not in the Mediterranean); has relatively large eyes.

● *T maccoyii*, southern bluefin tuna; up to 7 feet 6 inches long; found worldwide south of 30°S.

● *T atlanticus*, blackfin tuna; up to 39 inches; found only in the West Atlantic from Massachusetts down to Brazil, most commonly taken in the Caribbean region.

● *T alalunga*, longfin tuna or albacore (in English, but note that in French this same name refers to the yellowfin tuna); up to 4 feet long; found worldwide in the Atlantic and Indo-Pacific; has long pectoral fins.

● *T albacares*, yellowfin tuna; can be over 7 feet long; record angling weight 375 pounds; found worldwide in tropical and sub-tropical seas but not in the Mediterranean; dorsal and anal fins and finlets bright yellow.

Of of all various species, skipjack tuna accounts for the largest share, by weight, of the catch, with yellowfin not far behind. The albacore and big-eye tuna come next. Northern and southern bluefin tuna are much less important.

All tuna meat is firm, compact and rather heavy. The best part is what the Italians and Spaniards call *ventresca*, a cut from the belly. In Japan, tuna meat of the finest quality is prized for eating raw as *sashimi*. Tuna steaks can be broiled or a larger piece can be bought and braised.

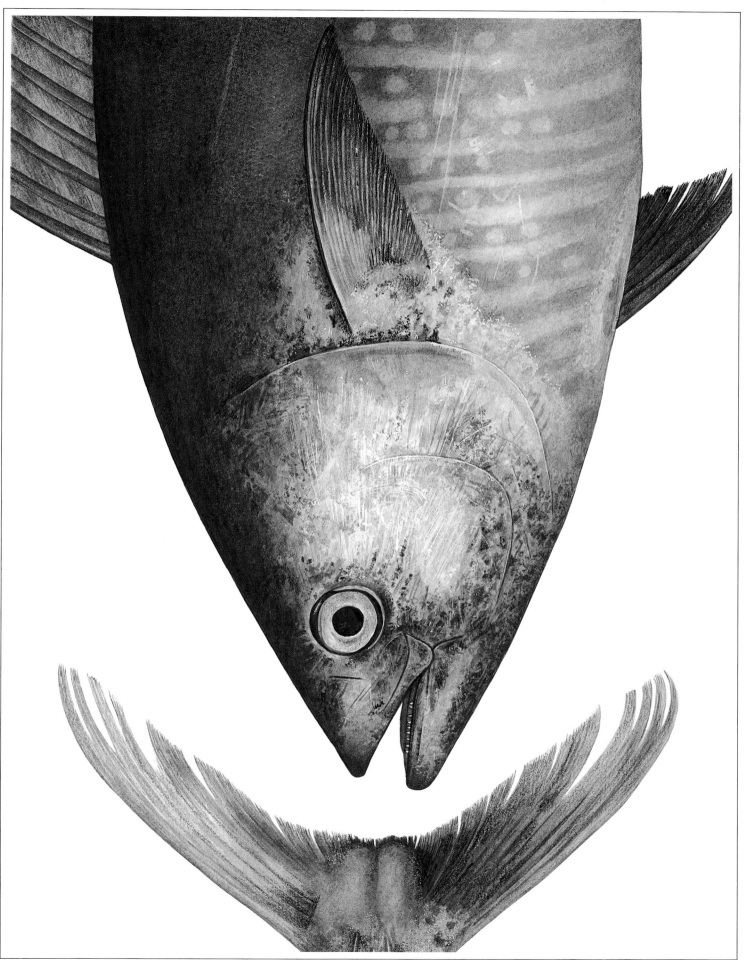

Bluefin tuna, *Thunnus thynnus*

Swordfish

88

One of the fish which range right around the world in warm, temperate waters is the swordfish, *Xiphias gladius*. It is a big fish, with a maximum length (including the sword) of 13 feet.

Most of the common names for this fish refer to its sword, which is not for driving holes through the bottoms of wooden boats (although there are many tales of this happening), but for flailing around among banks of smaller fish, thus killing or stunning its prey. The name broad-billed swordfish is sometimes used to distinguish the species from marlins and others like them, which can also be loosely described as swordfish.

Although they are so large and so formidably equipped, swordfish often laze on the surface of the water and can be harpooned. In classical times, as now, this was a common method of capture. Swordfish are also taken in tuna traps.

A traveller in Sicily in the eighteenth century recorded that the Sicilian fishermen used a Greek sentence as a charm to lure the fish towards their boats; if the fish overheard a word of Italian it would plunge underwater at once and make off. A possible explanation of this legendary phenomenon is that the Sicilians, in whose waters swordfish abound, are notoriously better than Greeks at catching them.

Although the swordfish is cosmopolitan, it is not at all prominent in Asia, as can be inferred from the paucity of vernacular names. It occurs in Australasian waters, and the Japanese have taken quantities from New Zealand. The swordfish is rare around southern Africa, but more common off the Atlantic coast of the Americas and off the Pacific coast from Oregon southwards.

In Hawaii, the swordfish used to be esteemed more for its supposed magical powers than as food. The rule was that a swordfish could belong only to a chief and was to be sacrificed on an altar in the same manner as a tiger shark. In the same manner? What was that, I wondered, and was horrified to learn that it meant in company with a human sacrifice; also that human bait was used for both.

The flesh of the swordfish has a very compact structure which shows up well when a steak is cut from it. A broiled steak, dressed with a little olive oil and plenty of lemon juice, is particularly good. A pleasant lunch dish can be made by poaching a large steak and then, when it has cooled, encasing it in a wine aspic, suitably garnished. Because the flesh is so compact, a smaller quantity of it can be served than of other fish (a point which also applies to tuna).

Smoked swordfish, a traditional preparation in Turkey and now increasingly common elsewhere, is a delicacy. But the Turks also have plenty of ways of preparing fresh swordfish, for example grilling pieces of them on skewers with slices of lemon and tomato, or marrying the fish with tomato, as in this recipe.

Kılıç Domatesli

$\frac{1}{2}$ pound swordfish in steaks or slices
4 moderately large tomatoes
4 tablespoons olive oil
2 teaspoons salt
4 tablespoons fish stock or water

Peel, seed and chop the tomatoes. Heat the olive oil in a deep pan, add the tomatoes and salt and cook for five minutes, stirring often. This produces a kind of tomato sauce. Spread half of it over the bottom of a shallow baking dish, arrange the pieces of fish on this bed and pour the rest of the sauce over them. Add four tablespoons of water (or fish stock). Cook in the oven at 350° uncovered, for 30 to 40 minutes, depending on the thickness of the fish. Serves four.

Swordfish, *Xiphias gladius*: tail (top left); dorsal fin (bottom left); head (center); and the "sword" (top right)

Gurnards

Gurnards
ENGLISH-SPEAKING COUNTRIES

rascasse
FRENCH

Drachenkopf
GERMAN

scorfano
ITALIAN

rascacio, cabracho
SPANISH

cap-roig
CATALAN

rocaz, rascasso
PORTUGUESE

scórpena
GREEK

iskorpit
TURKISH

bou keshesh
ARABIC

90

It is a pity that the common English name for fish of the family Triglidae should be gurnard. It has an unattractive ring to it, suggestive somehow of a creature with a surly disposition, or prematurely aged. In Scotland they have better names: crooner, croonack, gowdie. "Croon" there means not to sing in the style of the 1940s but to emit a croaking noise, which these fish do. Consider this pleasing description of the gray gurnard by the nineteenth-century ichthyologist Couch: "Its habits are social so far as regards its own species, for not only do they commonly keep together in companies, but sometimes in the fine weather of summer they will assemble together in large numbers, and mount to the surface over deep water, with no other apparent object than the enjoyment of the season; and when thus aloft they move along at a slow pace, and rising and sinking in the water for short distances, and uttering a short grunt, as if in self-gratification."

The gurnard family is well represented in the temperate and warm waters of the Atlantic and Mediterranean, and it also includes a few Indo-Pacific species. Its members all have relatively large heads, covered with bone. It is rare for them to reach a length of more than 20 inches and many are so small as to be suitable only for fish soup.

In North America, where the name "sea robin" is often used, the gurnards are little used for food. In Europe, the larger species are brought to market, especially *Eutrigla gurnardus*, the gray gurnard, and *Trigla lucerna*, the tub gurnard, the largest of all. There is also a rosy red gurnard, the piper, *Trigla lyra*, and another red one, *Aspitrigla cuculus*, which is shown in the painting. The streaked gurnard, *Trigloporus lastoviza*, is of so bright a red that its name in several languages means "drunkard". The best Indo-Pacific species is *Chelidonichthys kumu*, another red one. It is found in southern Africa, Australasia, Japan and China, and is a good food fish.

Gurnards tend to have rather dry flesh, but it is firm and white and yields good fillets. These may be fried. A large gurnard may be stuffed, and then baked, with very pleasing results. I greatly enjoyed a gray gurnard *Farci à la Boulonnaise* (see page 190). The recipe presented below is a Turkish one, which is ideal for people with access to really fresh almonds.

It used to be the practice to preserve fried fillets in vinegar, but they cannot have been greatly esteemed if we are to judge by Shakespeare's Falstaff, who said: "If I be not ashamed of my soldiers, I am a soused gurnet."

Gurnard with Almond Sauce

I whole gurnard, weighing 3 pounds	generous ½ cup olive oil
court bouillon, enough to cover the fish	juice of ½ lemon
for the sauce	salt and pepper
I cup freshly blanched almonds	slices of lemon and chopped coriander,
I slice white bread, with crusts removed	for garnish

First have the gurnard cleaned, then cook it in a *court bouillon* (see page 177). While it is cooking, prepare the sauce as follows.

Pound in a mortar, or blend very thoroughly in an electric blender, the freshly blanched almonds with the white bread, adding enough cold water to produce a creamy paste. Add the olive oil, mixing all the time, and then the lemon juice and seasoning to taste. Be careful not to add too much lemon juice – the sauce should have the consistency of thick cream. Serve it cold with the fish, which may be cold too or hot. Garnish the fish liberally with thin lemon slices, and sprinkle chopped coriander over the sauce. Serves four.

Alternative Fish
parrotfish (p 70)
mullet (p 78)

Alternative Recipes
Bapsetek Ikan (p 80)
Baked Fish Spetsai Style (p 68)

A red gurnard, *Aspitrigla cuculus* (left); and a sea robin of North American waters, *Prionotus carolinus* (right)

Scorpion Fish
ENGLISH-SPEAKING COUNTRIES

grondin
FRENCH

Knurrhahn
GERMAN

poon
DUTCH

cabra
PORTUGUESE

rascacio, cabracho
SPANISH

cap roig
CATALAN

capone
ITALIAN

capóni
GREEK

kırlangıç
TURKISH

trigla
RUSSIAN

djaje, serdouk
ARABIC

knurhane
DANISH

kurek
POLISH

knorrhane, knot
SWEDISH

knurr
NORWEGIAN

urrari
ICELANDIC

shek kau kung
CHINESE

kanagashira, hobo
JAPANESE

Scorpion fish, mainly of the genus *Scorpaena*, occur all around the world, but it is in the Mediterranean and especially in Provence that one of their number, *S scrofa*, has achieved fame as an essential ingredient for *bouillabaisse*. It is the largest of its genus, with a maximum length of 20 inches. The color varies, but red or orange is usual. As the painting shows, this is a fish of arresting appearance, always a focus of attention in a market display. In life, the mottled and irregular appearance of the fish enables it to rest invisibly on the sea bottom, supporting itself on its ventral fins and waiting for suitable prey to come within range. When this happens, the scorpion fish moves extremely fast and its mouth opens very wide.

Large specimens of *S scrofa* are normally cooked whole, usually baked with aromatic herbs, and they make a noble dish. It is the smaller specimens which are used for *bouillabaisse*, but it is a moot point whether they are really better for this purpose than their minor relations such as *S notata*, which bears names such as *petite racasse* or *scorfanotto*. Referring to another of these (the *rascasse noire*, *Scorpaena porcus*), the poet Méry romantically suggested that, swimming among the rocks close to shore, it somehow managed to absorb the aromatic essences of the herbs growing on the clifftop. If this inshore species could really achieve this feat, it would have the edge over *S scrofa*, which prefers deeper waters. However, it is perhaps best – and it is certainly prudent if one is in the company of people from Provence – to stick with the idea that *S scrofa* is the one and only rascasse for *bouillabaisse*.

The late A J Liebling once daringly suggested in the *New Yorker* that people thousands of miles away from the waters in which rascasses swim might still make a satisfactory *bouillabaisse* by using related species, for example the redfish of North Atlantic waters (see page 94). I would add, as an interesting possibility, the cabezon and other large sculpins (all of which have a certain rascasse look) of the Pacific coast of Canada and the USA. There are also true scorpion fish which could be tried out in, for example, the Caribbean (where *S plumieri*, the spotted scorpion fish, is the largest and the most common) and in Australasian waters, but I haven't yet experimented myself. Nor have I had an opportunity to explore the potential of the various "stingfish" or scorpion fish found in Japanese waters. They mostly belong to the genera *Sebastes* (see page 94) and *Sebastodes*, and several of them are highly prized, but the various and special Japanese ways of preparing them bear no relation to *bouillabaisse*.

Don Nicolas Magraner Garcia of Palma on the island of Majorca gave me the recipe below.

Cap-roig con Salsa de Almendra
(Scorpion Fish with Almond Sauce)

$1\frac{3}{4}$ pounds of rascasse (cleaned weight)	1 cup roasted almonds
seasoned flour	4 medium tomatoes
4 tablespoons olive oil	2 chicken livers
	$\frac{1}{2}$ cup sherry

Alternative Fish
small turbot (p 100)
trigger-fish (p 110)

Alternative Recipes
Fish Baked with Tahini (p 187)
Pargo con Salsa de Aguacate
(p 44)

Cut the fish into eight pieces (two per person), dip them in seasoned flour then brown them lightly in a pan of hot olive oil.

Grind the roasted almonds. Peel, halve and broil the tomatoes. Broil the chicken livers briefly. Mix all this together, add the sherry and mix again.

Place the pieces of fish in a heatproof earthenware casserole and pour the sauce over them. Cover and cook gently for about 30 minutes. Serves four.

The finest scorpion fish (French rascasse) of the Mediterranean, *Scorpaena scrofa*

Ocean Perch & Rockfish

Ocean Perch, Redfish
& Rockfish
ENGLISH-SPEAKING COUNTRIES
(Names for northern Europe
apply to Sebastes marinus, *for*
southern Europe to Helicolenus
dactylopterus, *for the orient to*
various Sebastes *species)*

chèvre, rascasse du Nord
FRENCH

Rotbarsch
GERMAN

roodbaars
DUTCH

cantarilho
PORTUGUESE

gallineta
SPANISH

scorfano di fondale
ITALIAN

mosrskoĭ okun'
RUSSIAN

stor rødfisk
DANISH

karmazyn
POLISH

iso kuninkaankala
FINNISH

rödfisk
SWEDISH

uer, raudfisk
NORWEGIAN

karfi
ICELANDIC

mebaru, hatsume, etc
JAPANESE

Alternative Fish
Mediterranean sea breams,
porgies (pp 40, 42, 44)

Alternative Recipes
Tilefish Wakasa (p 59)
Gefilte Fish (p 198)

Within the large family Scorpaenidae, whose most fearsome-looking members are represented on page 92, there is a large group of fish which are of medium size, have bony cheeks (as do the scorpion fish), belong to temperate waters rather than to the tropics, and are generally good to eat. Many are red, and some are indeed called redfish, but the range of colors and names is extensive, as is the geographical spread. All these factors tend to obscure the close relationship between these fish. (I should add, as an example of further potential confusion, that it took me a while to find out that the fish exported as "orange roughy" from New Zealand, does not belong to this group, as I had thought, but to the family Trachichthyidae. It is the same species which can be fished in the Atlantic, *Hoplostethus atlanticus,* where it has even less attractive names such as "slime head".)

However, back to the family we started with. The best known Atlantic species are the bluemouth, *Helicolenus dactylopterus,* and the species which is called ocean perch (in the USA; it is redfish in Britain), *Sebastes marinus.* The latter can be as long as 40 inches, although its market length is rarely as much as half of that. A smaller relation, *Sebastes viviparus,* bears the misleading name "Norway haddock". In Britain, these fish are often used for making the "fish fingers" which are viewed with dismay by gastronomic purists (quite why, I do not know, since they are convenient and tasty and the Japanese, who are above criticism in seafood matters, have long enjoyed such products).

But this is far from all. The Indo-Pacific tropics do not contain such fish, but the North Pacific certainly does. There are quite a few species in Japanese waters, and, as for the Northwest Pacific coast of the USA, this seems to be their headquarters (or perhaps one should say headwaters) and a fish market there is a real eye-opener for Europeans in this respect. It dawned on me after I had been in California for a while that the whole host of "rock cod" (well over 50 species, all in the genus *Sebastes*) which one meets there, often under the general name "rockfish" (also "Pacific snapper" and "red snapper"), all belong to this group. With so many to choose from, and with some of them having several common names, what is the cook to do? A good answer is to study *The California Seafood Cookbook,* whose three authors (see under Cronin in the bibliography) comprise one writer, one chef and one person concerned with fish marketing: just the right combination for this particular problem. They do not list all edible species, but they have helpfully grouped the better known ones into categories, best first. They comment that in general there is a correlation between depth of body and excellence; and they direct particular attention to the following as being of "fancy" quality:

● *Sebastes auriculatus,* the bolina, with which they bracket the gopher rockfish, the copper or barriga rockfish and the China rockfish (the last of which has an interesting pattern of yellow on near-black).

● *S ruberrimus,* the goldeneye rockfish, plus the flag or tree rockfish and the canary or fantail rockfish.

Their last category – species whose flesh is less well adapted to the lifting of firm fillets – includes the bocaccio, *S paucispinis,* and the attractively named chili pepper, *S goodei,* which I like well. They do not categorize the largest, the cowfish or cowcod, *S levis,* although this is a great prize for sport fishermen.

Although this whole group of fish includes none of sensational merit, with the possible exception of a couple of Japanese species which I have yet to taste and which Japanese authors praise, it is an important group. Many of its members lend themselves well to any sort of fish cookery. Since they vary in their particular merits, I have no single recommendation for the whole tribe, but suggest that those of "fancy" quality be treated like sea breams or porgies (see pages 40-44) and that others be used for making really good fish balls (see pages 197) or fish cakes.

"Norway haddock", *Sebastes viviparus* (top); and redfish, *S marinus* (center and bottom)

White Pomfret

Butterfish & Harvestfish

Pomfret is a name used usually for two deep-bodied narrow fish found in Asian coastal waters. These have many characteristics in common, but belong to different families. The white pomfret, *Pampus argenteus*, is in the family Stromateidae; whereas the so-called black (brown-gray in reality) pomfret, *Formio niger*, is the one and only member of the family Formionidae. The pomfrets, when adult, have no pelvic fins – a family characteristic.

The white pomfret, shown in the upper part of the painting, is the larger, with a maximum length of 20 inches; the black pomfret reaches only 12 inches. In each instance, average market length is about half the maximum.

The white pomfret is the most highly esteemed fish for serving at honorific meals in Malaysia, where the excess of demand over supply makes it expensive. Indeed it is everywhere expensive. Its firm white flesh divides readily into fillets, and the soft anal fin and tail fin should be eaten too. The black pomfret (referred to by some authors as "German fish", I know not why) is also good.

Pomfret is also the English name for a fish found in the Mediterranean and East Atlantic, *Stromateus fiatola*. It has oval golden marks running in interrupted bands from front to back, so is a pretty fish; but it is less good to eat than its Asian relations, having flesh which is too soft.

Some other members of the same family are of greater interest, notably the butterfish of the Northwest Atlantic, *Peprilus triacanthus*, shown bottom right in the painting. This is the butterfish, also known as dollarfish, shiner, pumpkin-seed, and harvest-fish; but the last of these names is better reserved for *P alepidotus*, which has a more southerly range. It is the fish shown bottom left.

Howard Mitcham has a lovely chapter on "The Beautiful Butterfish" in his *Provincetown Seafood Cookbook*. " . . . this", he writes, "is one 'trash' fish that the fishermen do not throw back. They save every one of them and pass them out to their relatives and friends. Sometimes a fisherman will bring a bucket of baby butterfish into Cookie's, and Joe and Wilbur will put on a fish fry. They'll fry these babies and the customers will sit there all afternoon nibbling the fish and washing them down with beer."

The name butterfish is used of other species too. In Hong Kong, *Oplegnathus punctatus* is the "spotted butterfish"; it has a deep, thin body, with a parrot-like beak for tearing food off rocks, and is highly esteemed. The name is also used in California for fillets of sablefish, *Anoplopoma fimbria*.

Given what I said above about Malaysia, it seems right to choose a Malay recipe for the pomfret. It will work just as well for the butterfish and harvestfish, but not for the Mediterranean species.

Pangang Ikan Bawal
(Barbecued Pomfret)

4 pomfret, each large enough for one person, cleaned and scaled	8 small fresh red chili peppers, de-seeded
2 medium onions	1 cup coconut cream
4 cloves garlic, peeled	(first extraction, see page 177)
	1 lime or lemon

Chop finely the onions, garlic and chili peppers, and mix them with the coconut cream. Pour this over the fish and leave them to marinate for several hours.

Remove the fish from the marinade and grill them over a charcoal fire. Keep the marinade warm by the fire and use it to baste the fish, frequently.

When the fish are ready (which will not take long, since small pomfret are not thick), serve them with a squeeze of the lime or lemon juice. Serves four.

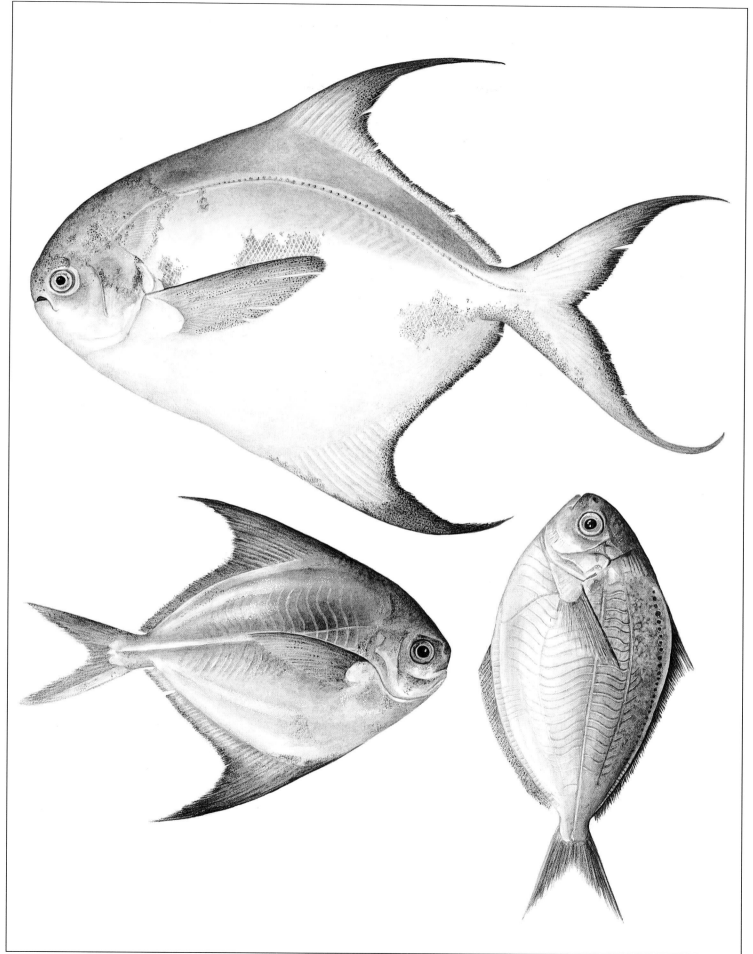

White pomfret, *Pampus argenteus*; below: harvestfish, *Peprilus alepidotus* (left) and butterfish, *P triacanthus* (right)

John Dory

H ere is a fish of remarkable shape: deep and thin in the body, belonging to the genus *Zeus* (after the Greek god). It occurs in the Mediterranean and Northeast Atlantic as *Z faber*, in Australasian waters as *Z australis* and in the northern part of the Pacific from Japan to southern Korea as *Z japonicus*. Less well known species are found in the western North Atlantic and on the Pacific coast.

The maximum length of these fish is around 2 feet, and a large specimen may weigh as much as 7 pounds. Market size is usually about half as large. The thin body serves a purpose. This fish cannot swim very fast, so is unable to catch its prey by speed. Instead it uses stealth, approaching head-on with an almost invisible outline and then shooting out its huge, retractable jaws to engulf its prey.

The John Dory's mouth, so ingeniously hinged and capable of opening very wide, includes some bones of striking shape. The configuration of these has suggested, at least in Turkey where the fish's name means "carpenter", a set of carpenter's tools.

The black marks on each side of the fish are responsible for many of its common names, signifying an association with St Peter, whose fingers are supposed to have left the marks. One tale is that this is the fish which he took up on the instructions of Christ, to find in its mouth the silver which he was to pay as tribute. But this can't be so, since the incident took place by the Sea of Galilee (fresh water) and the John Dory is a marine fish. The alternative story is that St Peter threw a John Dory back into the sea after it had engaged his sympathy by making distressed noises. That is possible.

The large head and gut account for nearly two thirds of the weight of this remarkable fish, so there is a lot of waste. It is, moreover, a thin fish. Despite this, the John Dory yields excellent fillets. It is a prized fish in Australian waters (especially New South Wales) as well as in the Mediterranean. An alternative French name for the fish, *poule de mer* (sea chicken), is an indication of the esteem in which it is held in France.

In Britain its popular estimation, previously low, was boosted by the remarkable partiality for it shown by the eighteenth-century actor John Quin, who flourished in Bath, where his celebrity "as the prince of epicures was well known, and where his palate finished its voluptuous career". Kitchener reports that, in considering which sauce best suited his favorite fish, Quin eventually announced "the Banns of Marriage between delicate Ann Chovy, and good John Dory", a pleasing conceit.

Filetti di Pesce Gallo al Marsala
(Fillets of John Dory cooked with Marsala)

Marsala is a wine much used in Sicilian cooking, whence this recipe comes (although not from a Sicilian, who would use olive oil instead of butter).

1 whole John Dory weighing 2 pounds or more
a little flour
$\frac{1}{2}$ stick butter
$1\frac{1}{4}$ cups Marsala
$1\frac{1}{4}$ cups strained fish stock

Wash and dry the fillets and coat them lightly with flour. Fry them gently in butter until they take color on both sides, then add the Marsala and fish stock.

Continue cooking gently, covered, until the amount of liquid is reduced by half. Then serve the fillets in their sauce. Serves four.

John Dory, *Zeus faber*

Turbot

100

I f one were to say that the two finest flatfish in the world are the so-called Dover sole (see page 104) and the turbot, it may seem like an unduly European point of view, since both species are exclusively European. However, that's the way it is, in my opinion, and the turbot, *Psetta maxima*, scores two points over the Dover sole. First, it is generally bigger: large specimens may be as long as 40 inches, and have considerable breadth and weight. Secondly, it has been honored by having a special utensil, the *turbotière*, created for it. (I have not been able to determine when the first *turbotière* was made, but it was evidently long after Roman times, if we are to believe the familiar anecdote about how the Emperor Domitian called upon the Roman Senate to debate what sort of vessel should be used to cook a huge turbot sent to him from the Adriatic. The alleged behavior of Domitian has been a favorite target for moralisers as recently as in nineteenth-century England, but his question seems to me just as good a one for Senators to consider as how to conquer the Parthians and that sort of thing.)

Although confined to European waters, the turbot has an extensive range: from the Black Sea through the Mediterranean and up the Atlantic coasts as far as the Arctic Circle. The color of the back is generally grayish or sandy brown, and it is covered with tiny bony tubercles. In the Black Sea region, these tubercles become much more prominent, indeed larger than the fish's eyes. This accounts for the vernacular names there (meaning "nail-head"). The great breadth of the turbot's body accounts for an old Scots name, "bannock-fluke" (bannock being a round oatcake, and fluke a name for left-eyed flatfish).

The main fishery for the turbot in Atlantic waters is in the North Sea. The numbers caught are small in relation to the demand. The firm white flesh is highly esteemed and is often honored by restaurants with an expensive sauce. I remember from the years when I lived in Brussels how often it was served there with Sauce Mousseline (see page 202), and I must say that this is an excellent accompaniment. The French writer Brillat-Savarin has a memorable anecdote about the procedure devised for steaming a giant turbot – the cook finished up using a laundry boiler. This is a useful reminder that steaming is an excellent way of cooking turbot. However, slices cut across and fried, with the skin still on, are also delicious as I found in Bulgaria. Various authorities have urged the desirability of eating the skin and an idiosyncratic Scots cookery writer, Jenny Wren, asserts in her book of 1880 that the fins should on no account be discarded as they are the true "tid-bit". My recipe is from Tom Jaine (*Cooking in the Country*, 1986); he combines knowledge with imagination and flair.

Turbot with Lime and Green Ginger

4 fillets of turbot, each of 6 ounces	1 teaspoon green (ie fresh) ginger, grated
1 lime	salt and pepper
2 tablespoons butter	$\frac{1}{4}$ cup white wine

Pare the lime in strips, without the pith, and blanch the peel. Remove the pith from the rest of the lime and cut the fruit into sections. Finely shred the blanched peel.

Put the turbot fillets on a buttered dish, arrange the lime sections on top, sprinkle the grated ginger over all and add the shredded peel. Season with salt and pepper and add the wine. Bring to the boil on top of the stove, then transfer to the oven at 160°, cover with foil and leave until done. Then remove the fillets and reduce the juices to form a sauce. (Or, adds Tom Jaine, coat the whole dish with a hollandaise sauce, "whose unctuousness is enjoyable in contrast to the taste of ginger and lime"). Serves four.

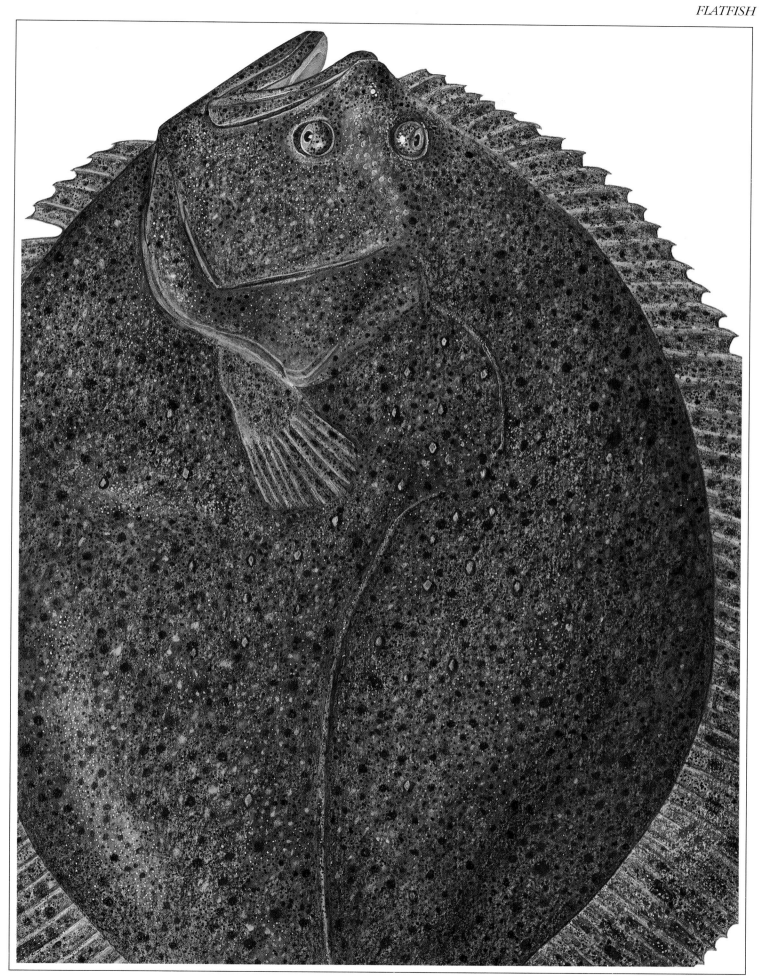

101

Turbot, *Psettus maximus*

Plaice

102

Large red or orange spots on the brown "back" (more correctly "eyed side") of the plaice make it instantly recognizable. And it is anyway one of the most familiar fish in European fish shops, being abundant on the continental shelf over a wide range, from the western Mediterranean up to Iceland and Norway. Indeed it is the most important flatfish of the European fisheries.

Pleuronectes platessa, to give it its scientific name, has a maximum length of 3 feet, but it is unusual to find a plaice measuring more than 20 inches.

Yarrell, a nineteenth-century writer on fish, was moved by the appearance of the plaice to indulge in some philosophizing characteristic of his time:
"The want of symmetry so unusual in vertebrated animals is the most striking and distinctive character of the fishes of this family; the twisted head with both eyes on the same side, one higher than the other, not in the same vertical line, and often unequal in size; the mouth cleft awry, and the frequent want of uniformity in those fins that are in pairs, the pectoral and ventral fins of the underside being generally smaller; and the whole of the color of the fish being confined to one side, while the other side remains white, – produce a grotesque appearance: yet a little consideration will prove that these various and seemingly obvious anomalies are perfectly in harmony with that station in nature which an animal possessing such conformation is appointed to fill."

Yarrell also points out that, while these fish remain "flat" on the seabed, they are capable of swimming very fast in a vertical position.

The esteem in which this fish is held varies considerably, since its quality as food depends not only on the season (spring is best) but also on the ground from which it is taken. Plaice from sandy bottoms are excellent, with firm and sweet flesh, while those from mud or gravel are likely to be poor fare.

Danes and Swedes are among the greatest enthusiasts for plaice, and the former at least prefer to buy their plaice alive. It happens that the plaice is very tenacious of life (Francis Day, the Victorian ichthyologist, recorded that one remained alive for 30 hours after being removed from the water) so this is not as difficult as one might think, though it may seem a heartless procedure.

Plaice can be poached, fried, or broiled. They are naturally tender, and care must be taken not to overcook them. In Denmark I particularly enjoyed *Rodspaetter Skawbo*, fried plaice served with home-made cranberry sauce. However the recipe I have chosen is a German one, associated with Hamburg and the old fishing port of Finkenwerder.

Scholle in Speck Gebraten
(Plaice with Smoked Bacon)

4 small plaice, cleaned
1 lemon
6 ounces smoked streaky bacon, cut thick
salt and flour
sprigs of parsley

Sprinkle the juice of half the lemon over the fish and leave them for ten minutes while you dice the bacon and fry it in a pan. Remove the bacon when done, but leave the fat in the pan. Season the plaice lightly with salt, dredge them in flour and fry them in the bacon fat for two to three minutes on each side, until golden-brown. Arrange the fish on a platter, white sides up, and sprinkle the diced bacon over them. Garnish with sprigs of parsley and the second half of the lemon, cut into wedges. Serve with boiled potatoes. Serves four.

103

Plaice, *Pleuronectes platessa*

Soles

104

True soles belong to the family Soleidae. They are dextral flatfish, which means that they have their eyes on the right hand side. If anything else is presented as a sole, forget it.

The name *solea* is from the Greek, "as the Greeks considered it would form a fit sandal for an ocean nymph" (Day, 1880-84). Fit praise for fish which are generally of superb quality, although not all of equal merit.

I shall not be thought chauvinist – for I have never come across disagreement on this point – when I say that the Dover sole, *Solea solea*, is the best sole. In any case, despite its name, it is not peculiar to the waters near Dover, England, nor even to the English Channel and the North Sea. On the contrary, it ranges all the way from the Mediterranean to the south of Norway, although the best fishing grounds for it are the North Sea and the Bay of Biscay. The fact that in Britain it is often distinguished from its lesser relations by being called "Dover sole" is simply the result of Dover having in the past been the best source of supply to the London market of freshly caught specimens.

The maximum length of this fish is 20 inches. The color of the eyed side is sepia, marked in life by darker blotches. Wheeler (1979) has described the habits of the sole thus: "The sole is found on sand, mud, and even fine gravel. During daylight it lies buried with only the eyes and gill cover exposed. At night-time, or during very dull days it is active, and large specimens are not infrequently seen swimming at the surface of the sea. The best catches of soles are usually made at night." The sole is to some extent migratory, moving into shallow water in spring and summer, and offshore when the sea cools during winter. The North Sea being at the northern end of its range, it may be driven during winter to seek refuge in the few deeps which this sea offers, such as the "Silver Pits", so called because of the concentration of soles there during really cold weather.

The name sole may also be correctly applied, but usually with a qualifying epithet (for example "French" sole for *Pegusa lascaris*), to other species of the family Soleidae. There are several in European waters, but they do not include the so-called "lemon sole" which belongs to a different family. Nor are most of the "soles" of North America true soles. There are none on the eastern seaboard of the USA. On the Pacific coast there are at least two left-eyed flounders and a dozen right-eyed ones to which the common name sole has been given; but none is a sole. (That is not to say that they lack merit. The petrale sole, the rex sole, the "English sole" and the "Dover sole" are all deservedly popular.)

There are some true soles in Asian waters, for example the widely distributed Oriental sole, *Euryglossa orientalis*, which is a favorite of Hong Kong restaurateurs. The Japanese are unfortunate in having only inferior species, such as *Zebrias zebra*, the striped sole: "not tasty", says the great expert Okada.

The true sole keeps relatively well, and many authorities hold that it is at its best a day or two after death, the theory being that its flavor develops during this period, whereas that of other flatfish deteriorates.

A whole sole, broiled and served with nothing more than lemon wedges, is as good a dish as one could have. However, it is a fish which is well adapted to being filleted, yielding cohesive, firm fillets of a good thickness, and many of the classic sole recipes are for fillets. These are sometimes masked in an over-elaborate sauce which could well be done without. I would agree however that a home-made Sauce Tartare (page 201) complements fried fillets nicely, and I even go along with the famous *Sole à la Normande*, which involves a complex garnish but works.

The recipe which I particularly recommend (Sole au Glui, see page 179) is an unusual one, and distinctly homespun. It simply enhances, in a subtle way, the intrinsic fine flavor of the fish.

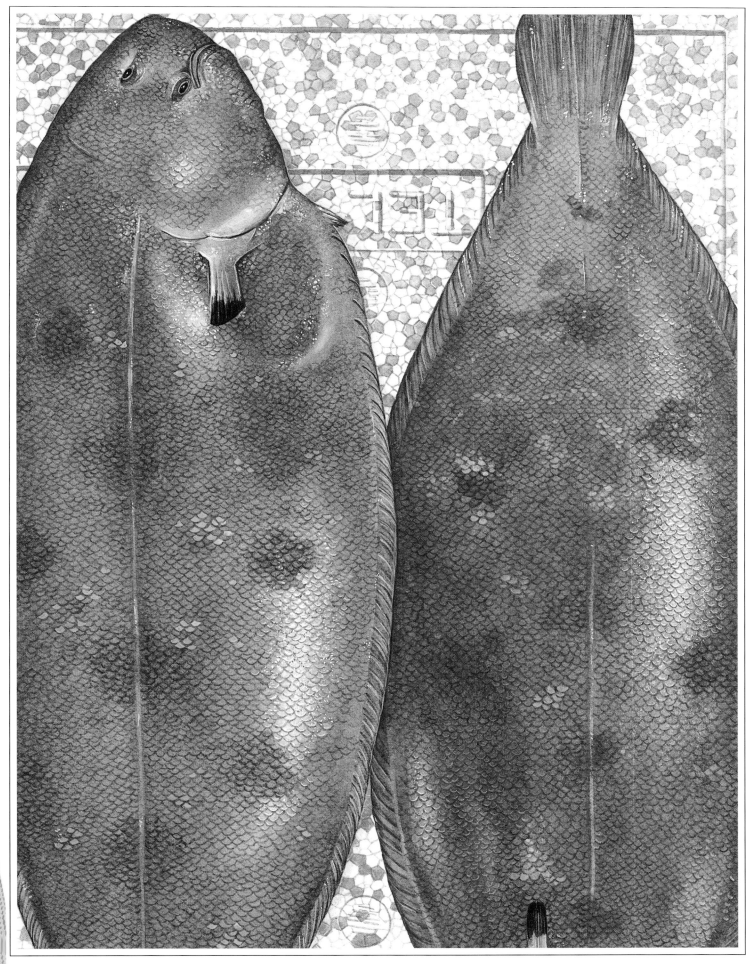

Dover sole, *Solea solea*

Halibut

106

There is no doubt about which is the largest of the flatfish. The halibut, *Hippoglossus hippoglossus*, has been known to reach a length of 8 feet and a weight of over 650 pounds. It is, moreover, a creature of extraordinary vitality and a strong fighter. At the beginning of this century, when halibut were still fished by trawl or line from frail dories launched by a "halibut schooner", some epic struggles took place over the hauling in, gaffing and clubbing of the giant fish. When anglers whose prey is relatively small fish talk of their struggles with "great fighters" or "worthy opponents", the implied picture of some sort of equal contest may seem unreal. Few anglers have perished in their efforts to land a trout. But deep-sea fishermen who pursued the halibut were engaged in a real combat, and their boats might even have been capsized and lost.

The halibut is a fish of the North Atlantic, ranging from the cold waters of the Arctic down to New Jersey and Scotland. It is less common further south. The color of the eyed side is greenish-brown or dark brown.

The name used to be spelled "holibut", and "holy" forms part of its name in several languages. The reason for this is not clear. The flesh of the halibut tends to be dry, and in large specimens, coarse. It has always enjoyed high esteem in Norway and in Greenland, where it has been an important element in the diet: strips of the flesh are dried and preserved for future consumption.

The reputation of the halibut in West Europe has fluctuated. Nineteenth-century authors record references to the halibut as "workhouse turbot", evidently a term of disparagement, and generally describe it as a fish which could be sold only when nothing better was available. However, a Mr Rowell, writing in *Land and Water* (16 July 1881) said that at Newcastle-upon-Tyne the halibut was prized, and that it cost more than twice as much as cod or ling. As if to defend this unusual preference, he continued: "Let any one get a piece of halibut from a small one, season it with nutmeg, pepper, and salt, and bake it in the oven, and I know nothing so fine."

Mr Rowell was anticipating a change in the fortunes of the halibut which has become obvious in the twentieth century, now that it commands a fair price and is definitely in demand. One region where it is not in demand, because it is not present, is the Caribbean. However, my suggested recipe comes from there.

Fish Steaks in Cream and Lime Juice

This is a wonderfully adaptable recipe, says Cristine MacKie in *Trade Winds*: "try it with red snapper, swordfish, . . . or any firm fleshed northern fish."

5-6 ounces steaks of halibut or any firm-fleshed fish	1 teaspoon black pepper
2 tablespoons olive or coconut oil	1 tablespoon ground coriander seeds
1 large onion, finely chopped	4 drops tabasco sauce
1 clove garlic, crushed	2 tablespoons lime or lemon juice
3 cups tomato juice	1 teaspoon sugar
	generous $\frac{1}{2}$ cup heavy cream

Heat the oil and fry the onions and garlic until soft and golden. In another pan, heat the tomato juice to boiling point then add it to the first pan along with the black pepper, coriander seeds and tabasco. Simmer for 15 minutes. Then stir in the lime or lemon and sugar and simmer for five minutes more. Pour the cream into the center of the pan and do not stir but cover and simmer very gently for five minutes.

Place the fish steaks in the sauce. Cover again and cook very slowly for eight to ten minutes until the steaks are cooked through. Serve with plain or coconut rice. Serves four.

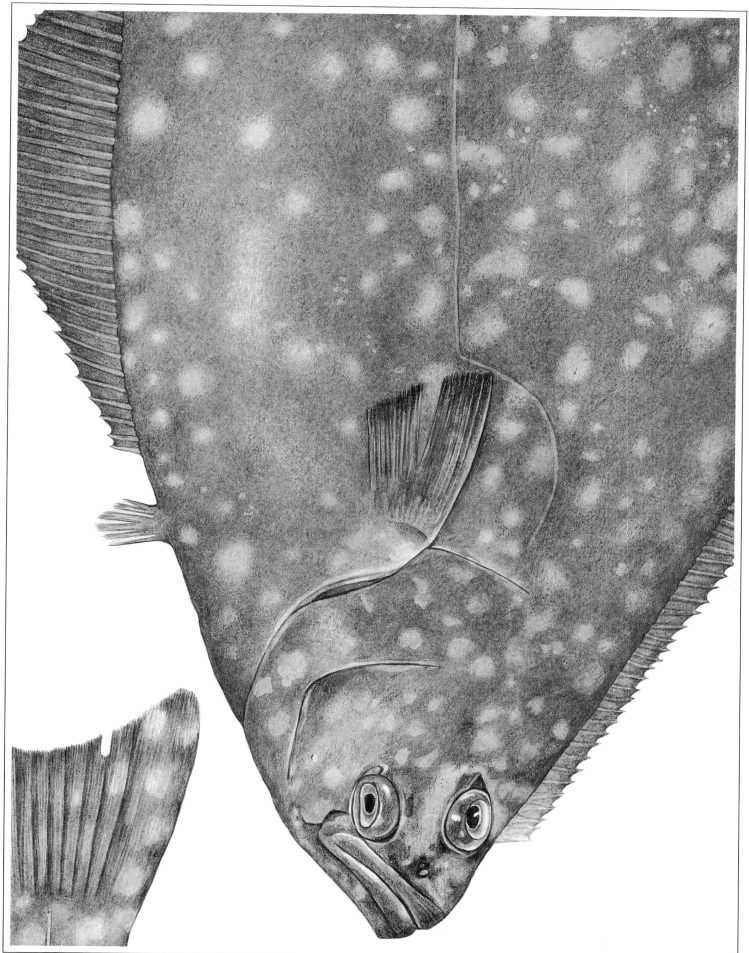

Halibut, *Hippoglossus hippoglossus*

Rabbit Fish

108

Rather few fish are named after land animals. The French name "rat" (see page 72) for the stargazer is one. Rabbit fish, applying to members of the family Siganidae, is another.

These fish used to be described as belonging to Indo-Pacific waters, where numerous species were listed. Now, however, following the gradual fall in the salinity of the Bitter Lakes which punctuate the Suez Canal, some Indo-Pacific fish have been able to swim through the Canal and establish themselves in the East Mediterranean. Foremost among these is *Siganus rivulatus*, which has now acquired local Mediterranean names as far west as Malta; but its path has been followed by *S luridus*, so two of them are now part of the Mediterranean fauna.

The rabbit fish, so-called because its rounded head and general appearance is thought to resemble a rabbit, may also be called "spinefoot". This is because it has sharp spines not only at the front of the dorsal fin, and in the pelvic fins, but also underneath in the anal fin. These spines can inflict painful wounds; it is thought that a mucus associated with them is venomous.

In the Seychelles, whence come the trio of rabbit fish in the painting, the name generally used for them is the French name *cordonnier*. *S rostratus* reaches a length of 15 inches; the other two are a little smaller (12 inches).

The flesh of these fish is firm and palatable. That from the underside is preferred. After a visit to the west coast of the Malayan peninsula, I noted that fried rabbit fish served on a bed of papaya pickle was a very successful dish. I don't suppose that there was any special magic about the papaya, but it is generally a good idea to serve a moderately sharp pickle with fried fish of this sort.

The recipe proposed is a Vietnamese one for fried fish with bamboo shoots, which are readily obtainable in cans. The only other ingredient which might cause problems is the *nuoc mam*. This is the Vietnamese name for the fish sauce found in so many Southeast Asian countries. By fish sauce is meant a sauce made from fermented fish, not a sauce made exclusively to accompany fish. Vietnamese will tell you that theirs is the best. I remember that when I was in Saigon shortly before the end of the Vietnam War, a charming lady who owned a *nuoc mam* factory presented me with a bottle of one of her finest vintages. It was amazingly good. I recalled the words of a mysterious French writer of the 1930s who signed himself Nestour and of whose book only one copy is known to survive, in the public library at Hanoi, which is where I inspected it. He said that the art of making fish sauce is comparable to that of making cognac.

Cá Sào Măng Tuoi
(Fish fried with bamboo shoots)

I pound rabbit fish	$\frac{1}{4}$ cup pork fat or olive oil
salt and pepper	2 shallots, finely chopped
10 ounces bamboo shoots	fish sauce (*nuoc mam*)
$\frac{1}{2}$ cup dried mushrooms	scallion leaves, cut into sections

Clean, skin and bone the fish, so that you are left with only the flesh. Cut it into small pieces and season it. Cut the bamboo shoots into small pieces, cook them in boiling water and drain them. Soak the mushrooms in water.

Heat the pork fat (or olive oil) in a pan, then fry the shallots and the fish in it. Remove them, and replace them with the bamboo shoots and mushrooms, some fish sauce and a little more salt and pepper. After these have cooked briefly, return the fish to the pan and mix all well together. After a few minutes the dish will be ready to be garnished with the scallion leaves and served. Serves four.

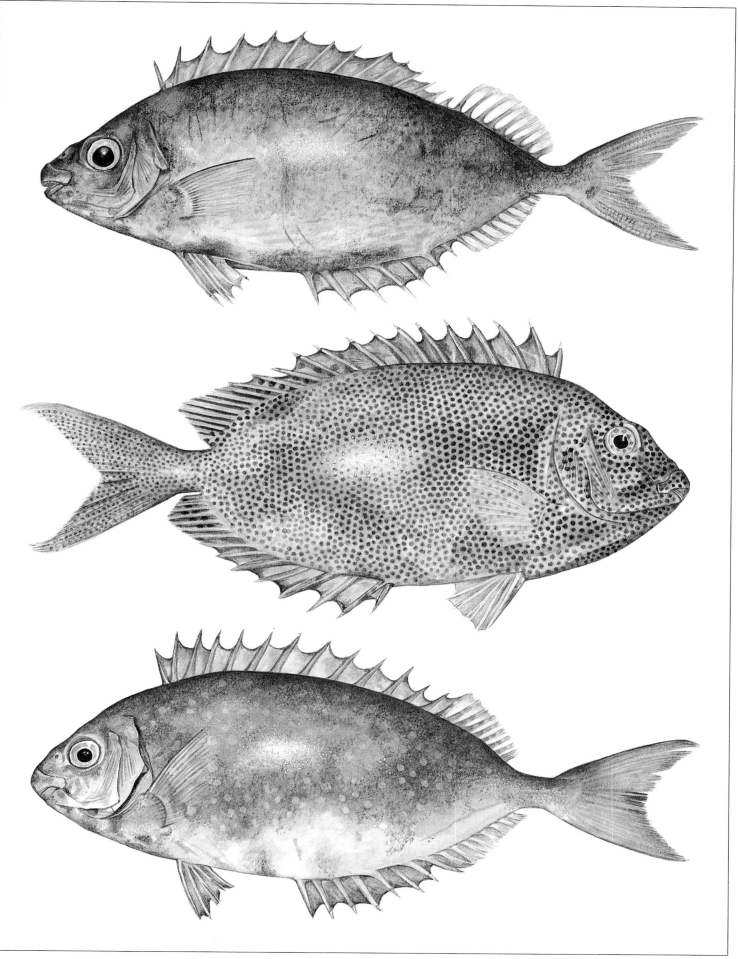

Three rabbit fish from the Seychelles: *Siganus rostratus,* cordonnier soule femme (top); *S stellatus,* cordonnier margueriete (center); and *S oramin,* cordonnier brisant (bottom)

Trigger-Fish

110

Fish of the family Balistidae may be called leatherjackets, in allusion to their remarkably thick and tough skins, but their most common English name is trigger-fish. The "trigger' is one of two little spines on the back, just behind the principal dorsal spine. By an ingenious system of fishy architecture this trigger can be used to lock the dorsal spine in an upright position, which makes the fish a less attractive morsel for any large predator.

Trigger-fish are said to swim around in pairs, so that if one is hooked the other can use its strong teeth to bite through the line. Further evidence of their crafty nature is given by Goode (1884-7): "Its manner of taking the bait is rather peculiar, I think, for instead of pulling the line backward or to one side it raises it upward so quietly that the fisherman does not perceive the motion, and then, by careful nibbling, cleans the hook without injury to itself."

The larger trigger-fish may reach a length of 24 inches or even a little more, but they are mostly smaller. The coloration of most (but not all) species is sombre. Although these fish are fairly short, they are deep-bodied, so have enough flesh to be worth eating, and this is good. They are often skinned before being sold.

Among the species brought to market are:
● *Balistes carolinensis*, of the West and East Atlantic and the Mediterranean; this is the one shown in the painting.
● *Monacanthus cirrhifer*, the most common species in Japanese waters and the most appreciated, especially in summer. Its liver is a delicacy.
● *Alutera monoceros*, a relatively large trigger-fish of the Indo-Pacific, which is grayish brown with yellow fins.
● *Abalistes stellaris*, another Indo-Pacific species, which Maxwell (1921) said was preferred to all other fish by many Malay, including fishermen. The reason given was the likeness between its flesh and chicken meat.

While not going so far as the Malay in my enthusiasm for these fish, I do think that they are greatly underrated as food, and when living in Tunisia and Southeast Asia I used to seek them out in the markets. The recipe given was adapted in the island of Phuket, in Thailand, from one for a chicken curry. The name refers to the tiny island near Phuket from which the cook who made the dish came.

Koh Lanta Trigger-fish Curry

1½ pounds skinned and cleaned trigger-fish
2 coconuts
2 pieces galingale
a generous bunch of lemon grass (about 10 stalks)
salt
12 small onions
1 large head of garlic
10 chili peppers
5 Kaffir lime leaves

Cut the trigger-fish into fairly large pieces.

Use the coconuts to make 1 cup of thick, and 5 cups of thin coconut cream (see page 177). Heat the thin coconut cream in a roomy pot, then add the fish and salt to taste. Cut the galingale into small pieces. Cut the lemon grass into lengths of about 1 inch and beat them to soften them and release the flavor. Add both ingredients to the pot. Peel and crush the small onions and the cloves of garlic, then add them and the chilis.

Simmer until the fish is tender – the time will depend on the size and shape of the pieces, but will not be more than 15 minutes. Then add the thick coconut cream and Kaffir lime leaves, bring just back to boiling point, remove from the heat at once, and serve. Serves four.

Alternative Fish
virtually all fish are suitable

Alternative Recipes
Ange de Mer au Four (p 120)
Moqueca de Peixe (p 190)

A trigger-fish, *Balistes carolinensis*

Puffer Fish

112

Puffer fish, or blowfish, which possess the faculty of enormously inflating their bellies so as to become outsize, prickly and unmanageable morsels from the point of view of a marine predator, also have a certain notoriety among human gastronomic predators.

Fugu, the Japanese name for some species of them, is a name associated with sudden death. Yet certain species are considered by the Japanese to be among the greatest of marine delicacies. These are *Fugu rubripes* (*torafugu*), and *F porphyreus* (*mafugu* or *namerafugu*).

These fish have to be prepared with great skill to avoid any possibility of the fatally toxic parts being eaten or contaminating the flesh. There are whole books in Japanese – I have one – devoted to the necessary technique, and only cooks who have qualified in this are allowed to deal with the fish. Even so, instances occur of Japanese dying from *fugu* poisoning, usually because someone without the necessary skill has attempted to prepare the fish. It is certainly no matter for amateurs, since the location of the toxin varies and years of training and experience are needed if all the signs are to be read correctly. *Fugu* are most often eaten in Japan in the form of *sashimi* and *nabemono*.

Puffer fish in other parts of the world are less dangerous, although it is well to treat all with caution. The species found off the eastern seaboard of the USA, *Spheroides maculatus*, has various names: puffer, swellfish, blowfish, toadfish and blowtoad. It has also been called "sea squab" for marketing purposes. It yields fine white meat, which it may be convenient to buy ready dressed. (If you buy a whole puffer, wear gloves; then cut off the tail and head and dorsal fin; detach the head; peel the skin back like a glove, after which the innards will drop out, leaving the flesh attached to the backbone. Discard everything except the white meat, and under no circumstances risk eating even a small piece of the liver.)

Of the various authors who have written about blowfish cookery in and around New Jersey, my favorite is Hugh Zachary. He gives, in a breezy style, exact instructions on how to clean a puffer (much as above, but he makes a cut through the thick skin all the way along the back and then peels the skin downwards on each side, exposing the white meat and backbone ready to be lifted out). He also supplies advice on cookery, including the much-debated question (much debated, anyway, in the circles in which he moves) whether the meat is better when cooked on the bone or when removed as fillets.

It is a version of Zachary's recipe which I give below. He remarks that the flavor of blowfish is so delicate that it is highly desirable to use fresh oil for the frying. Recycled oil, being used for the second or third time, will not produce really good results.

Fried Blowfish

4 blowfish fillets or steaks, off the bone	1 teaspoon paprika
generous $\frac{1}{2}$ cup milk	$\frac{1}{2}$ teaspoon salt
$\frac{3}{4}$ cup all-purpose flour	black pepper to taste
$\frac{3}{4}$ cup fine cornmeal	3 tablespoons cooking oil

Combine the flour, cornmeal and paprika, salt and pepper. "Meal" the fish fillets or steaks by dipping them in the milk and then rolling them in the flour mixture.

Heat the oil in a skillet until smoke begins to rise from it, then fry the fish for two or three minutes a side. Serves four.

Puffer fish of the Northwest Atlantic, *Sphoeroides maculatus*

Goosefish

114

The goosefish (British name angler-fish) is a fish of bizarre appearance and considerable size with a maximum length of 6 feet 6 inches. It is also known in Britain as monkfish, which is confusing as the name monkfish properly applies to the angel shark, a quite different fish. The principal species, *Lophius piscatorius*, has an extensive range from the Black Sea through the Mediterranean and up to Iceland. On the American side of the North Atlantic it is matched by its close relation, *L americanus*. Of the several Indo-Pacific species, *L litulon* is prized by the Japanese, so much so that there is a restaurant in Tokyo which serves nothing but various parts of this fish.

The goosefish is a master of camouflage, concealing itself in a manner well described by the Duke of Argyll in the nineteenth century, and quoted by Goode: "The whole upper surface is tinted and mottled in such close resemblance to stones and gravel and seaweeds that it becomes quite indistinguishable among them. In order to complete the method of concealment, the whole margins of the fish, and the very edge of the lips and jaws, have loose tags and fringes which wave and sway about amid the currents of water so as to look exactly like the smaller algae which move around them and along with them. Even the very ventral fins of this devouring deception, which are thick, strong and fleshy, almost like hands, and which evidently help in a sudden leap, are made like two great clam-shells . . ."

Thus disguised, the goosefish agitates the "fishing-rod" above its head and prepares to engulf in its vast mouth the smaller fish that come to investigate. It even has a spare fishing-rod. The main one projects forward and has a piece of tissue on it which serves as "bait". But in case this is bitten off, there is another in reserve.

The ability of the fish to swallow large prey is astonishing. A goosefish 26 inches long was found with a codling 23 inches long inside it. Naturally, such a remarkable creature has attracted many interesting vernacular names. The name "goosefish" (bestowed because it stuffs itself) is matched by bellyfish, allmouth (North Carolina) and lawyer in parts of New England.

The tail of the goosefish, or rather the tail-end of its body, is the part which is skinned and marketed. In the Netherlands it is sold as *ham* or *hozemondham*. The merits of the goosefish are now widely acknowledged in Europe but its acceptance as human food in North America has been advancing more slowly.

The flesh is so firm and white that it invites comparison with that of the lobster. Indeed there have been instances of a lot of goosefish being used to supplement a little lobster. The fishmonger in Marseilles who gave me the recipe for *Flan de Baudroie* – see below – commented that those who ate the result often thought it was a lobster dish until his wife told them the truth.

The tail-end of the goosefish may be poached or steamed, or opened out butterfly-fashion and broiled. Slices can be fried. The head, not often obtainable, makes a good soup and the roe is considered a delicacy in Japan.

Flan de Baudroie

2 pound tail end of goosefish
2 pounds ripe tomatoes

2 tablespoons olive oil
8 eggs

Cut the fish into large slices and poach these in simmering water for 20 minutes or so, depending on their thickness. Meanwhile, peel, chop and de-seed the tomatoes and soften them in the olive oil.

Cut up the cooked fish finely and mix it with the tomato. Beat the eggs into the mixture. Put it into a buttered mould and cook it in a *bain-marie* for an hour in the oven at 400°. Unmould and serve cold. Serves four.

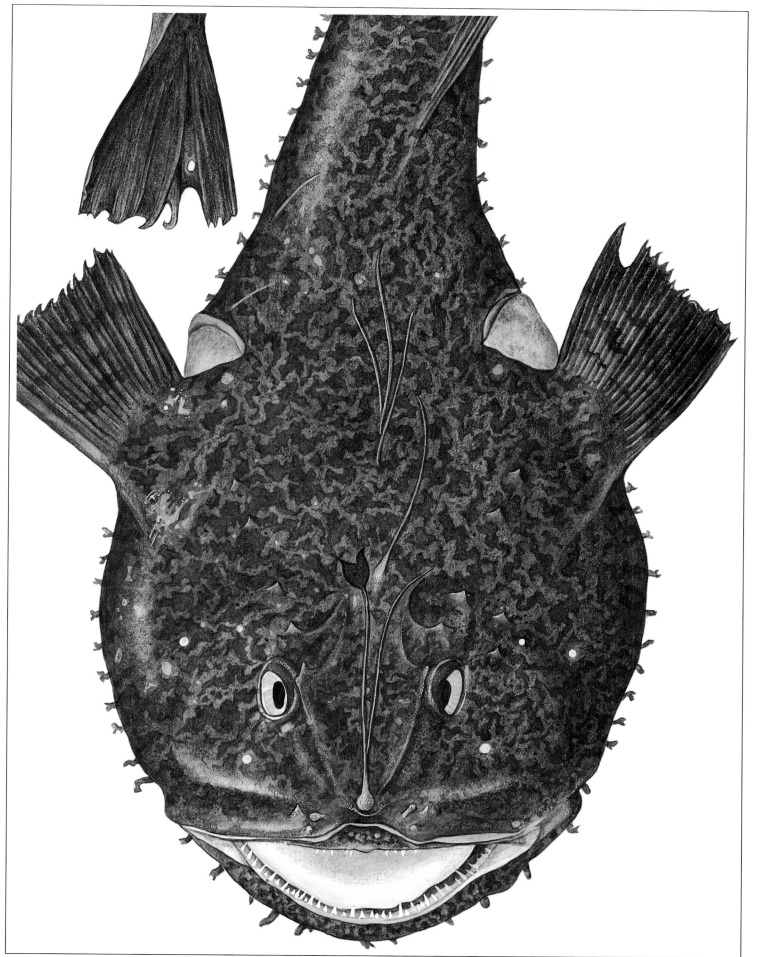

The goosefish of the Atlantic, *Lophius piscatorius*

Sturgeon

116

In the never-ending struggle for survival, sturgeon have done rather well. They are primitive fish and look it, with their "armor-plating" (rows of bony scutes along their sides) and their shovel-like snouts. These snouts are equipped with barbels for rooting about in search of food. The German name, from which many others are derived, is from the verb *störer*, meaning to root about. The tubular mouth is to the rear of the barbels, so that when the barbels detect food the sturgeon can shoot its mouth downwards, right onto the morsel, without checking its forward motion.

Sturgeon, of which there are about two dozen species, all in the family Acipenseridae, vary in their habitat and habits. Some species live at sea and spawn in fresh water, while others are purely freshwater species. They are all found in the northern hemisphere, and most of them in Central Eurasia.

They are a resource of considerable value, especially for their caviar. The fact that the rearing of young fish in a protected environment has proved possible in various places, including the Caspian Sea and the Northwest Pacific coast of North America, is likely to increase their importance.

The outstanding species, with the regions they belong to and their maximum lengths, are as follows:

● *Acipenser sturio*: the Mediterranean and Northeast Atlantic: 3 feet. Now rare, although populations still exist in the rivers Gironde and Guadalquivir and in the eastern Baltic.

● *A ruthenus*, the sterlet: fresh waters in the vicinity of the Black and Azov Seas, known also in Siberia: 20 inches. A small sturgeon, sometimes found at sea.

● *A gueldenstaedti*: the Black, Azov, and Caspian Seas. Its maximum length is 5 feet 6 inches. It has a short, blunt snout.

● *A stellatus*, the sevruga sturgeon: the Caspian and Azov Seas: 6 feet 6 inches. The main source of caviar in the Caspian.

● *A mikadoi*, the Japanese sturgeon: northern Japanese waters: 5 feet.

● *A transmontanus*, the white sturgeon: rivers in Northwest America: 15 feet.

● *A oxyrhinchus*: the eastern seaboard of North America: length as for *A sturio*, with which some authorities think it identical.

The quality of the caviar obtained from these species varies considerably. Beluga caviar has the most delicate flavor. It is gray, as is sevruga; whereas osetra is brownish or yellow-gold. Malossol caviar is not taken from a particular species; the name simply means that it has been very lightly salted.

As fish to be eaten, all sturgeon are good. Their flesh is fairly rich in fat, and it is possible to roast "joints" of them like meat. Alternatively, slices can be broiled or fried, and preferably served with a sharp dressing. Smoked sturgeon is a delicacy.

My recipe is a nineteenth-century one from the learned British author Piscator, who also had immense practical knowledge of fish and fish cookery.

Stewed Sturgeon

"Sturgeon should be cut up in slices of about an inch, or a little more, in thickness, which, being half-fried, should be placed in a stewpan with some good veal broth, an onion, and a bundle of sweet herbs, and be allowed to stew until it becomes perfectly tender. Having then fried an onion or two in the butter in which the fish was previously fried, put this, and also the gravy in which the fish was stewed, into a sauce pan, adding to it a glass or two of wine, some butter rolled in flour . . . and a spoonful of ketchup . . . As soon as the whole has boiled up well together, strain it through a sieve . . . and pour it over the fish. Garnish with sliced lemon." Serves four.

Alternative Fish
nothing suitable

Alternative Recipes
Ange de Mer au Four (p 120)
Mérou Blanc with Rosemary
Sauce (p 36)

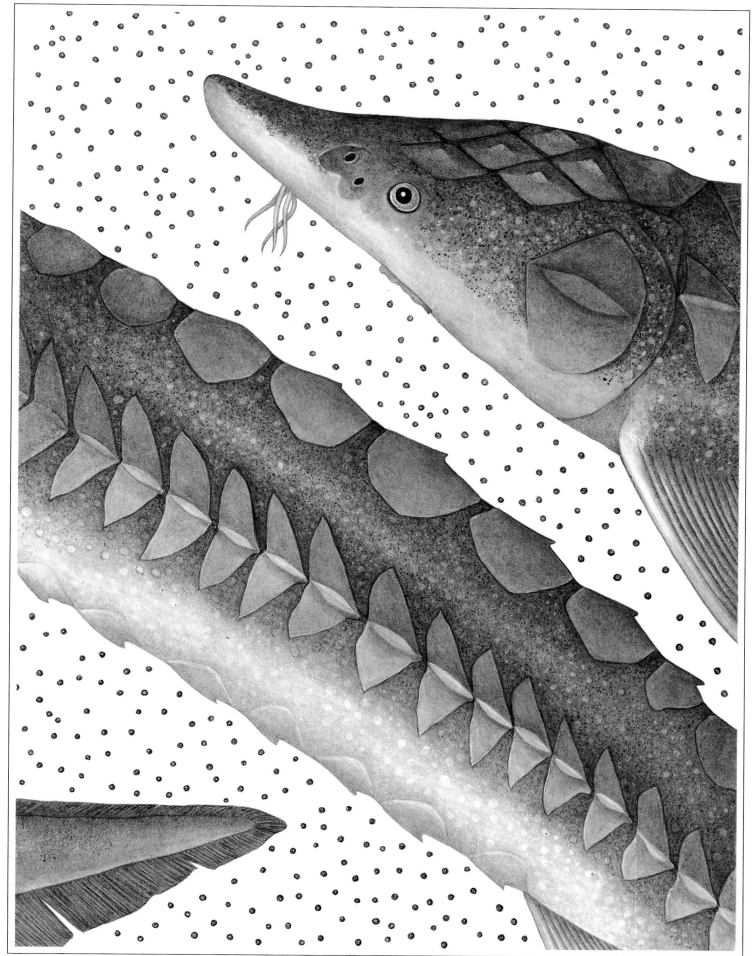

Atlantic sturgeon, *Acipenser sturio*, with Beluga caviar

Dogfish

118

Why are many of the smaller species of shark called "dogfish" in many different languages? The question is perplexing, all the more so since the doggy theme not only crosses species boundaries (thus *Squalus acanthias* is "spur-dog" and *Mustelus mustelus* is "smooth hound") but also extends laterally (newly born spur-dogs are called a "litter" of "pups").

This system of names does not extend to larger sharks, except for the porbeagle (*Lamna nasus*). The species to which it applies are those that have maximum lengths of anything from 24 inches to twice that. Most of them have tough, rough, sandpapery skins. They are regarded as a nuisance by fishermen in North America, and sometimes also in Europe; but everywhere except in North America they are seen as a marketable commodity. Whereas special techniques are needed for catching large sharks such as the porbeagle, the mako and the tiger shark, dogfish come up frequently in trawls. A few of the many species are:
- *Squalus acanthias*, the spur dog, found in the Mediterranean, the North Atlantic (both sides), and the North and South Pacific.
- *Mustelus canis*, the sand shark, common in warm waters of the West Atlantic.
- *M asterias*, the principal Mediterranean and Northeast Atlantic member of the genus; known as smooth hound.
- *Scyliorhinus stellaris*, the nursehound or huss, with a similar range. The painting shows an Irish specimen of its smaller relation, *S canicula*.

Whatever the true explanation of the name "dogfish", it was not bestowed in

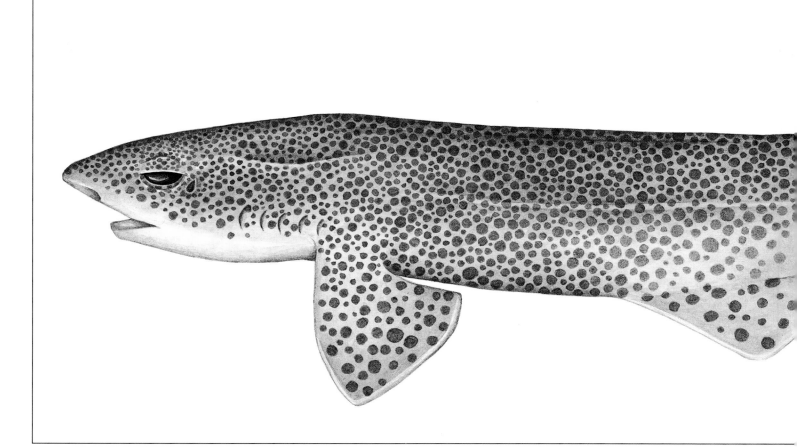

order to make these fish seem attractive to consumers. Indeed fishmongers have consistently rechristened them by more flattering names, some of which, like the British "rock salmon" or the Venetian *vitello di mare* ("veal of the sea"), are outrageously misleading. However, in so far as these euphemisms work, fine, since there are two reasons for encouraging consumption of dogfish. One is that they breed fast and are voracious predators, feeding often on smaller, more valuable species. The other is that they are good to eat, if properly prepared.

Like all sharks, dogfish have no true bones but make do with a cartilaginous skeleton. This is good from the cook's point of view, since there are no tiresome small bones to contend with and it is easy to lift off fillets of whatever size seems suitable. Dogfish do not have a delicate flavor, but this simply means that they do not need to be cooked in a delicate way; they are fine in fish and french fries, or covered with a robust sauce. The recipe below came from an Englishman who became one of the great experts on fishing and fish cookery in Turkey.

(A) kalb bahr, (B) ktat
ARABIC

(A) rødhaj, (B) glathaj
DANISH

(A) rödhaj, (B) glatthaj
SWEDISH

(A) raudhå, (B) glatthai
NORWEGIAN

(C) hangawr (Be), Kamot (Ur), corungun sorrah (Ta)
INDIAN LANGUAGES

hoshizame
JAPANESE

(C) pla chalam
THAI

(C) yu pasir, yu jereh
MALAY

(C) cucut pisang
INDONESIAN

(C) pating, bongalonon
PHILIPPINES

Mr Whittall's Dogfish

4 fillets or steaks of dogfish	2 bay leaves
4 tomatoes, peeled	I lemon, thinly sliced
2 small onions	4 tablespoons olive oil
pinch of salt	4 tablespoons parsley, chopped

Chop up the tomatoes and onions quite finely, place them in a large skillet, add just enough water to cover, and cook until a fairly thick sauce is formed. Remove from the heat, add the salt, bay leaves, most of the lemon slices, and the olive oil. On the bed thus prepared lay the fish, with the remaining few slices of lemon on top and a generous layer of chopped parsley over all. Cover and cook over a moderate heat for 20 minutes or until the fish is done.

Mr Whittall pointed out that this *basse cuisine* recipe permits the addition of almost anything you fancy. He recommended Worcestershire sauce. Serves four.

Alternative Fish
nothing suitable

Alternative Recipes   119
Fish and Chips (p 182)
Fried Drum Southern Style (p 50)
Anguille au Vert (p 184)

A common European dogfish, *Scyliorhinus canicula*

Angel Shark

120

T he angel shark, often called "monkfish", is *Squatina squatina* in the Mediterranean and Northeast Atlantic, but it has relations in warm waters elsewhere. It is a fish of unusual features and interesting names. It is correctly termed a shark, having cartilaginous rather than true bones and possessing most of the other characteristics of sharks. But in the view of scientists it represents a sort of evolutionary stage between sharks and rays. A glance at the small shark shown on page 119 and at the ray on page 123 will be enough to demonstrate that the angel shark occupies an intermediate position.

The whole question of which fish are more advanced, in evolutionary terms, than others is an interesting one. All fish without true bones – that is all sharks, rays and sturgeon – are considered to be primitive by comparison with the great majority of fish, which have true bones. But that is not to say that they have lacked staying power in the battle for survival. Sharks and rays have proved to be highly successful in this respect and my guess is that the same would apply to sturgeon but for the fact that their habitat renders them highly vulnerable to man and to the pollution created by man.

The angel shark certainly does not look like a conventional shark. On the contrary, it is generally agreed to present an ecclesiastical appearance. Medieval sages saw its large pectoral fins as wings and its tapering body and tail as angelic robes. From being an angel, it was later demoted to the rank of monk by the Norwegians who, according to Rondelet (1588) were impressed by a specimen washed up on the shore and noted that "it had a man's face, rude and ungracious, the head smooth and shorn. On the shoulders, like the cloak of a monk, were two long fins . . .". It is still often called monkfish, although promoted to bishop by some authorities; and an Australian species even came to be known as the archbishop fish.

In view of this ecclesiastical history, it does seem appropriate to reserve the name monkfish for this species, but it is often used for the quite different goosefish (see page 114). Since neither fish is normally sold whole, it is necessary to be aware of the potential confusion when setting out to buy either of them.

The Western Atlantic species is *S dumeril*. Both it and *S californica* of the Eastern Pacific are comparable in size, with a maximum length of about 5 feet, and eating quality (better than most people realize), to *S squatina*. Generally, an angel shark can be treated like a ray (see page 122), but it is always a safe bet to bake a sizable chunk of "wing" with added flavors. The recipe I give is from Tunisia.

By the way, if you have bought a whole fish and have a cabinet-maker among your friends, he or she will be glad to have the dried skin, which is excellent for polishing wood.

Ange de Mer au Four

4 thick slices of angel shark	I green bell pepper, de-seeded sliced
salt and pepper	2 tablespoons lemon juice
butter	2 medium eggs
3 tomatoes, sliced	2 tablespoons flour

Season the pieces of fish and lay them side by side in a buttered oven dish. Dot some more butter on top, then cover with the sliced tomatoes and green bell pepper rings. Pour the lemon juice over this and cook in the oven at 350° for 25 minutes or so.

Meanwhile beat the raw eggs well into the flour, pour this mixture over the dish and return it to the oven for a further 15 minutes. Serves four.

Angel shark, *Squatina squatina*

Rays & Skates

122

Ray or skate? In America and England the terms are more or less interchangeable, although the latter tends to be used of the bigger fish with long snouts. Americans are less apt to use the term ray. In addition there is a relatively newly-coined name, rajafish.

Like sharks, these are fish with no true bones; but they are of a very different shape, being flat and thin. They live on the sea bottom, where the coloring of their backs camouflages them successfully.

The rays and skates of the Mediterranean and North Atlantic are of the familiar kind, but in the tropical waters of the Indo-Pacific and Caribbean they are largely replaced by less appetising species such as sting-rays (which can reach a gigantic size), eagle rays, shovel-nose rays, and others.

Which is the best ray? Many would say *Raja clavata*, the thornback ray, but *R montagui*, the pretty ray shown in the painting, is also of good quality. So is *R radiata*, which belongs to the Arctic, but ranges some way south on both sides of the Atlantic.

There is a prejudice against rays in various parts of the world. A Filipino fisheries expert once lamented to me that he could not persuade his fellow countrymen to eat the creatures – he hated to see "all that protein going to waste".

Among possible causes for their unpopularity is the ammoniac odor which they give off. This results from the breakdown of the urea which they maintain in their blood. They need this to ensure that the salt water in which they live does not drain away the less salty water in their bloodstreams and tissues by osmosis. Rays are best kept for a couple of days before being eaten, and the ammoniac odor signals the departure of unwanted urea from them, so is welcome. Lemery, writing his *Treatise of All Sorts of Food* in 1745, had all this figured out: "The Thornback . . . should not be too fresh. It must be kept for some time, during which there is a little fermentation wrought in it, whereby some dull and viscous matters . . . are insensibly attenuated and destroyed: and therefore those that live at Paris . . . eat the Thornback in a better condition than those near the sea-side . . ."

Fricasseed Ray or Skate

2½ pounds "wing" of ray or skate	½ stick butter
½ teaspoon mace	4 tablespoons flour
a pinch of grated nutmeg	I cup light cream
a *bouquet garni*	¾ cup white wine
salt	

If what you are cooking is a section of a large "wing", dress it so that you have clean pieces, free of cartilage, about 1 inch across and 2 inches long; but don't worry about the exact size or shape. If dealing with a small "wing", just cut it along the lines of the fibers, from the thick side to the thin side, into 1 inch strips. The flesh will slip off the cartilage easily after it is cooked.

Place the fish in a heatproof casserole and add 3 cups water. Add also the mace, grated nutmeg, *bouquet garni* and salt. Bring to a boil, cover and leave to simmer for 15 minutes. Then discard the *bouquet garni*, remove the fish, slipping out any remaining cartilage, and keep it hot. You will find that you have about ¾ cup of cooking liquid left in the pot.

Melt the butter, stir in the flour, add the cooking liquid and a very little salt. Then add the cream and the white wine. Bring this mixture back to the boil and let it simmer gently and thicken for three to four minutes. Replace the pieces of fish in the sauce and serve hot. Serves four.

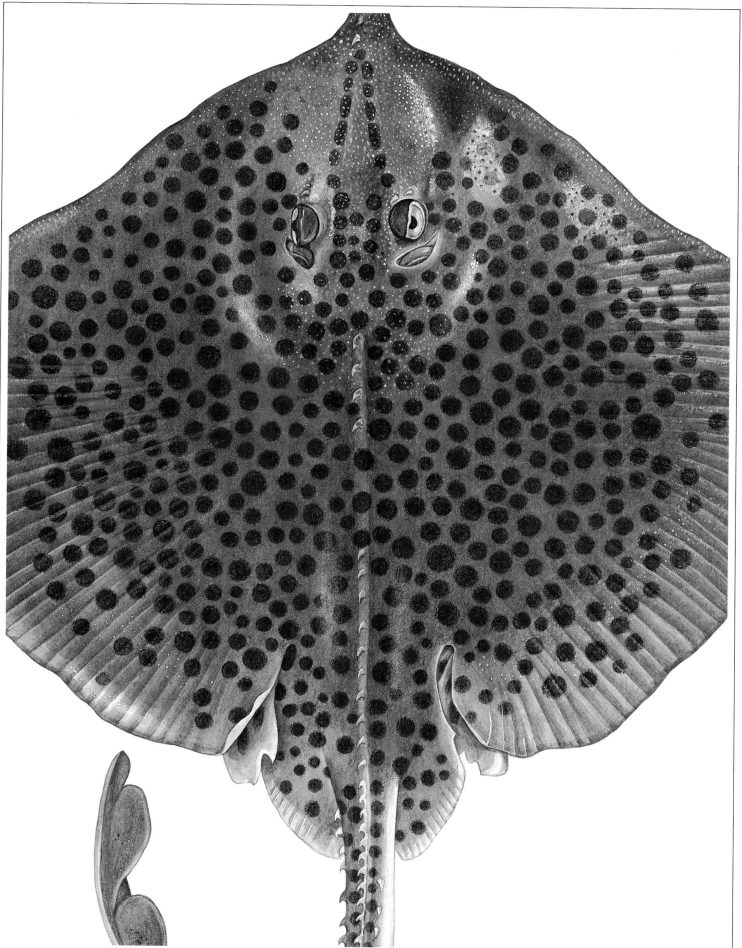

123

Spotted ray, *Raja montagui*

Lobster

124

*H*omarus gammarus and *H americanus*, the outstanding crustaceans of North Atlantic waters, are very similar. The situation is that what is essentially the same creature, the lobster, has developed in slightly different forms on the two sides of the North Atlantic, so is classified as two species, not one. The difference is that the American lobster grows slightly larger than its European brother. It is, however, difficult to give maximum dimensions. Before the lobster fisheries became as intensive as they are now, some lobsters lived to a great age and attained extraordinary sizes. For example, one taken off the coast of Virginia in the 1930s was over 39 inches long and weighed about 45 pounds Nowadays a lobster half that size would be considered a giant.

The color of the live lobster varies according to its habitat, but is usually dark blue or greenish. After being cooked, when the red pigment in its carapace is, so to speak, "released", it turns bright red; "like a cardinal's hat", as a French writer put it.

The range of the European lobster is from the far north down to the Mediterranean. The American lobster occurs as far south as South Carolina. Their habits are such that they can be caught only in special lobster pots, and the fishery for them is a relatively expensive and arduous one. Partly for this reason, the lobster has become one of the most costly seafoods in the world. In North America it is the Maine lobster which is most famous, but this fact merely reflects the hard work put in by Maine publicists. The Canadian catch is far greater.

W B Lord (1867) tells a strange tale about canned lobster, which "travels about to all parts of the known world, like an imprisoned spirit soldered up in an air-tight box. It has been said that during the Indian war a box of regimental stores belonging to our forces fell into the hands of the enemy, who thinking that a great capture of some kind of deadly and destructive ammunition had been made, rammed the painted tin cases, with goodly charges of powder behind them, into their immense guns, aimed them steadily at the devoted British troops, and then with a flash and a thundering roar, preserved lobster, from Fortnum and Mason's, was scattered far and wide over the battlefield".

There are various well known ways of preparing lobster, including Lobster Newburg and *Lobster à L'armoricaine* (or is it *à l'Americaine?*). Here I recommend one from Myrtle Allen at Ballymaloe House in County Cork.

Hot Buttered Lobster

4 pounds lobster	generous $\frac{1}{2}$ cup white wine
I carrot	a bouquet of herbs
I onion	I$\frac{1}{2}$ sticks butter
4 cups water	I lemon

Slice the carrot and onion and place in a saucepan with the water, wine and herbs. Bring to the boil, add the lobsters and cover with a tight-fitting cover. Steam until the lobsters are beginning to change color and speckle with red. Remove the pot from the heat and drain the lobsters. (Keep the cooking water for a sauce or soup.)

Open the lobster and put the meat from the body, tail and claws, together with all the green juices, into a warm bowl wrapped in a kitchen towel. Heat plenty of butter in a skillet until it is foaming. Add one helping at a time of the meat and green juices and toss in the butter until the meat is cooked and the juices turn pink. If necessary, re-heat the lobster shells gently in the oven or under hot running water. Spoon the meat back into the warm shells. Finally, put the remaining butter into a pan, heat and scrape up any remaining bits. Pour into a hot sauce boat or individual lobster dishes. Serve with quartered lemon and a green salad. Serves four.

Lobster, *Homarus vulgaris*

Spiny Lobsters

Spiny lobster is the correct name for crustaceans of the family Paniluridae; greatly preferable to the name crawfish which is sometimes used but invites confusion with crayfish, which are freshwater creatures.

The spiny lobsters are indubitably lobsters, but they differ from the archetypal lobster of the North Atlantic (the "common lobster", see page 124) in having no claws and in belonging to warmer waters. Indeed they are most abundant in the tropics, although their range extends into temperate waters in some regions, for example up to Southwest England. Their size and the excellence of their meat ensures that they are in strong demand, although the question whether they are better than or inferior to the common lobster is and will no doubt for ever be debated. Such debate is complicated by the fact that the established recipes for the Atlantic lobster, generally speaking, have been those of classical French cuisine plus the more robust traditions evolved in North America; whereas the spiny lobster, with its worldwide range in warmer waters, has attracted to itself a large number of recipes involving tropical or sub-tropical ingredients.

In the Mediterranean (mainly in the western basin and the central parts) and southwestern Europe, the two species are *Palinurus elephas* and *P mauritanicus*. They are brown or reddish in color and have a maximum length of 20 inches. There are certain places, such as Menorca and the Tunisian island of Galita, where they find a congenial habitat and are much more common than elsewhere.

In the Caribbean there are at least three species:
- *P argus*, which can grow to the exceptionally large size of 24 inches and may weigh as much as 30 pounds. Color varies. This is the *lagosta comun* of Brazil.
- *P guttatus*, a smaller and darker species, sometimes called "spotted crawfish" or "Guinea lobster". In French it is *langouste brésilienne*.
- *P laevicauda* is of a bluish green or purplish color, with white spots on the sides of the tail. This is the *lagosta cabo-verde* of Brazil.

In the Mediterranean region most ways of preparing spiny lobster are such as one would expect: that is to say, they involve the use of garlic, tomatoes, and Mediterranean herbs. Thus the provision of *Salsa Romesco* (see page 201) to go with broiled spiny lobster would be one attractive option. In the Caribbean, as the recipe from Kendal A Lee (see Barrow and Lee in the bibliography) demonstrates, there are parallel but different preparations. Lee says that he has three kinds of basil in his garden, described as: the regular green-leafed kind; the purplish or opal kind, which is stronger in aroma; and fine-leafed Greek basil, which has an anise aroma. He doesn't mind which you use.

Spiny Lobster with Buttered Basil Sauce

4 "tails" of small spiny lobsters	2 cloves garlic, minced
1 tablespoon corn oil	2 tablespoons fresh basil leaves, minced
2 sticks butter	1 tablespoon chives, chopped
2 tablespoons shallot, minced	1 lime, cut into wedges

Halve each lobster tail lengthways and arrange the halves, meat side up, in an oven-proof dish.

Heat the oil in a pan with a quarter of the butter and gently fry in it the shallot and garlic until they are transparent. Add the salt, then spoon the mixture in equal quantities over the lobster meat. Place the meat in the center of the oven at 400° for ten to 12 minutes. Meanwhile melt the remaining butter in a saucepan and mix into it the basil and chives. Serve the lobsters hot with this sauce, and accompanied by lime wedges. Serves four.

A Mediterranean spiny lobster, *Palinurus elephas*

Asian Spiny Lobsters

128

If a beauty competition were held in an Asian fish market, the finalists would undoubtedly be some of the numerous spiny lobsters which are found in the Indo-Pacific, especially in Southeast Asian waters. Their colors, unlike those of certain beautiful fish such as the dolphin fish, do not fade on death – and anyway they are often sold alive. Unlike the Atlantic lobster, with its sober hue and heavy claws, the spiny lobsters have a fairy-like lightness and rainbow coloration. It is not surprising that in some places the fisherfolk laboriously remove everything from inside the finest specimens and mount the gorgeous creatures in large glass cases trimmed with tin. (Nor was it surprising, although it remains a matter of keen regret to me, that when I was poised to buy one at the tiny airport in Phuket, Thailand, my family intervened with a veto, pointing out that any hope of transporting such a thing intact to England was doomed.)

The best known are:

● *Panulirus polyphagus*, the species shown in the painting, whose green and brown livery is relatively restrained, but pleasingly accented by the white cross-bands which mark off the segments of the tail end.

● *P penicillatus*, at first glance somewhat sombre, the carapace predominantly brown but prettily dappled, the sea-green legs bearing delicate white lines right along their length, and the tail shading delightfully from pale jade to deep violet.

● *P longipes*, usually dark purple, but with amber-colored legs dashed with white and tipped with pale orange feelers, also jewel-like white and black spots in charming arrangements on thorax and abdomen.

● *P versicolor*, whose abdomen and tail are green, the segments of the abdomen being marked off by broad black cross-bands with narrow white ones running across them, and whose carapace is a beautiful medley of pink, pale green, buff, black and white markings.

● *P ornatus*, which has the most striking appearance of all; the legs are banded in cream and maroon, the spines on top of the body are orange at the base and green at the tip, and the general effect is like that of a delicately colored butterfly.

Mention should also be made of *P interruptus*, found on the American Pacific coast southwards from South California. In California it is generally known as "langosta". Its maximum length is 35 inches.

These spiny lobsters can, of course, be prepared according to Mediterranean recipes. However, if one is in Asia, one is naturally inclined to use at least some Asian ingredients, and the recipe which follows is one which I worked out myself when following this inclination.

Spiny Lobster with Pineapple

I cooked spiny lobster, large enough for four people
2 small pineapples
other tropical fruit (optional)
I cup mayonnaise
black pepper

Cut the lobster meat into bite-size pieces.

Halve the small pineapples lengthways. Cut out the flesh, reserving most of it for some other purpose, but incorporating a dozen or so small cubes of it in the mayonnaise. If you wish, add a few small pieces of some other tropical fruit. Incorporate the pieces of lobster in the mayonnaise.

Fill the scooped out pineapple halves with the mayonnaise, dust with black pepper, chill and serve. Serves four.

An Asian spiny lobster, *Palinurus polyphagus*

Norway Lobster

130

Shall we call it Norway lobster or Dublin Bay prawn, or use the Italian name *scampo* (plural *scampi*))? Whichever we choose, it will remain for scientists *Nephrops norvegicus,* a small lobster which is found from Iceland down to Morocco, and in the western and central Mediterranean.

Because of its relatively small size, this little lobster is sometimes confused with large shrimp. Its maximum length, not counting the claws, is 9-10 inches. The carapace is pink, rose or orange-red, often quite pale but sometimes (in some places off the north coast of Spain, for example) quite dark, and its claws are banded red and white. It lives on a muddy sea bottom, in burrows, from which it emerges at night to seek food.

The name "Norway" lobster is easily explained; the species is abundant on the Norwegian coast. Its second name is more puzzling. It seems to be due to the circumstance that fishing boats coming into Dublin Bay often had a catch of it on board, which was disposed of to street vendors who hawked it as Dublin Bay prawns. But some authors hold that they were caught in Dublin Bay itself; so a veil of Irish mystery hangs over the subject.

The Irish were apparently ahead of the British in eating the creature, since it was not until the 1950s that British fishermen began to think it worthwhile to land the creature. That statement, however, may be both true and misleading. I noticed recently that the nineteenth-century author W B Lord (*Crab, Shrimp and Lobster Lore*) referred to very substantial imports of Norway lobster being sold at Billingsgate Market, London in his day. He reckoned that in a typical season 150,000 regular lobsters were sold there and 600,000 Norway lobsters. Be that as it may, it remains true that it is only since the 1960s that the Norway lobster has become a cliché of British menus under the name "scampi". This reflects the fact that Italians in the Adriatic had long appreciated it, and had many recipes for scampi cooked in various ways which, in turn, became familiar to tourists.

In Central and South American waters some related crustaceans of the genus *Nephropsis* occur, and these are sometimes marketed as "lobsterettes".

Norway lobsters can be cooked like large shrimp. Brushing them with olive oil and broiling them is a good method. The recipe I have chosen is from the Dalmatian coast of the Adriatic.

Rižot od Skampi

8-12 Norway lobsters, according to size	I cup rice (*Arborio* if possible)
4 tablespoons olive oil	salt (very little) and pepper
2 cloves of garlic, chopped	I tablespoon wine vinegar
2 sprigs of parsley, chopped	I or 2 tablespoons grated Parmesan cheese
2 tomatoes peeled, de-seeded and chopped	

Cut off the tail ends of the lobsters, peel them and cut the meat into bite-size pieces. Crush the claws, heads, carapaces and other debris and set all this to boil in lightly seasoned water to produce a little broth.

Heat the olive oil in a large pan, add the garlic and parsley to cook for just a couple of minutes and then add the lobster meat and tomato. When all this has cooked over a medium heat for three or four minutes, add the rice, seasoning, and vinegar. Turn up the heat and as the rice cooks, pour in the broth, a little at a time. Stir frequently. The rice will absorb the broth and will be ready in about 15 minutes.

Turn off the heat, let the dish rest for a couple of minutes, then serve with a light sprinkling of Parmesan cheese. Serves four.

Alternatives
jumbo shrimp (p 136)

Alternative Recipes
Grilled Norway Lobsters (p 180)
Shrimp with Egg-white and Peas (p 136)
Shrimp Badum (p 181)

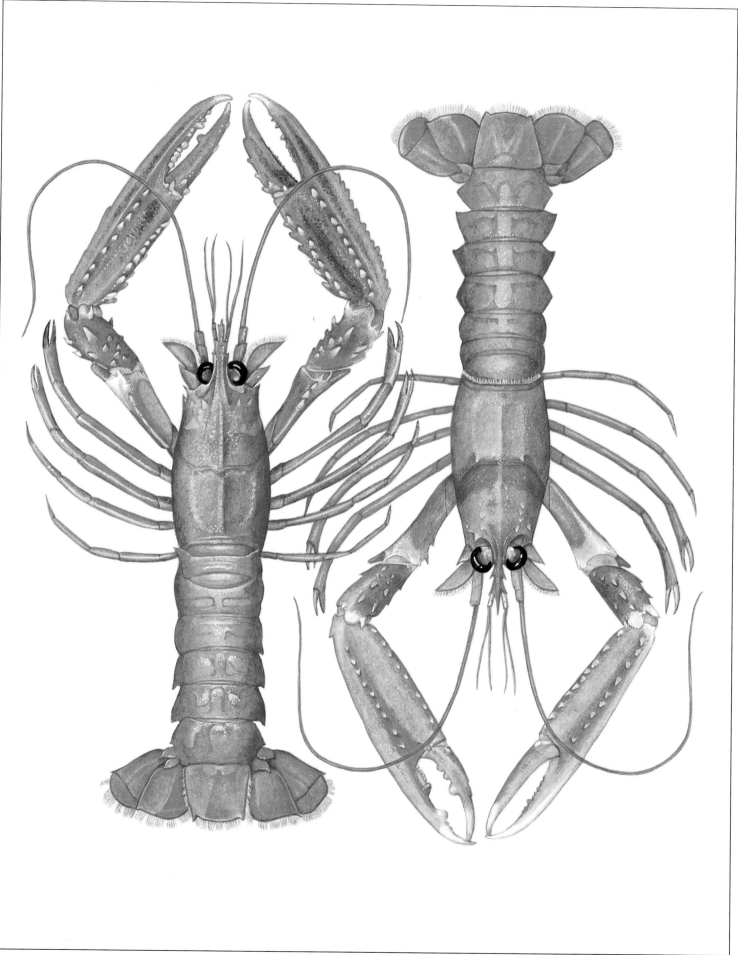

Norway lobsters (Dublin Bay prawns), *Nephrops norvegicus*

Slipper Lobsters

Slipper lobster, flat lobster, flathead lobster and shovel-nose lobster are all English names for crustaceans of the family Scyllaridae, species of which are found all around the world. Their French name, *cigale de mer* ("sea cricket"), echoed in Italian and Spanish, is given to them because they make a snapping cricket-like noise in the water, plainly audible to underwater fishermen.

They all have the same shape and general characteristics, but vary in color and size. *Scyllarides latus*, of the Mediterranean, may be up to 18 inches long, while *Scyllarus arctus*, the principal species of the East Atlantic, is only half that size.

In the Indo-Pacific, *Thenus orientalis* is the main species and it measures up to 10 inches. It has a slightly smaller relation, *Ibacus ciliatus*, which is distinguished by its bright red back.

These crustaceans offer palatable meat but have not been sought after by commercial fishery in the same way as true lobsters or shrimp. Indeed the species present on the eastern seaboard of the USA, including the large *Scyllarides aequinoctialis* which grows to up to 12 inches, seems to be ignored except by some discerning amateurs in Florida. However, the toll taken by the local artisanal fisheries and by underwater sport fishermen in the Mediterranean has made them scarcer there than they used to be. And in recent decades *Thenus orientalis* has achieved some fame in Australia under the name Moreton Bay bug ("Bugs in a Basket" was the attention-catching name of a dish I enjoyed in Townsville, Queensland) while its southerly relation *Ibacus peronii* has become known as the Balmain bug. Lesley Morrissy, a leading Australian expert on crustaceans and their cookery, says that the Moreton Bay bug is considered to have a better flavor than the Balmain bug. She adds that the name "prawn killers' is sometimes given, incorrectly, to these creatures in southern Australia.

In the Mediterranean countries these lobsters, the smaller specimens at least, are used mainly in fish soups. In some places in the south of France and in Italy, however, large specimens of *Scyllarides latus*, which may weigh up to 4 pounds, are esteemed almost as highly as the spiny lobster (see page 126) and are prepared in the same ways.

The smaller species of the Indo-Pacific are not, in my experience, often prepared separately, except in Australia. It is thus no surprise that the Australian expert Lesley Morrissy is among the few authors to have given specific recipes for them, and I have chosen one of hers here.

Creamed Bay Bugs

12 slipper lobsters	4 tablespoons sliced mushrooms
1 stick butter	1-2 tablespoons dry sherry
salt and pepper	pinch of cayenne pepper
juice of half a lemon	1 cup cream
1-2 tablespoons brandy	

Take the tail meat out of the shell and slice it thinly. Melt the butter in a heavy pan, add the lobster meat, salt and pepper and lemon juice and cook gently for five minutes.

Pour the brandy into a heated ladle, ignite it and pour flaming over the mixture. Shake the pan until the flames die down then add the mushrooms, sherry and cayenne and let it cook for two or three minutes. Finally, add the cream and continue cooking over a low heat, stirring, for another five minutes. Serves four.

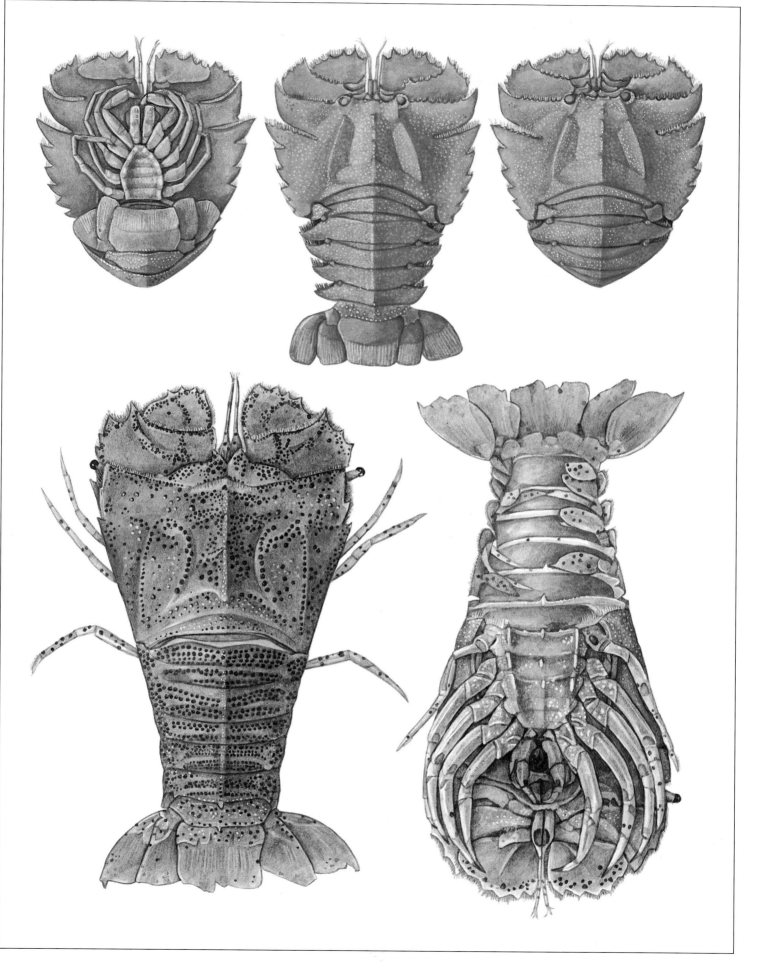

133

Slipper lobsters: above, *Ibacus peronii*, the Balmain bug of Australia, cooked; below, *Thenus orientalis*, the Moreton Bay bug, uncooked

Shrimp/Prawn

The names shrimp and prawn are used in different ways on the two sides of the Atlantic, and I had better start by explaining this, following the lucid exposition in the Food and Agriculture Organization *Catalogue of Shrimps and Prawns of the World*: "... we may say that in Great Britain the term 'shrimp' is the more general of the two, and is the only term used for Crangonidae and most smaller species. 'Prawn' is the more special of the two names, being used solely for Palaemonidae and larger forms, never for the very small ones. Compare with the *Oxford English Dictionary*, which defines prawn as 'a marine crustacean-like large shrimp'".

"In North America the name 'prawn' is practically obsolete and is almost entirely replaced by the word 'shrimp' (used for even the largest species, which may be called 'jumbo shrimp'). If the word 'prawn' is used at all in America, it is attached to small species (Webster's Dictionary gives the meaning as 'a small crustaceous animal of the shrimp family')."

Anyway, everyone in Britain would agree on attaching the name shrimp to the small shrimp of the family Crangonidae, of which the most familiar member is the common brown shrimp, *Crangon crangon*. This is the shrimp used in the potted shrimp of England, of which the most famous comes from the Morecambe Bay area. It is also the shrimp which is still fished by a few of the traditional horseback fishermen at Oostduinkerke in Belgium. Its range extends to the Mediterranean.

This brown shrimp, not to be confused with its larger namesake on the American side of the Atlantic (see next page), is small and likes to live in sandy ground. It has the ability to change its color to match that of the sand it is on (or in, since it often burrows into the sand, leaving only its antennae projecting). Hence the fact that in English it is called brown shrimp, whereas it is gray shrimp in some other languages. It has a close relation on the American side of the Atlantic, *C septemspinosa*, found all the way from Baffin Bay down to Florida.

While alive, these creatures are translucent. They turn opaque when given a brief boiling, which is all the cooking they need. Some people are then prepared to eat them whole, but the custom in most places is to pick out the meat from the tiny tail end, a laborious job. When enough meat has been assembled, the best thing to do is to make a shrimp paste, as explained below, but it can also be used to advantage in making a shrimp sauce (see page 203).

The small shrimp of the Indo-Pacific region are also commonly made into something called shrimp paste, but this is a different product; it is fermented, and has a stronger flavor. It can be found in oriental provision stores under names such as *patis* (from the Philippines) or *blachan* (Malaysia and Indonesia), and plays an important part in many South East Asian dishes.

English Shrimp Paste

½ pound uncooked shrimp
½ pound flaked raw fish (any white fish)
1 teaspoon powdered mace

½ teaspoon cayenne pepper
2 drops anchovy sauce
1½ sticks butter

Shell and remove the heads from the shrimp, and then boil this debris in enough water to cover it. Drain, discard the heads and shells, and use the broth to cook the flaked fish until tender. Drain again, and when cool, pound the fish into a smooth paste with the seasoning of mace, cayenne, and anchovy sauce. Add most of the butter and work all into a paste again. When this is completely smooth, add the shrimp meat. Heat it all thoroughly, then press it into pots, pouring the remaining butter, melted, on top as a seal. Serves four.

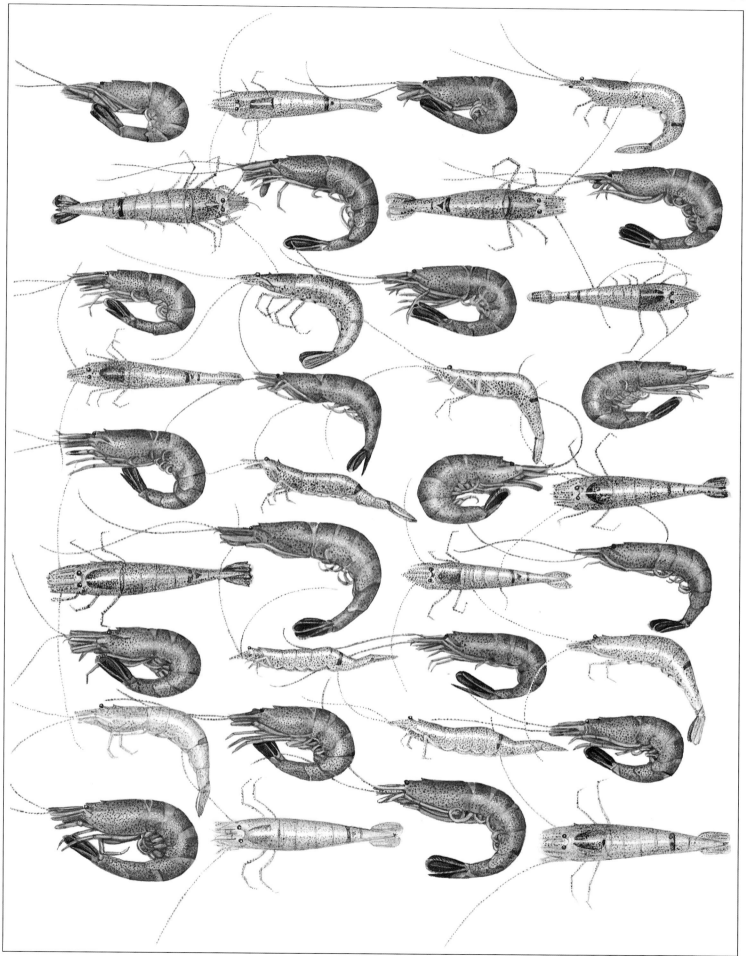

Common brown shrimp, *Crangon crangon*, cooked and uncooked

Jumbo Shrimp

Now we move on from small shrimp to the realm of those larger crustaceans which are called prawns in Britain and most other English-speaking countries, but shrimp or jumbo shrimp in North America. From the many species I have selected a few of particular interest.

The smallest of these are no bigger than large specimens of the shrimp described on the preceding page, but the largest are very much bigger. In the Mediterranean, one which deserves special mention is *Penaeus kerathurus*, the Italian *mazzancolla*. Measuring up to 9 inches, and usually brownish in color, it is especially good. Other large Mediterranean shrimp are of comparable quality, and usually pink or red in color. But it takes an expert to distinguish between them unerringly, and there is no need for the cook to do so.

The common shrimp of the North Atlantic, *Palaemon serratus*, is almost without color in life, and relatively small. In the far north, a rather bigger red shrimp, *Pandalus borealis*, or "northern shrimp", is fished extensively by the Norwegians.

On the American side of the Atlantic, the brown shrimp (not always brown), *Penaeus aztecus aztecus*, and the white shrimp (translucent white), *Penaeus setiferus*, have pride of place from the Carolinas southwards; but down in the Gulf of Texas and the Caribbean they yield to the pink shrimp (not always pink), *Penaeus duorarum duorarum*. On South American coasts, species proliferate.

The tropical and sub-tropical waters of the Indo-Pacific are also rich in shrimp. The largest is *Penaeus monodon*, the giant tiger shrimp, which reaches a maximum length of 13 inches. It and other members of the genus *Penaeus* may be distinguished from other shrimp by the fact that they have a rostrum (beak) which is serrated both above and below. The yellow shrimp, the greasy-back or school shrimp (*Metapenaeus ensis*), and the rainbow shrimp (*Parapeneopsis sculptilis*) belong to other genera and are mostly smaller.

The shrimp which may ultimately prove to be the most important commercially, because they are easy to farm, are those of the genus *Macrobranchium*. These are large shrimp, that like fresh or brackish water (so do not, strictly speaking, count as seafood). They are already of great importance in Southeast Asia, and several species occur in the West Indies, among which *M carcinus* is the finest.

This recipe, from Hong Kong, provides small helpings for four.

Shrimp with Egg-white and Peas

$\frac{3}{4}$ pound fresh shrimp (peeled weight)
2 tablespoons peanut oil for stir-frying
whites of 6 eggs
1 tablespoon flour dissolved in 1 tablespoon water

4 tablespoons chicken soup
20 cooked green peas
2 teaspoons salty Chinese cooked ham, finely chopped
2 teaspoons soy sauce (optional)

Heat the oil in a wok until it begins to smoke. Stir-fry the shrimp for three minutes or so in the oil, then pour in the egg whites and continue stirring until they set, which will take just another minute or two. Drain the shrimp and egg white.

Now pour the chicken soup, the flour solution and the peas into the empty wok. Cook for two minutes, then return the shrimp and egg white to the wok and sprinkle the ham over all. Serve at once (with the addition of the soy sauce, if you wish). The shrimp will be swimming, so to speak, in a clear liquid consisting of the chicken soup and such oil as was left on the shrimp and egg white. The pale glassy aspect of this liquid contrasts beautifully with the pink shrimp, the creamy white of the egg white and the green peas. Serves four.

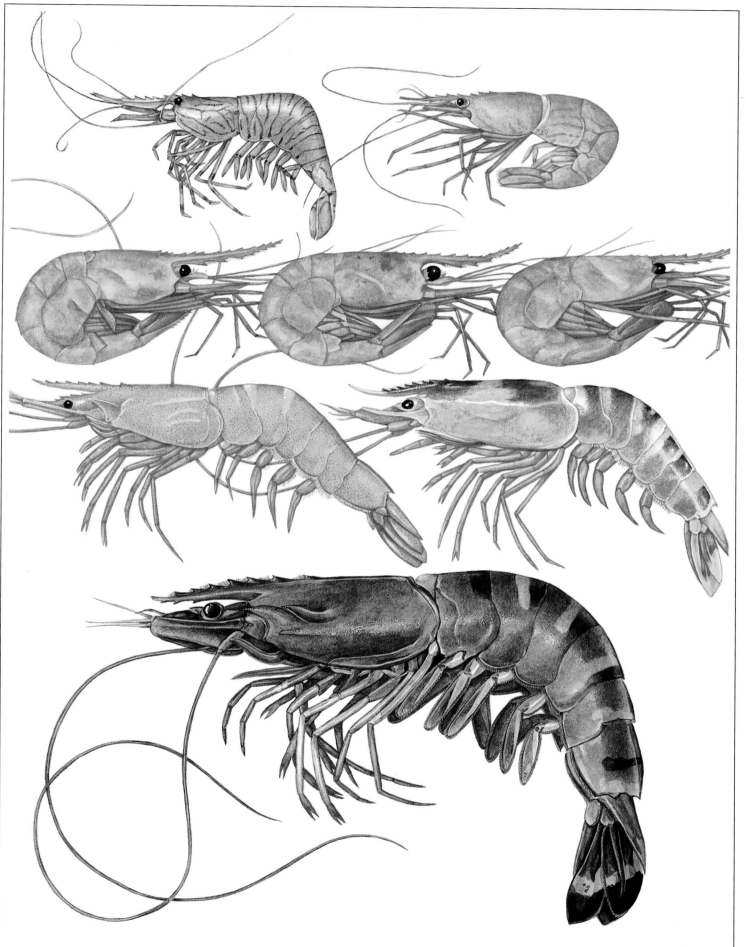

First row, common shrimp uncooked and cooked, *Palaemon serratus*; second, northern shrimp, cooked, *Pandalus borealis*; third, greasy-backed shrimp, *Metapenaeus ensis* and rainbow shrimp, *Parapeneopsis sculptilis*; below, tiger shrimp, *Penaeus monodon*

Blue Crab

The blue crab, *Callinectes sapidus*, would be the most famous American crab even if its fame had not been increased by a remarkable book devoted to it: *Beautiful Swimmers – Watermen, Crabs and the Chesapeake Bay* by William W Warner. This has all the information anyone could want about the blue crab and the people who live by catching or dressing it.

The natural range of the blue crab extends down the eastern seaboard from Delaware Bay to Florida and beyond, but it is mainly caught in the Chesapeake Bay area. It has now been introduced into the eastern Mediterranean.

Adults are large. The marketing authorities in Maryland define the sizes of the blue crab in its "soft" state thus: "whales" or "slabs" are over 5 inches wide; then in descending order come "jumbos", "primes", "hotels", and "mediums".

They are handsome crabs, as the painting shows, and their scientific name is suitably honorific: *Callinectes* means "beautiful swimmer" and *sapidus* means "tasty". Warner remarks that it was Dr Mary J Rathbun who gave it its specific name and that, although in her long career she identified 998 new species of crab, this was the only case in which she alluded to culinary quality.

The first step in dealing with a blue crab (assuming that it has been taken in the "hard" state – see below for dealing with soft-shell crabs) is to steam or boil it until the meat is cooked through and the claws have turned red. The claws yield excellent white meat, which can be taken out relatively easily once cooked and firm. The back-fin meat ("jumbo lump") is very good too. From the body comes the usual brown meat. At the annual Hard Crab Derby at Crisfield in Maryland, the champion crab-pickers can pick a whole crab in 40 seconds.

The marketing of soft-shell crabs is a major part of the industry in Chesapeake Bay. The blue crab is very soft indeed when it has shed, and will normally take refuge in some relatively safe nook for a day or so while its new shell becomes reasonably hard. Since it is not feasible to catch the crabs while they are soft, they are caught in advance and kept in special floats until they shed.

It is only at the moment of emergence from the old shell that the crab is a soft crab in the full sense of the term. Soon afterwards, as a slight hardening becomes apparent, it is termed a "paper shell". Further hardening turns it into a "buckram" or "buckler"; at this stage the new shell is still flexible, but too firm for the crab to be treated as a soft-shell crab. Within 24 hours or so of shedding, the new shell will be hard and the crab can resume a normal life.

Soft-shell crabs must therefore be conveyed to market with extreme rapidity if they are to be sold fresh, and most are frozen in the soft state. They are suitable for frying, preferably in clarified butter, or broiling.

As for regular crab meat, I like it very well in crab meat cakes. Those prepared "Norfolk style" have nothing added but butter and seasoning, and are very rich. The Maryland version, which includes breadcrumbs, is a lighter dish.

Maryland Crab Meat Cakes

1 pound cooked crab meat	2 teaspoons Worcestershire sauce
$\frac{1}{2}$ cup each milk and light cream	3 drops tabasco sauce
2 cups fresh breadcrumbs	fine dry breadcrumbs
$\frac{1}{2}$ teaspoon cayenne pepper	oil for deep-frying
1 teaspoon dry mustard	

Mix all the ingredients, except for the last two, thoroughly and form the result into eight patties, two per person. Roll them in the fine dry breadcrumbs and deep-fry them until they are golden-brown. Drain and serve. Serves four.

Blue crabs, *Callinectes sapidus*

Common European Crab

140

The common crab of western and northern Europe, also called the edible crab (as though there were no other edible ones!) is *Cancer pagurus*. It may occasionally be found in the western Mediterranean, but this is doubtful. The maximum width of the carapace is over 10 inches and the weight of the largest specimens can be as much as 11 pounds. The usual color of the carapace is pinkish or reddish brown, with black tips to the claws.

These edible crabs are of great importance in commerce, being more abundant than lobsters and yet, in the opinion of many, including myself, producing meat of comparable quality. White meat comes from the claws only. The body produces brown meat, including the exceptionally large liver, which is a delicacy. On average the yield of meat from a crab will be one-third of its whole weight; about two-thirds of this yield will be brown meat.

The white meat is fibrous, but in a pleasing way. The quality of the meat in general, both white and brown, varies according to a number of factors. The flesh of the male, which has larger claws than the female, is generally preferred. The sex of a crab can be easily determined by looking at the tail, which is curled up under the body. That of the female is broad and round, while that of the male is narrower and pointed (see the drawings on page 178).

A crab should feel heavy for its size; and, if it is shaken, there should not be a sound of fluid swilling round inside. The large claws should be tightly tucked up against the body, not hanging loose.

All this applies equally to related crabs in other parts of the world, of which the most notable is the Dungeness crab of the Pacific northwest of the USA and Canada, renowned for its fine flavor. It is only a little smaller than the edible crab of Europe; the carapace may measure 8 inches across. It is moderately common from Central California to Alaska, but its numbers fluctuate markedly. There are regulations allowing that only fully adult males to be kept and sold.

It is usual to sell all these large crabs cooked, to which end they are steamed in huge containers. This used to present a dramatic sight at the old Billingsgate Fish Market in London.

Cornish Crab Pasty

Cornish pasties are famous, and not just in England; they have penetrated deep into the State of Michigan in the USA, for example. They usually contain meat and vegetables, but variants with seafood are known and seem to me to constitute a really successful combination.

I pound crab meat, cooked and flaked	8 ounces lard or suet
lemon juice	(or a mixture of the two)
parsley, chopped	$\frac{1}{2}$ teaspoon salt
for the pastry	water to mix
4 cups flour	

Make up the pastry, roll out to $\frac{1}{4}$ inch thick and use a plate to cut it into rounds about 6 inches diameter.

Have the cooked crab meat ready, moistened with lemon juice and mix with some chopped parsley. Take a round of pastry and put it on a floured board. Put a helping of the crab mixture on one side, then fold the other side over to make a semi-circular pasty. Crimp the edges down neatly and make a slit in the middle of the top.

Then bake the pasties in the oven at 430° for about 20 minutes. Serves four.

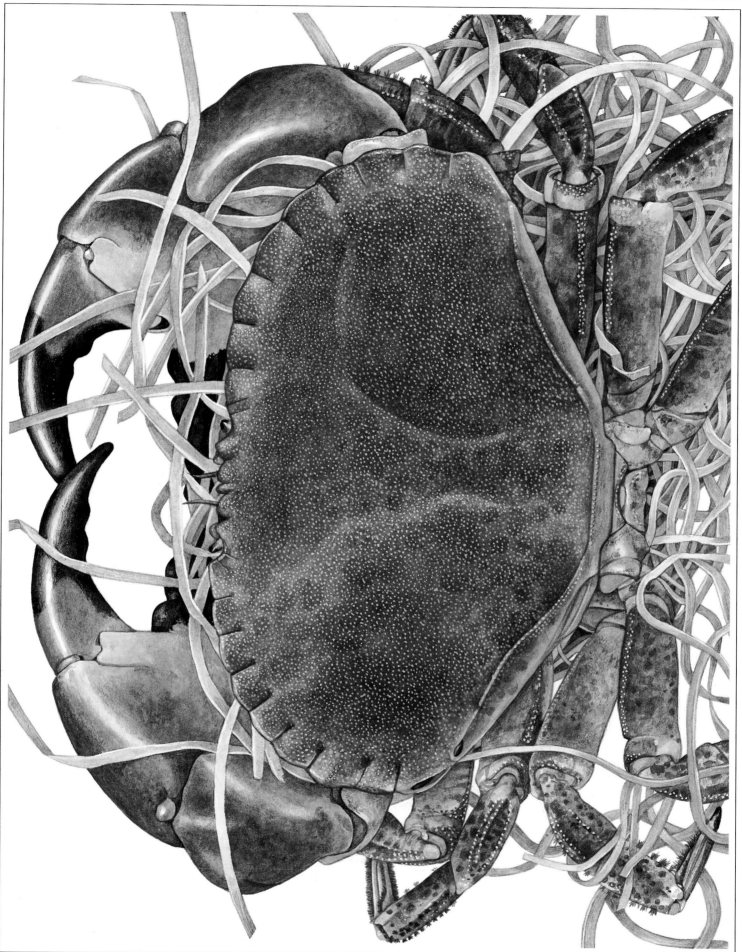

Common European crab, *Cancer pagurus*

Spider Crab

142

A denizen of the Mediterranean and Northeast Atlantic (as far north as the south of Britain) the aptly named spider crab, *Maja squinado*, takes its English name from the spider-like arrangement of its legs. It is reputed to hibernate, emerging in May (hence *Maja* in the scientific name: *squinado* comes from the Provençal name).

The carapace is reddish-orange to brown (the specimen shown in the painting is not a cooked crab, as one might think, but a freshly caught one from Cornwall, England) and may measure 8 inches across.

This crab's remarkable ability to camouflage itself gives it a high degree of protection from predators, for it often looks like a small rock encrusted with natural growths. The naturalist Edward Step, who studied it in Cornwall, described in detail how "Gran'f'er Jenkin" (a Cornish name for it) uses his nippers to break off bits of seaweed or other suitable items, "kisses" these to coat them with gummy saliva, and then "plants" them among the prickles and hooked hairs on his back. "The intelligence of the action may be further seen in the fact that Gran'f'er picks and snips only from those things that will grow when cut and transplanted. He knows, too, which is the 'business end' of his cuttings and plants them in the manner best calculated to enable them to 'root' easily." Nor is this all. The marine garden planted on the crab's back is an attractive habitat for many small forms of animal life, which take up residence there and contribute further by their presence to the camouflage.

There are many other spider crabs around the world, but almost all have such small bodies and such thin long legs that they are not worth eating. Even *M squinado* used to be disdained by fishermen in the west of England, who were irritated by its behavior in the traps they had set for more valuable creatures such as lobsters. The "spiders" would bustle about anxiously and deter lobsters from coming in to join them.

These crabs also have the disconcerting habit of forming themselves into conical heaps some distance below low tide mark. These may be several feet high and are said to comprise as many as a thousand individuals, and the crabs can stay in this posture for weeks or even months on end. Inspection reveals that the smaller crabs are on the inside, and it is thought that the habit is a form of self-protection against predators such as the octopus. It may be an effective aid to survival, but it certainly sounds like a boring way of life.

Whatever English fishermen used to think of it, this is an excellent edible crab; it is particularly appreciated in France and Spain and at the northern end of the Adriatic, where *Grancevola alla Veneziana* is a well-known dish.

One really large spider crab could serve two, but one per person is the norm. The female is slightly smaller than the male and is the better buy, especially at the beginning of the year, when she is carrying eggs – about 75,000 of them, so the cost per egg is quite low!

Preparing dressed spider crab, according to the Venetian recipe mentioned above, is straightforward; indeed it corresponds almost exactly to the recipe for Dressed Crab on page 199. A more ambitious dish, which I enjoyed at the restaurant of Sr Don José Castillo at Beasain in the Basque country, is *Txangurro Relleno*, for which full instructions are given on page 190.

If you would like to prepare spider crab, or any other crab, in a distinctly Oriental way, try the Filipino *adobo* method, as follows. Cut the crabs in half and put them in a saucepan with two parts vinegar to one of water and plenty of crushed garlic. Bring this to the boil and keep cooking until the crabs are just about ready and much of the liquid has evaporated. Add the same amount of coconut cream (see page 177) as was used of vinegar and continue cooking for just one or two minutes more, then serve the crabs in the sauce.

A European spider crab, *Maja squinado*

Snow Crab & King Crab

Snow Crab
ENGLISH-SPEAKING COUNTRIES
tarabagani
JAPANESE

144

As one moves up towards the North Pole, the crab population on the seabed changes and so do the methods of fishing for them. The targets now become the snow crabs, of the genus *Chionocoetes*, and the king (or red king) crab, *Paralithodes camtschatica*. These crabs have quite extraordinarily and inconveniently long legs, but have become an important and valuable food resource.

The more compact edible crabs of temperate waters are caught in pots, the only feasible method on rocky or irregular bottoms; or by trawling (which works on smooth muddy bottoms, especially if a "tickler chain" is dragged along in front of the trawl to disturb the crabs). In contrast, the specialized Russian and Japanese fishing boats which seek out snow and king crabs in the icy Arctic waters have used tangle-nets. These are of considerable size, perhaps 160 feet long and constructed with buoys and weights in such a way that they form "walls" on the seabed. The snow crabs become entangled in them as they try to move past, and the best catches are made at the time when the crabs are moving into deeper waters for breeding purposes. This has become a really big operation, with one lot of boats for laying the nets and another for picking them up and a factory ship attending each fleet.

The meat is usually frozen or canned in the factory ship, since the great length of the relatively thin legs (those of the king crab are shown in the painting) and the distance of the fishing grounds from the markets would make any other procedure too expensive.

In waters less far north there are other long-legged crabs which live in deep water and are at present under-exploited, but have commercial possibilities. The red crab, *Geryon quinquedens*, is one such. It has a range from Nova Scotia all the way down to Cuba, and is delicious, as I found when sampling it at a research station near Gloucester, Massachusetts. It is in the waters off southern New England, at depths of 900-2,800 feet, that experimental fisheries have been established on a small scale. Although the legs are very thin, which is a disadvantage, the meat slips out of them readily.

Incidentally, the name red crab is also used for a Pacific coast crab, *Cancer productus*, which is not often found in the markets but is large and very good, so good that there are those who rate it above even the Dungeness crab (see page 140). Another interesting red crab, the centolla or southern king crab, *Lithodes antarcticus*, is being fished in large quantities off the coast of Chile.

Before leaving the subject of crabs, I have to mention the smallest edible crabs of all, the pea or oyster crabs which live inside the shells of oysters and also some other bivalves. In this protected environment the tiny pink creatures remain permanently soft-shelled and become incapable of anything but sluggish and minor movements. In times gone by they were regarded as great delicacies, and it is said that the first President of the USA liked them so well, floating on top of oyster stews, that there was a proposal to rename them "Washington crabs". I have one book published in Philadelphia in 1901 which contains no fewer than 16 recipes for preparing them. Nowadays, few people know about them, and those who do are likely simply to fry the little morsels.

Reverting to the long-legged crabs, their succulent meat, which has a sweetish taste, may be used for any of the standard crab preparations. Shredded, it is a wonderful addition to certain soups and, since it is quite expensive, this is a good and economical way to enjoy the flavor and texture. Otherwise, I recommend using it for a crab *soufflé*, or for dressed crab (see page 199). Some may think it inappropriate to serve the meat of one kind of crab in the carapace of another, but I defend the procedure. A seafood lover will do well to have a battery of really fine carapaces of various sizes and species, for this kind of dish.

Alternatives
nothing suitable

Alternative Recipe
Tempura (p 183)

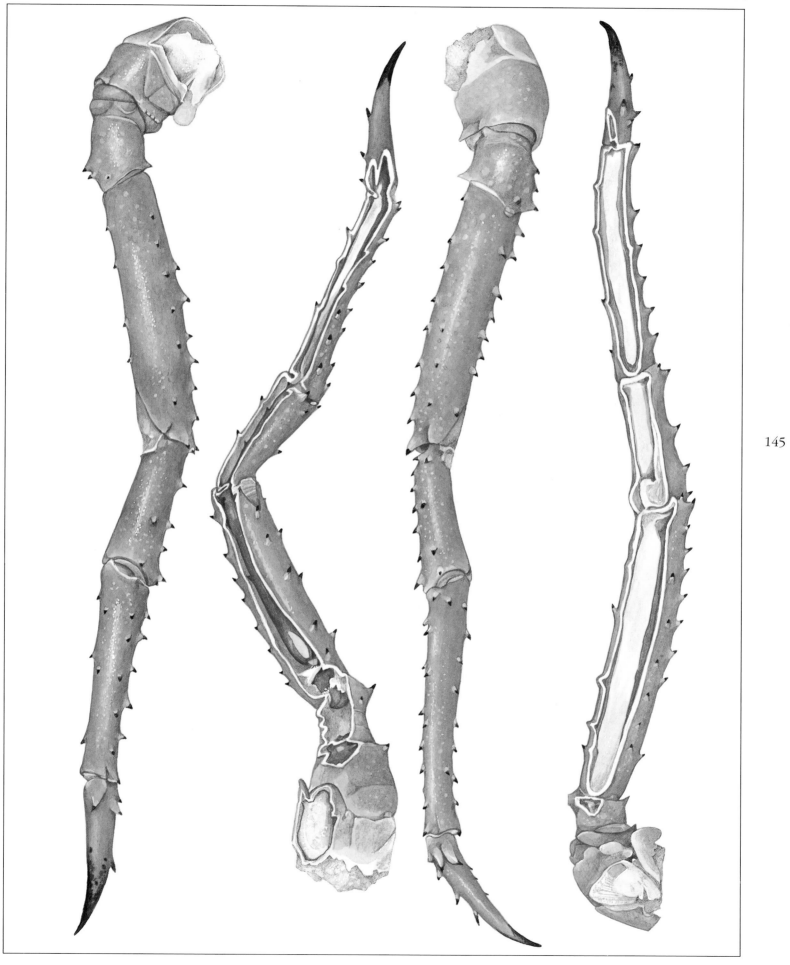

Legs of the king crab, *Paralithodes camtschatica*

Stone Crab

Stone Crab
(this species has very few names in other languages)

The stone crab provides an example of how a desirable species which has quite an extensive distribution may be "appropriated" by one state in the USA. Just as Maine has taken the Atlantic lobster to itself (including the Canadian catch, which is larger than the Maine catch), so Florida has annexed the stone crab. The reason is simple: it makes very good eating, and any state would be proud to own it.

Damon Runyon, who was responsible for the most dogmatic pronouncements ever made on the matter, described the stone crab as "an ornery looking critter that hangs out around the Florida Keys and nowhere else in the world", and went on to suggest that it was really the property of Dade County alone, not of the whole state, and that stone crabs were too good for mere visitors. "A certificate of at least four years' residence should be required of every person desiring stone crabs," he said. This was a remarkably proprietorial statement, considering that Runyon himself acknowledged that up until 1920 no one in Dade County bothered much about these crabs, and that it was only when a visiting Harvard professor saw some boys about to throw the crabs away and remonstrated with them that their merits became apparent. Anyway, none of this deterred me from eating stone crab claws with considerable pleasure when visiting Miami and no one questioned my credentials, although I was patently a visitor.

The range of this crab, whose scientific name is *Menippe mercenaria*, extends from the Gulf of Texas to the Carolinas; and it is also known in many parts of the Caribbean area. It is dark brownish red, mottled with gray when adult and its carapace may measure 5 inches across.

The stone crab has relatively large claws, one bigger than the other, which are tipped with black. Fishermen sometimes simply detach the larger of the two claws from a crab they have caught and toss it back in the water, since it can grow a replacement (a practice which echoes that of Portuguese fishermen with another crab which has similar regenerative powers).

Stone crabs live in burrows in muddy bays or harbors or among rocks in tidal creeks and estuaries.

Although the backfin meat of this crab is edible, the commonly accepted idea is that everything is waste except for the claw meat and it is only the claws which are sold. These may of course be prepared according to any of the standard methods for crabmeat. It is not essential that the whole claws be brought to table, but their appearance is so striking that this is the almost invariable practice. In those restaurants in Miami which have built their reputation on this crab, there are a number of pleasing rituals associated with the manner in which the claws are presented.

For the recipe, and a lesson in vivid and concise recipe-writing, let's stay with Runyon.

Damon Runyon's Recipe

"The stone crab is cooked by boiling. A lot of people have tried to think up better ways, but boiling is best. It is served cold with hot melted butter with a dash of lemon in it on the side.

Probably the right place to eat stone crabs would be the bath-tub. The fingers are used in toying with them. Some high-toned folks use those little dinky oyster forks, but the fingers are far speedier and more efficient."

Alternatives
large claws of the blue crab (p 138)
common European crab (p 140)

Alternative Recipe
Tempura (p 183)

146

Claws of the stone crab, *Menippe mercenaria*

Asian Crabs

148

Crabs belonging to the Indo-Pacific are an interesting and handsome collection, and it is noticeable that the pattern of consumption is different in Asia. Until I went to live in Southeast Asia and was exposed to the menu-making of a Vietnamese cook, I hadn't realized that "Crab and Western Bamboo Soup" would become a staple dish in our family (Western bamboo is asparagus).

The family Portunidae, all of whose members are swimming crabs, includes one genus, *Scylla*, which is a notorious source of puzzlement to taxonomists; but this doesn't matter, since these are all quite big and handsome crabs and make fine eating. The same applies to the blue swimming crab, *Portunus pelagicus*, shown in the painting, and its close relation, *P sanguinolentus*, which bears three large purple spots on its greenish carapace. In exploring the ways of Thai cooks with these crabs, I came across an interesting practice in the south of the country: the meat of the crabs is "candied" in palm sugar syrup and eaten as a sweetmeat.

The crabs which are picked off trees are mangrove crabs, relatively small ones of the genus *Sesarma*; they occur in the West Indies too. Crabs of this sort have rather square, box-like bodies with eyes protruding very noticeably on stalks. Mangrove swamps are their habitat, and it is at high tide that they perform their tree-climbing act. Meanwhile, down on the ground, the "fiddler" crabs which are also typical of mangrove swamps throughout the tropics, wave their single big claws like violinists at passers-by.

However, the strangest crabs which are eaten in Asia are surely the beetle or horseshoe crabs, of the family Xiphosuridae. They have a large, rounded, outer shell as a form of protection, and a spike protruding at the rear, so that the general effect resembles that of a circular gun turret moving across the sea bottom. Or, I should say, a pair or string of gun turrets, since the male horseshoe crabs, reputedly blind, have to cling to the females, one of whom may be leading a "crocodile" of dozens of males, when they want to go anywhere. The male of the biggest species, *Tachypleus gigas*, is said never to leave go of the female at all. The eggs are very good fried, especially if mixed with the light blue blood of the crab.

My chosen recipe comes from Malaysia, and is an easy one to make. I precede it by this mini-recipe for the delicious Crab and Western Bamboo Soup referred to above. Its Vietnamese name is *Mang Cua*.

Start with the meat of one large crab, cooked and flaked. Bring $4\frac{1}{2}$ cups of good chicken broth to a boil, lower the heat, add the crabmeat and at least a dozen asparagus tips. Thicken the soup with 3 tablespoons of manioc (tapioca) flour, then stir into it, thoroughly, 2 beaten eggs. Season and garnish with chopped coriander and chopped scallion, both in discreet amounts.

Malaysian Baked Crab

I pound cooked crab meat
4 large empty crab shells
vegetable oil, for both pan- and deep-frying
4 small red onions, finely chopped

I tablespoon chili sauce (from a bottle)
2 scallions, finely chopped
4 tablespoons grated coconut
salt and pepper to taste
2 egg whites, stiffly beaten

Heat a little oil and fry the onion until golden, then transfer it to a mixing bowl, add the crab meat and then all the other ingredients except the egg whites. Mix thoroughly. Spoon this mixture into the crab shells and coat each one with the beaten egg white. Fry the stuffed shells in plenty of hot oil for about three minutes, or until the tops are golden brown. Serves four.

An Asian swimming crab, *Portunus pelagicus*

Goose-necked Barnacles

150

This extraordinary creature, *Mitella pollicipes* (still widely known as *Pollicipes cornucopia*) is best known under its Spanish name, *percebes*. It is a marine delicacy which is unknown in many countries but appreciated with enormous enthusiasm in others.

The goose-necked barnacle is a crustacean (not a mollusc, as one might think at first glance) but very different from creatures like crabs and shrimp. Its classification as a crustacean was belated, since its internal structure was misunderstood for some time. It is indeed puzzling; one natural historian described the barnacle as "lying on its back, holding on by its head, and kicking its food into its mouth with its heels".

The adjective goose-necked is questionable, since the name was originally just "goose barnacle" and was not given because of anything to do with the creature's neck (if it has one). On the contrary, it represented a medieval myth according to which barnacles grew on trees or on logs in the water and, on reaching a certain size, fell off and became geese or ducks. So ancient and powerful was this myth that the great naturalist Linnaeus, when he devised the binomial system of scientific names for everything in the plant and animal worlds, gave the specific name *anatifera* (goose-bearer) to this barnacle, although he himself cannot have believed the myth. In more recent times an explanation for the myth has been given. It seems that the breeding habits of barnacles, because of the difficulty of studying them in their habitats, were not really known until the early part of this century. There was a similar mystery about the breeding of certain geese, which took place on inaccessible cliffs in the Arctic region. The young goslings would fall or scramble down to the water, appearing as if by magic from places where there were known to be barnacles. Thus the erroneous inference was made.

Anyway, to return to the goose- or goose-necked barnacle, it consists of what might be called a tube, as thick as a finger, with a dark parchment-like skin bearing tiny scales. On this is mounted a sort of hoof – a pair of white bony pads, from between which emerge the creature's feet.

What one eats is, so to speak, the "inner tube". If the outer skin is pinched near the hoofs, it can be prised off, revealing a stalk-like protuberance which is bitten off entire. Percebes may be eaten raw, but are usually cooked briefly before being offered in Portuguese and Spanish bars. They are considered to be at their best in the summer when they are bearing eggs.

The distribution of *M pollicipes* is quite limited: they are found only on the coasts of Spain, Portugal, Morocco and Senegal. The difficulties and dangers involved in gathering these barnacles ensure that they will always be expensive. They have to be plucked from the base of wave-battered cliffs, the rugged habitat which suits them best.

There are related species in various parts of the world, but few are ranked as edible, still less as delicacies. *Lepas anatifera*, which is one, has a global distribution, including the Mediterranean and even Antarctica. It is eaten, but with less enthusiasm. It is what the French call *anatife*.

The other gastronomically outstanding species is found chiefly in Chile, but also in Peru. This is *Megabalanus psittacus*, called *picoroco gigante* in Spanish, but known in Chile simply as *picoroco* or *balanido gigante*. Its normal size is 4 inches, but it may grow much larger. It is considered locally to be a quite exceptional delicacy. The species shown also belongs to the East Pacific, whence it is now exported to New York and elsewhere.

There are no recipes for percebes. They will normally be bought cooked, and you just eat them as described above. If you were to have some uncooked ones, you would simply boil them for between five and ten minutes according to their size (perhaps longer for a real giant from Chile).

Goose-necked barnacle, *Pollicipes polymerus*, from Colombia

Cuttlefish

152

Like the squid and the octopus, the cuttlefish is an eminently edible mollusc which belongs to the group called cephalopods. This name, literally, means "head-footed" and refers to the way in which the arms and tentacles of the creatures sprout directly from their heads. The convolutions of their tentacles, especially those of the octopus, may be repellent to some, but were a frequent theme in classical art and a source of aesthetic pleasure to such authors as Athenaeus, who referred to their "wondrous curls".

All cephalopods have ink sacs, from which a dark ink can be ejected to screen the creature's escape from a predator (or, as some believe, to form an insubstantial likeness of the cephalopod, which turns colorless and slips away while the predator attacks its inky look-alike). The cuttlefish and squid (see page 154) are "ten-footed", while the octopus (see page 156) is "eight-footed".

The species familiar in the Mediterranean and eastern Atlantic is *Sepia officinalis*, which has a maximum body length of about 10 inches and is usually dark in color with markings of the sort shown in the picture. Like other cephalopods, it has ink sacs and its ink was formerly used to produce the color sepia. Both cuttlefish and squid may be called inkfish.

In the Indo-Pacific area the species of cuttlefish most commonly consumed are:
- *Sepia pharaonis*, slightly larger than *S officinalis* and most abundant off the Arabian peninsula, although its distribution extends across to Japan and Australia.
- *S esculenta*, a smaller species found in Korean and Japanese waters.
- *S latimanus*, the region's largest cuttlefish (up to 20 inches long).

Japan is by far the most important market for cephalopods, and the Japanese generally pay more for cuttlefish than for squid or octopus; but this may be partly because supplies are limited.

The Chinese, remarking that "the cuttle has ink in its bosom", have called it "the clerk of the god of the sea". Other names in use in Hong Kong include *mak mo* (nanny inkfish) and *foo ban woo chak* (tiger-blotched black thief).

There are also some very small cuttlefish, such as *Sepiola rondeleti* and *Rossia macrosoma*, in the Mediterranean. They are only 1-2 inches long, and are often offered for sale ready cleaned and fried. They make delicious morsels. It is these which the French call *suppions* and the Spaniards *globitos* or *chipirones*.

Cuttlefish can be cooked like squid or octopus, but need no special treatment to make them tender. This recipe, from Thailand, is for the very small cuttlefish.

Khao Tom Pla Muk
(Stuffed Baby Cuttlefish)

24 tiny cuttlefish (1-2 inches)
½ pound ground pork
2 teaspoons garlic, chopped, plus 2 teaspoons for garnish
salt and pepper

2 teaspoons coriander root plus leaves for garnish
2 cups fish stock
2 teaspoons uncooked rice
2 tablespoons Chinese mushrooms, soaked and finely sliced

Wash and remove the ink sacs from a dozen of the cuttlefish. Combine the ground pork with a pounded mixture of the garlic, salt, pepper and coriander root. Stuff this mixture loosely into the fish and steam them until cooked.

Bring the stock to the boil and add the pounded (but not pulverized) rice and the mushrooms. Cook for ten minutes. Put three inkfish into each soup bowl and pour the hot soup over them. Garnish with garlic, which has been fried crisp and golden in plenty of oil, plus pepper and coriander leaves. Serves four.

Alternative
squid (p 154)

Alternative Recipes
Squid Sauté with Pineapple
(p 181)
Moqueca de Peixe (p 190)
Soho Fish Pie (p 194)

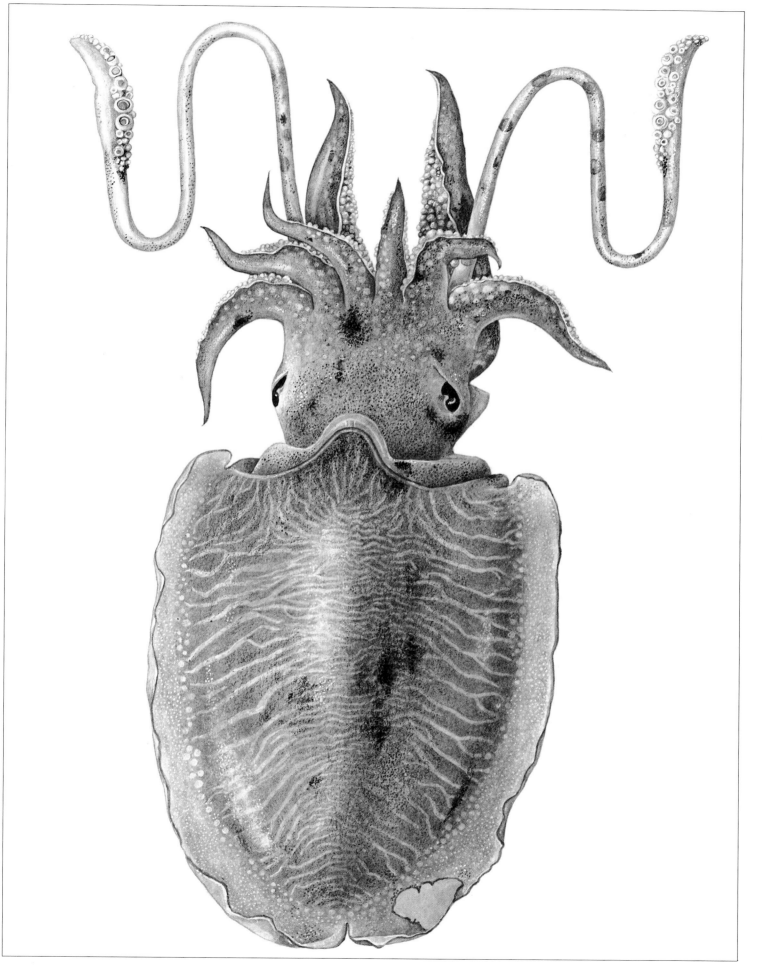

The common cuttlefish, *Sepia officinalis*

Squid

154

Squid, one of the major marine food resources and possibly the most important of those which are not yet fully exploited, occur in all oceans and seas except the Black Sea. The world catch had risen to over one million tons (live weight) by the early 1980s. However, like other cephalopods (cuttlefish and octopus), squid are eaten less than they might be in some parts of the world because people are repelled by their appearance and ignorant of how to prepare and cook them. This certainly does not apply in Japan, which takes about half of the world catch, nor to the Mediterranean peoples, who are perhaps further advanced than any others in the art of preparing squid dishes.

The architecture of a squid is simple. The body has swimming fins projecting from it at the rear. At the front is the head, and projecting from this are two long tentacles and eight "arms". Since squid swim near the surface of the water and any predator would be likely to attack them from below, they are nearly transparent and thus hard to see; but they can blush a brownish color.

There are numerous species in a dozen families, two of which accommodate all the edible species. The so-called flying squid, which constitute about three-quarters of the world catch, belong to the family Ommastrephidae and are oceanic; whereas members of the family Loliginidae are inshore creatures.

Loligo vulgaris is the principal squid of the Mediterranean and of the East Atlantic as far north as the English Channel. *L forbesi* is the most common edible squid of the Northeast Atlantic. On the other side of the Atlantic, common from Cape Cod to Venezuela, is *L pealei*, known in the USA as long-finned or bone or winter squid. The market for it in the USA remains limited, although Americans of Mediterranean descent buy it. Similar species inhabit Asian waters.

Turning to the "flying" squid (they don't really fly, though they can propel themselves out of the water and glide briefly), we find that the most important, *Todarodes pacificus*, belongs to the Pacific, ranging from Canada to China. *Illex illecebrosus*, or the short-finned squid in the USA, occurs in slightly different forms on both sides of the North Atlantic. *Todarodes sagittatus*, a species of the Northeast Atlantic and Mediterranean, is the one which the French call *calmar*.

Squid of whatever species might have been specially designed for the cook to stuff. It is easy to pull out the innards, which include the single "bone" (this is really a vestigial shell which has migrated to inside the creature) leaving the body empty. The head (minus eyes) and tentacles can be chopped up to form part of the stuffing; the rest can be almost anything – rice, chopped meat, vegetables or herbs.

However, this is not the only way to prepare squid. If the body is sliced across, this will produce rings, and these are deep-fried with the tentacles to form an important part of the traditional Italian *Frittura Mista*.

Squid with a Smoked Ham Stuffing

4 squid of ½ pound each
3-4 ounces smoked ham
2 ripe tomatoes, peeled
salt, pepper, parsley

1 medium to large onion
2-3 tablespoons olive oil
2 cloves garlic

Clean the squid. Chop the tentacles finely with the ham and tomatoes, and add salt, pepper and chopped parsley to make a thick mixture. Stuff the squid with this, but not quite full, and fasten each with a toothpick. Chop the onion and cook it gently in the oil with the whole cloves of garlic. Add the squid and cook them gently over a low heat for 20 minutes, adding a little water (or wine) towards the end if the sauce is drying up. Serve on a bed of rice. Serves four.

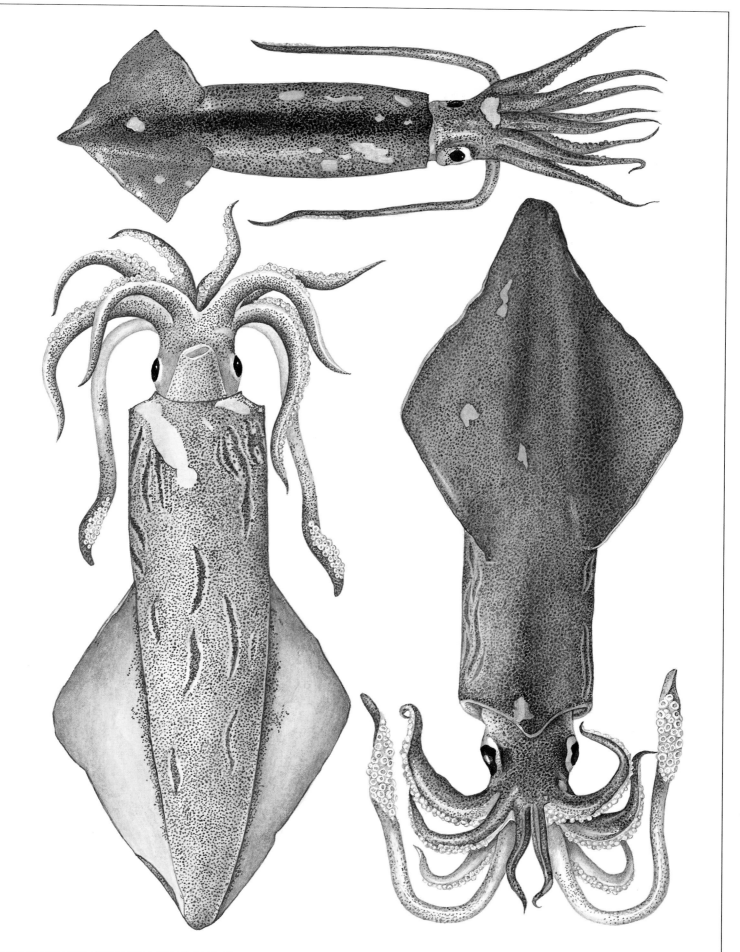

155

Short-finned squid, *Illex illecebrosus* (top) and views from below and above of *Loligo forbesi* (bottom)

Octopus

156

Consumption of the octopus, *Octopus vulgaris*, and its relations has been inhibited, except in the Mediterranean countries and the Orient, by the alarming appearance of the whole creature; by its largely undeserved reputation as a peril to divers – it is known as devil-fish in the USA; and by the need to tenderize the flesh before cooking.

O vulgaris belongs to the Mediterranean, where it thrives to such an extent that it has greater commercial importance than squid or cuttlefish. It also lives in the warm waters on both sides of the Atlantic up to, for example, the English Channel and Bermuda, but not normally beyond. This is the octopus which is often depicted on classical Greek vases, testifying to the popularity and respect it enjoyed in antiquity. Modern Greeks continue to eat it with enthusiasm and import dried octopus from North Africa; but their consumption per capita is less than that of the Spaniards, who are the most prolific consumers and producers of octopus in Europe. Only about a sixth of the world catch is European: about a half of it is accounted for by the Japanese. The oriental and other relations of *O vulgaris* are numerous.

The octopus passes the winter in deep water but approaches the coast in early spring and spends the summer in inshore waters. It is a solitary creature, living in a crevice in the rocks or, quite endearingly, in a house fashioned for itself from an old pot or tyre or other piece of debris on the sea floor.

The usual market length of *O vulgaris*, including its tentacles, is 20-40 inches and the maximum length is three times greater. It has a double row of suckers on each tentacle, a point to look out for when buying octopus. *O macropus*, smaller and with relatively longer and thinner tentacles, is found in warm waters round the world and is called *sui gwai* or "water ghost" by the Chinese. *Eledone cirrosa*, the curled octopus – which is smaller still, is distinguished by having only a single row of suckers on each tentacle and is less good. The common name comes from the way in which the body is curved back on itself. *Cistopus indicus* is the principal commercial octopus in Asian markets, but not the best, as one can guess from the fact that the Chinese in Hong Kong call it *laai por*, meaning "muddy old woman". The names they give to other species are more flattering and poetical: for example, the relatively small *Octopus aegina*, which has a wide range from the Red Sea to western Pacific waters, is known as *saa lui*, meaning "sand bird".

Various methods of tenderizing octopus are proposed. Some sound more like folklore than practical suggestions, for example the advice to add a cork to the cooking water. Others are known to be effective but are tedious, such as beating the octopus energetically on rocks. The Japanese method is to put the cleaned octopus in a bath of finely grated *daikon* (giant white radish) and to knead it with the fingers.

Octopus as Cooked in Naples

2 pounds small octopuses	4 tablespoons parsley, chopped
½ cup olive oil	2 tablespoons lemon juice
2 cloves garlic	salt and pepper

Have the octopuses cleaned by the fishmonger. Cook them in salted boiling water for between 20 and 45 minutes (the time will depend on how small they are).

Drain them, cut them into small pieces and season with the oil and other ingredients. Leave for two hours or so before serving so that the seasoning will have time to take full effect. Serves four.

Common octopus, *Octopus vulgaris*

Abalone

158

The abalone has the distinction of being just about the only single-shell marine mollusc which is regarded as a real delicacy, especially in the Orient and on the Pacific coast of North America. It is also, so far, the only single-shell that has been the subject of aquaculture. Although abalone is the common name generally used, "ormer" and "ear-shell" are other English names. For scientists, all species of abalone around the world belong to the genus *Haliotis*.

An abalone can be regarded as a kind of limpet, using the term in its general sense. Indeed it is the largest and most highly evolved sort of limpet. It has up to seven holes in its shell through which it exhales the water drawn in to be filtered through a pair of gills, and a very large oval "foot" or adductor muscle by which it adheres firmly to its rock.

It is the foot which is the edible part. Obtaining the creature is not easy, since it often lives at a depth which makes it necessary to dive and then prise the shells away from the rock. However, the rewards are commensurate with the task, since abalone fetches a good price. The Chinese and the Japanese are the greatest enthusiasts for it, and the finest and largest abalones are found in the Pacific off the coasts of Japan, Australia, New Zealand, and California. In Japan they are traditionally fished by women known as *ama*; and these now go about their task with the aid of neoprene suits.

The various species on the coast of California are afforded some protection by State regulations. They include black, red, green, white, and pinto abalones. The premier species, which used to be the only one for which there was a commercial fishery, is the red abalone, *H rufescens*. It may grow up to a size over 10-11 inches, but overfishing has made it increasingly difficult to find large specimens. The result is that other, smaller, species are now also gathered by commercial divers. The smallest is the pinto abalone, *H kamtschatkana*.

The species familiar in the Mediterranean and on the European Atlantic coast as far north as the Channel Islands is *H tuberculata*, which may measure as much as 5 inches. The "sea ear" has been esteemed since classical times when Aristotle described it, but it is not a noticeable feature of Mediterranean cuisine. It is more common on the Atlantic coast of France, and its reputation in the Channel Islands is high. A nineteenth-century writer said: "Tis much bigger than an oyster, and like that, good either fresh or pickled, but infinitely more pleasant to the gusto, so that an epicure would think his palate in paradise if he might but always gormandize on such delicious ambrosia."

However, the meat of abalone is tough, and will certainly not seem like ambrosia unless tenderized by beating with a mallet before cooking.

Dried or canned abalone is widely used in the Orient, and everywhere expensive, although fresh abalone costs even more. Abalone meat is also available in tenderized, frozen form.

Pop's Recipe

Abalone cookery is usually a simple business. In his excellent work, *The Abalone Book*, Peter Howorth quotes the classic recipe of "Pop" Ernest Doelter, who was the pioneer, at his Monterey restaurant in the first decade of this century, in presenting abalone to Californians as a delicacy.

Pop was a man of few words. He thought that the important point was to get the tenderizing right. "Without a properly spirited pounding, the abalone is too tough to eat, but, if assaulted too savagely, it becomes mush. The slices are dipped in beaten egg thinned with dry sherry, then fried in butter in a heavy skillet, one minute to a side."

Three species of abalone: ormer, *Haliotis tuberculata* (left); red abalone, *H rufescens* (center); and black abalone, *H cracherodii* (right)

Oysters

160

Of all marine molluscs, the oyster has been the most prized and, until it was overtaken by the mussel, the most cultivated. There are numerous species, but only half a dozen are important as food. First, for historical reasons, comes the European oyster, *Ostrea edulis*, but nowadays it has been outstripped or matched in importance by the Portuguese oyster, the American oyster and the oriental oyster. The small Olympia oyster of the Northwest Pacific coast of America and Australian rock oyster are also now prominent.

The oyster presents several surprises. Once a staple food of the poor (in England, for example), it has become almost everywhere a luxury food. The various species were formerly established in discrete populations in different parts of the world; but it is now possible to find several species being cultivated in one small area. Yet in some places where oysters abounded in the wild they are now almost extinct (I think of Trinidad and the mangrove oysters, for example, which used to be hawked by the plateful in Port-of-Spain).

Alone among the molluscs, the oyster has been the subject of a book at once scientific and poetic. This is by an American author, Eleanor Clarke, writing in France about *The Oysters of Locmariaquer*. Her description deals as much with the oystermen and oysterwomen as with the oysters, and would apply with little change to ostreiculture elsewhere.

Oysters produce millions of larval oysters in the form of "spat", which are at first free swimming but soon attach themselves to some support, and would in the normal course of events stay put until they had grown to their full size, lived out their allotted span, and died. Man, however, provides supports in the form of "collectors", which in the south of Brittany are special hollow tiles treated with lime. These are placed in the water at a carefully calculated time in June, when the fall of spat and the temperature are favorable. The larval oysters which quickly encrust them are allowed to stay on them for eight to ten months. The tiles are then retrieved and the tiny oysters stripped off them and transferred to "parks" or basins (known as "claires") where they can be shielded from some of their predators, such as starfish and whelks, while they grow. Each year they are moved to a fresh park; and this whole procedure constitutes what the French call *élévage*. When they are three or four years old, the oysters are transferred to ideal conditions for the stage of *affinage* (refinement); and, finally, they undergo the process of *expédition*, which means training them to survive for ten days or so out of water, and packing them up for despatch to the markets.

Oyster terminology can be bewildering, since names may refer either to a species, or to their region of origin, or to the locality or manner in which they have been prepared for marketing. In France, *plates* refer to oysters of the species *Ostrea edulis*; if they come from specific parts of Brittany they will be called *Belons* or *Armoricaines*. *Huîtres creuses* refer to *Crassostrea* species. *Fines de claire* is the name for oysters raised in special basins, for example those of Marennes-Oléron, where 60 per cent of French oysters are produced. Those which acquire a greenish tinge (chlorophyll derived from a minute organism present in certain basins) are *Vertes de Marennes*. In Britain and on the northeast USA coast, oysters are usually identified by the place in which they are reared or to which they are transplanted for a final spell of nourishment: thus Whitstable ("Royal Whitstables" are English native oysters from there), Helford and Colchester in England, and Blue Point, Chincoteague and Cape (Cape Cod) in the USA.

My own preference is for eating oysters straight from the shell. I have hardly ever cooked them. But I freely admit that in times when they were plentiful, and in some places even now, it makes sense to introduce variety into their consumption by doing so. Having surveyed the literature quite fully, my conclusion is that the eastern seaboard of the USA is the region which has been richest in oyster recipes. A recipe from there is given on page 196.

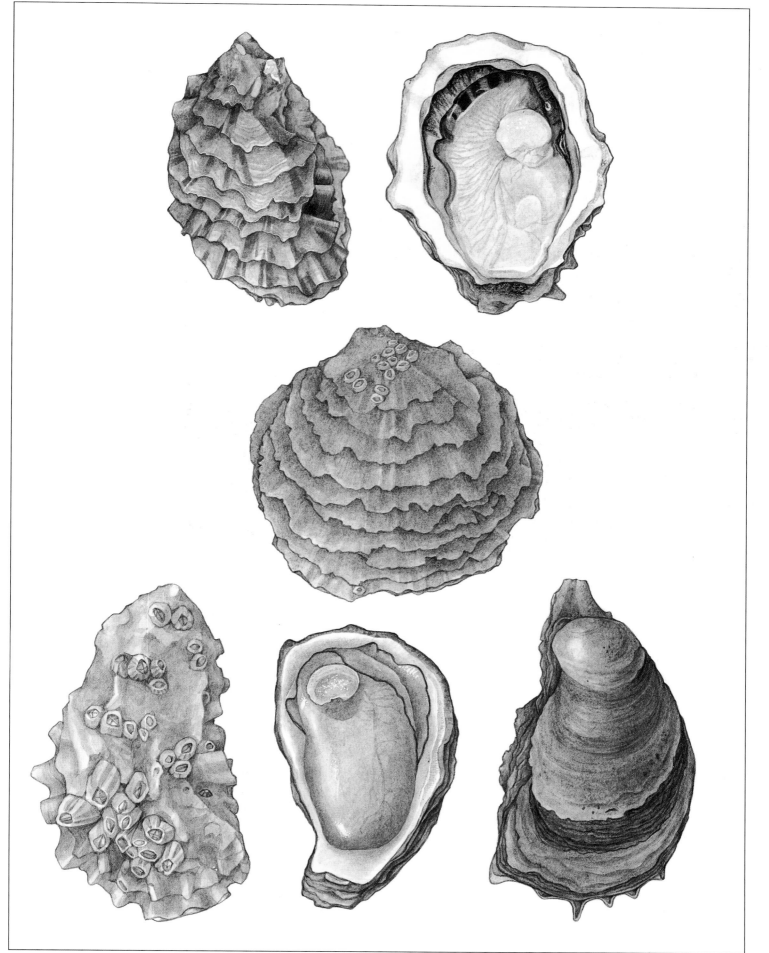

Portuguese oyster, *Crassostrea angulata* (top); European oyster, *Ostrea edulis* (middle); Pacific oyster, *C gigas* (bottom left); American blue point oyster, *C virginica* (bottom middle and right)

Mussels

162

Mussels are of worldwide distribution and importance. The painting, which shows side-by-side the principal European species, *Mytilus galloprovincialis* and *M edulis*, and the green mussel of New Zealand and Southeast Asia, *Perna viridis*, reflects this.

"Wild" mussels (if one can use the term for a creature of sedentary habits that feeds innocuously on the nutrients which it can filter out of sea water) have been gathered and eaten since remote antiquity. But the introduction of myticulture, as the culture of mussels is called, in France during the thirteenth century raised the consumption of mussels to a new level, and the development in Spain of a new method of rearing mussels on ropes suspended from rafts has transformed the industry in the latter part of the twentieth century.

Mussels grow in clusters, attaching themselves by means of a "byssus" (numerous threads, produced by the mussel itself) to rocks or other supports such as jetties or gravel beaches. They can also attach themselves to the hulls of ships, and it is by this means that the main European species and the very similar Mediterranean mussel, *M galloprovincialis*, have been spread all over the northern hemisphere. Other species important as food, or potentially so, are *M californianus*, a slightly larger species off the Pacific coast of North America and *Perna canaliculus*, the principal mussel of the Orient (not just New Zealand, though that is the country which has developed an export trade). This has a greenish-black shell which turns yellow after exposure to the sun and is larger still (up to 8 inches) but market length is usually only half that).

There are certain localities where "wild" mussels of exceptional quality are found, but in general these mussels tend to be skimpy and their consumption is sometimes risky for reasons explained below. The overwhelming majority of mussels brought to market are cultured, and these should always be plump, delicious and safe to eat. Their size, appearance and flavor vary according to species, age and place of culture. More than one place claims to produce "the best mussels in the world". One such is Wimereux, near Boulogne in France, where the mussels are relatively small but have an excellent flavor and remarkably clean, pretty indigo shells.

Mussels are a potential health hazard because they filter in an indiscriminate way the sea water passing through them, and can accumulate toxins from polluted waters or the notorious "red tides" created by concentrations of a certain dinoflagellate planktonic organism. They are not alone in this ability, but are so good at it that scientists employ them as unpaid monitors of water pollution. There is therefore some risk with "wild" mussels gathered from waters not known to be clean. But the risk is negligible with cultured mussels, which constitute over 99 per cent of those marketed, and which are subject to strict supervision.

Consumption of mussels varies greatly from one country to another. My subjective impression, after living there for some years, is that Belgium must be top of the league, *Moules et Frites* being a sort of national dish there.

Mussels can be eaten raw, but are usually cooked. They often feature in a Spanish *Paella*. Two famous French mussel dishes are *Mouclade* and *Moules Marinière*. Italians make a fine *Zuppa di Cozze*. A worldwide list of dishes prepared with fresh mussels would indeed be long.

Moules Nautile

I select for special attention a recipe which belongs to Toulon, famous for its mussels. It comes from the Hotel Nautilus, formerly the home of Jules Verne, in that great port. Since it needs to be set out at length, it will be found on page 186.

The Mediterranean mussel, *Mytilus galloprovincialis* (top row); the common mussel of western Europe, *M edulis* (left); and a New Zealand specimen of *Perna canaliculus*, the green mussel (right)

Scallops

Writing about one of the various scallops in American waters, Augusta Foote Arnold observed: "On clear, calm days the immature individuals of this species may often be seen in shallow water disporting themselves most gaily, skipping about and snapping their valves in great glee." A charming picture; and indeed scallops alive and in the water are remarkably different from what one buys.

Scallops do not crawl or burrow, so do not have a large "foot". Instead, they have a highly developed adductor muscle, by means of which they can open and close their shells and so propel themselves through the water. Not all of them exercise this ability. Some remain anchored by a byssus to some solid object. Others start life thus and then become free rangers, swimming or resting on the sea bottom.

Most but not all scallops are hermaphrodites, equipped with both an orange roe (or coral) and a whitish testis. Europeans eat these as well as the adductor muscle, but in North America they are usually discarded. Scallops are usually cleaned at sea, and only the adductor muscles (or muscles and roes) brought to market. But other parts, such as the mantle, are edible, and Canadian processors have canned scallop "rims and roes", for use in chowders.

Scallops belong to the family Pectinidae, in which the principal genera are *Pecten* and *Chlamys*. The principal species include:

● *Pecten maximus*, the "great scallop' of the North Atlantic, found from Norway down to the Iberian Peninsula: maximum diameter about 6 inches, 15 to 17 radiating ribs on the shell.
● *P jacobaeus*, the slightly smaller Mediterranean scallop; 14-16 ribs.
● *Chlamys opercularis*, the queen (scallop) or quin: maximum size 4 inches, about 20 ribs: *vanneau* in French, *volandeira* in Spanish. Color of the shell may be anything from yellow through pink to purple or brown. A species of deeper waters, fishery for which is increasing.
● *C varia*, a Mediterranean species, the French *pétoncle* and Spanish *zamburina*. About 30 ribs.
● *C islandica*, the Iceland scallop, a smaller species which is caught and marketed from both Iceland and Canada; its muscle is less white and tender.
● *Placopecten magellicanus*, the Atlantic deep-sea scallop, for which there is a growing North American fishery, is another large one.
● *Aequipecten circularis*, the speckled scallop, and *Pecten diegensis*, the San Diego scallop, are among the species of the American Northwest.
● *Amusium pleuronectes* is a large and common species of the Indo-Pacific.
● *Chlamys nobilis* is a dainty little scallop of various bright colors, cultured in the Pescadores Islands to the West of Taiwan.

Scallops are highly esteemed as food in most parts of the world, but not much in Southeast Asia. They are, however, caught and sold there to an increasing extent as a result of demand from hotels and restaurants catering for foreign visitors. The second Thai name cited in the list, *hoy shell*, shows what strange things can happen in linguistic practice. The Shell Company, which is active in Thailand as in so many other countries, displays its familiar scallop shell emblem there. Noticing the likeness, Thai people have taken to naming the scallop after the company.

As the popularity of scallops has grown, various ruses have been adopted for simulating them, for example by cutting out cylindrical pieces of goosefish or skate or (in Texas) the meat of the saw-toothed pearl shell. Or so they say: I've never myself met any such knavery.

How you cook scallops may well depend on where you are. In most places scallops are expensive; and this, combined with their delicacy of flavor, points to a rather delicate treatment, such as Scallops in Cider or Muscadet (see page 184). But in places such as Digby, the main scallop-fishing port in Canada, a more robust treatment is allowed, and they are made into a Nova Scotia Scallop Chowder.

Great scallop, *Pecten maximus* (top and bottom); queen scallop, *Chlamys opercularis* (left and right); *C nobilis* (center); bay scallops, *Argopecten gibbus* (loose)

Cockles

ockle is a confusing name which is applied to many edible bivalves in different parts of the world. How convenient it would be if it were reserved for members of the families Cardiidae (true cockles) and Glossidae (heart-cockles)! But no: there seems to be little hope of tidying up the nomenclature to this extent; but some encouragement may be gleaned from reflecting that the word cockle is derived from classical Greek and Latin words meaning "shell", and that its meaning has at least become narrower than that.

The species which can fairly be regarded as the archetypal cockle, and which is known as the common cockle, is *Cerastoderma edule*. This cockle has an extensive distribution from the Barents Sea and the Baltic to the Mediterranean and Senegal. As is true of most bivalves bearing the name cockle, it looks something like a human heart when viewed from the side.

The common cockle, which is what Molly Malone was selling when she called "Cockles and Mussels, Alive Alive-oh" in the streets of Dublin, has a maximum measurement of about 2 inches. The color of the shells is brown, pale yellow, or grubby white. It is a valuable and delicious food.

The spiny cockle, *Acanthocardia aculeata*, occurs in the Mediterranean and the eastern Atlantic coast as far north as the Channel Islands and Devon. It may reach a size of 4 inches. The creature inside the shell is red; hence the alternative name bloody cockle. The prickly cockle, *A echinata*, has a range extending further north to Norway. *A tuberculata* is a Mediterranean species, whose shell is covered with tubercles rather than prickles, and which also has a red inhabitant.

The edible cockles on the eastern seaboard of the USA are little exploited. On the Pacific coast confusion is rampant; the name cockle, often prefixed by such terms as "sea", "sand", "mud" or "bay", is used for a whole range of clams and Venus shells. However, there are also some true cockles present, notably the basket cockle, *Clinocardium nuttalli*, which can measure 4 inches.

In Britain cockles, which abound on sandy shores and in estuaries, provide the most valuable mollusc fishery. The cocklers of the Gower Peninsula in Wales are the most picturesque of the people engaged in the fishery, and the Welsh seem to have a wider range of cockle recipes than the English. But the best British cockles are generally held to be the Stiffkey (pronounced stookey) blues from Norfolk. These owe their blueness to the anaerobic mud which they inhabit.

The name cockle is sometimes given to arkshells, for example the "bloody clam" or "bloody cockle" of Southeast Asia. In New Zealand a common Venus shell, *Chione stuchburyi*, is called a cockle. Finally, the name "dog-cockle" is given to a sort of clam, *Glycymeris glycymeris*, of the Mediterranean and East Atlantic.

All cockles benefit from an opportunity to purge themselves before being eaten. Set them in clear sea water for this purpose. The smaller true cockles can be eaten raw or cooked, as in this Welsh recipe for cockles and eggs.

Cocos as Wyau
(Cockles and Eggs)

1 quart cockles	2 large eggs, beaten
2 tablespoons bacon fat	black pepper to taste

Put the cockles in a pot, cover with water and bring to the boil. Boil for a few minutes only, otherwise they will become tough. Remove them from their shells, wash them and lay them out on a large cloth to absorb excess moisture.

Heat the fat in a pan and lightly fry the cockles. Toss them well, pour the beaten eggs over them and stir with a wooden spoon. Season with pepper. Serves four.

Alternative
small clams (p 170)

Alternative Recipe
Zuppa di Cannolicchi (p 193)

The three small shells are of the common European cockle, *Cerastoderma edule*. Below is *Acanthocardia aculeata*, the spiny cockle; above, a pair of dog-cockles, *Glycymeris glycymeris*

American Clams

168

Here we meet the ill-defined clan of clams; ill-defined because the word clam is not used in a precise way. An attractive definition is "a marine bivalve whose hinged shells can close completely, or 'clam up'": but some bivalves that cannot close their shells completely are still called clams, while some which can close them are not. Fortunately, this does not really matter. North America is the best place in the world for clams, and the clams eaten there are such that no one has difficulty in figuring out which is which.

The soft-shelled clam, *Mya arenaria*, found on both sides of the North Atlantic (and accidentally introduced to the Pacific coast of North America in the 1870s), is greatly appreciated in Canada and the USA, but less popular in Europe. It is large (up to 6 inches) and has a brittle shell which gapes permanently at each end. Even so, it can survive for a long time out of water, even without oxygen, so can be marketed in good condition. Its double siphon is long, accounting for an alternative common name: long-neck. (A third name, steamer, is bestowed because it is judged to be particularly suitable for steaming.) On the European side, its range extends only down to the English Channel, but it does have some traditional Irish names such as Maninose or Nannynose.

Because they gape, these clams tend to be sandy and gritty, so are usually purged by being kept alive for a day or two in clean water, preferably with a little cornmeal. They are then ready for a clambake, or to become steamed soft-shell clams, or for use in certain clam chowders and clam pies.

The reputation of this clam rests also on its excellence when battered and fried. It was the first clam to be so treated, an event said to have taken place in Essex, Massachusetts, in the early twentieth century. However, nearby Ipswich became the headquarters of the clam processors and soft-shelled clams therefore became known also as Ipswich clams. They remain the most popular clams for battering and frying in New England.

The hard-shell clam (or quahog, or littleneck), *Mercenaria mercenaria*, is slightly smaller and has a much shorter siphon ("neck"). It is indigenous to North America, but colonies have established themselves, or been established by man, in Europe, for example in Southampton Water in England (where, it is thought, debris thrown over the side of transatlantic liners included some of these creatures, still alive), and in parts of France (where the French have adopted the name "clam" for it, thus making it a French word). There are various names for this clam, indicative of its size. In New York the list runs thus, the figures showing how many you can expect in a bushel: littlenecks, 450-650; cherrystones, 300-325; mediums, 180; chowders, 125. They have a slightly different system in Boston, where the larger specimens are called sharps. Those up to the size of cherrystones are best eaten raw; larger ones can go into clam chowders, or be stuffed.

The surf clam (or bar clam, hen clam or sea clam), *Spisula solidissima*, is larger and has a very hard shell. Seagulls pick up these bivalves, carry them to the nearest car park and drop them onto the surface of the car park in order to break them open and eat the contents. This clam (which has a European relation, *S solida*) accounts for something like three quarters of the clam harvest in the USA. It is usually shucked raw and minced for clam chowders. If preparing these clams yourself, remember that the large "foot" is tough (although strips of it can be deep-fried) and that the really delicious parts are the twin adductor muscles, (white and cylindrical, found just below the apex of the shell), and the juice (which can be strained and drunk as clam nectar).

Finally, the greatest American clam of all: *Panope geodosa*, the mighty geoduck of the Pacific northwest, so huge that it couldn't even try to fit itself inside its shell. It has to be skinned before being prepared for eating. Indeed its aspect is so repellent to some people that it is often marketed in fillets.

169

Surf clam, *Spisula solidissima* and soft-shelled clam, *Mya arenaria* (top); geoduck, *Panope geodosa* (middle); littleneck, cherrystone and quahog, three sizes of *Mercenaria mercenaria* (bottom)

More
Clams

Since my grandfather used a "cut-throat" razor, I have never had to wonder why the names razor clam or razor-shell are applied to the edible bivalves in the genera *Ensis* and *Solen*. The resemblance is striking. These shells are very brittle, usually covered by a thin glossy brown or yellowish outer covering; and they gape permanently at both ends.

Its long and powerful "foot" enables a razor clam to make its way through wet sand like a knife through butter, dodging danger by a swift descent. Hunting them in the intertidal waters where they lurk can be a frustrating business, and even perilous since the sharp edges of their shells can inflict severe cuts. In Orkney, where the cult of eating them is strongest, they are known as spoots. "Come spooting," said the Orkney schoolteacher with whom we were staying, and we did, but no spoots did we catch, although we tried all the approved techniques.

Opinions differ on how to make them emerge from their holes. Putting a teaspoonful of salt into the hole is said to work in some places but not in others. The comments of George Henry Lewes (1858) are apposite. "There is something irresistibly ludicrous in grave men stooping over a hole – their coat-tails pendant in the water, their breath suspended, one hand holding salt, the other alert to clutch the victim – watching the perturbations of the sand, like hungry cats beside the holes of mice."

The common species of European waters are *Ensis ensis*, which is curved; *E siliqua*, which is straight; and *Solen marginatus*, which is also straight. Maximum lengths are around 5-6 inches. On the eastern seaboard of North America *Ensis directus*, the eastern razor clam or Atlantic jack-knife, is the main species; while on the western coast, from Alaska to California, *Siliqua patula*, the northern razor clam, is the most prized species. In Asian waters *Solen grandis* is the species most commonly marketed.

Razor clams, once removed from their shells, may be eaten entire. Of the few dishes which specifically call for them, the Italian *Zuppa di Cannolicchi* (see page 000) is noteworthy, and can be adapted for any other clams.

Other clams worth eating, and better known, are numerous. There are those who put at the top of the class the relatively large (up to 12 inches) and agile *toheroa* of New Zealand, *Amphidesma ventricosum*, found only in certain localities and rigorously protected; and its little brothers, the *tuatua* and the *pipi*. But in the Pacific northwest of the USA, the pismo clam, *Tivela stultorum*, is considered the best in the world.

In Southeast Asia people are less chauvinist about clams, although there they have the truly named giant clam, *Tridacna gigas*, which can measure 40 inches across and weigh several hundred kilos! The meat on the border of the shells is good, although it has a rather strong flavor; and the huge adductor muscle can be boiled and dried and then used (in bits) in soups. But this giant has other uses: each shell can be turned into a very beautiful washbasin. The clams most appreciated (at least in the Philippines, where appreciation of clams is strong) are the large surf clam (or hen or trough clam) (*Mactra mera*) and the sunset/macoma shells (*Soletellina* species).

Back in Europe, the best clams are in the group known in English as venus or carpet shells, but often better known by their French names. The *palourde, Venerupis decussata*, has a maximum width of 3 inches, and is known in Italy as *vongola verace* (the true, or best, of the *vongole*). The slightly smaller *praire, Venus verrucosa*, has a more ridged shell, which shows up well in the painting; and the still smaller *clovisse jaune, Venerupis aurea*, one of the clams which has shells with patterns on the outside (the inside is golden yellow, hence *aurea*) which vaguely resemble certain carpets.

All these fine European clams can be eaten raw, but can also be cooked – usually by steaming them until they open.

Alternatives
any of the other clams on this page

Alternative recipe
Rappie Pie with Soft-shelled Clams
(p 195)

170

Two razor clams, *Ensis ensis* (top) and *E siliqua* (bottom); in the center, from left to right, palourde, *Venerupis decussata*, warty venus, *Venus verrucosa*, and smooth venus, *Callista chione*

Sea-Urchins

172

At first glance, sea-urchin seems like a strange common name for this sea creature of the order Diadematoida. Its outstanding characteristic is that, of all edible sea creatures, it provides the least amount of edible material for its volume; but that small part is a great delicacy.

However, there is no mystery about the name once one knows that it comes from an old English meaning of urchin: hedgehog. The sea-urchin does look like a small hedgehog, with spines sticking out in all directions from its "shell" (properly called test). These spines break off easily and are very difficult to extract from, for example, the foot of an incautious bather. Their purpose is to make their owner an unattractive mouthful for predators.

Inside the more or less spherical test there is little edible matter: in fact nothing but the five orange or rose-colored ovaries, also known as corals. These are revealed by cutting the sea-urchin open horizontally, preferably using the French implement designed for the purpose and called *coupe-oursin* (see page 178).

The sea-urchin of the Mediterranean, *Paracentrotus lividus*, is the best known, and the Mediterranean region is where these delicacies, marketed where they are landed, are most appreciated. This species may be found as far north as the south coast of Ireland. It measures up to 4 inches in diameter.

In the North Atlantic, all the way around from the English Channel to New Jersey, the species is *Strongylocentrus droebachiensis*. Indeed it has a circumpolar distribution. However, it is not marketed in many places. In North Europe, for example, it is largely ignored. It is abundant on the coast of Maine but is there called "whore's eggs" and regarded with abhorrence. Some are fished in the Bay of Fundy, and the taste for them may spread, but the unwieldy nature of the creatures makes it uneconomic to transport them unless they are going to fetch a very high price. On the whole, although they are now available at New York's Fulton Fish Market, it seems likely that they will continue to be exploited to only a limited extent, and only in certain places.

Further south in the West Atlantic there are smaller species, little eaten except for *Cidaris tribuloides* in the West Indies. And in Southeast Asia I was surprised to find that edible species such as *Diadema setosum* are consumed only in some localities, for example the Thai island of Kor Samuy, while in other areas no one gathers them. This may be because of the consequences which result from the skin being pierced by the exceptionally long (up to 8 inches) and sharp spines of *Diadema setosum*. Commenting that these may be venomous, a Singapore author states ominously: "Entry of the spine causes an initial searing pain which is followed by a deep ache and an ensuing general numbness in the immediate region of the injury, accompanied by swelling and redness of the skin." That is just the effect of one spine. This discomfort would at once turn into real danger if a naked bather fell heavily into a thickly clustered group of these urchins.

The giant sea-urchin of California, *Strongylocentrus franciscanus*, has been declared by Euell Gibbons (1964) to be the best of all, and to be greatly appreciated by Californians of Italian descent. It is sometimes as much as 5 inches in diameter. *S purpuratus* is smaller but more abundant, and its corals also have a fine flavor.

The corals, which need no cooking, make a delicious mouthful, with no accompaniment save a drop of lemon juice, and perhaps the little cubes of bread which one might eat with a soft-boiled egg. Some people, however, like to incorporate the corals in certain cooked dishes, for example an omelet or scrambled eggs (allow one sea-urchin for each egg). They can also be used to make an excellent sauce, by simply mashing up the corals from 2 pounds (six to 12, depending on size) of sea-urchins with a very little of the finest olive oil, and then beating this thoroughly into 1 cup of *Sauce Hollandaise*.

Paracentrotus lividus of the Mediterranean and East Atlantic (top and bottom), and *Strongylocentrus droebachiensis* of the North Atlantic (left and right)

Sea Cucumbers

174

W e end our display of seafood with a mysterious creature which belongs to the class Holothurians. Like the sea-urchins on the preceding page, these creatures are quite distinct from fish, crustaceans and molluscs. There are a lot of them (over 600 species) and they occur all around the world. Only a few species are used as food, however, and only in some regions, notably the Orient (where the principal markets are in Hong Kong, which is by far the most important, and in Korea, Singapore and Malaysia) but now also in Barcelona and its environs, and to a small extent in Provence and Istanbul.

A sea cucumber does resemble a cucumber in shape. It is distinctly phallic in appearance, a feature which is underlined by its habit of ejecting sticky threads (Cuvierian tubules) when squeezed. It does not swim around, but moves sluggishly about on the sea bottom extracting modest nourishment from the sediment. This sounds like a quiet life, and is, but it can be punctuated by a melodramatic piece of behavior. If severely disturbed, the sea cucumber will eviscerate itself (that is it will eject its entire apparatus of stomach and internal organs) and then regrow within the space of a few weeks the missing organs.

One end of the sea cucumber is its mouth, recognizable by a fringe of tentacles. The other end houses the anus, and also, quite often, an unwanted guest in the form of a small fish which backs into the hole and lives there, feeding itself by nibbling at the host's gonads.

These creatures have a great appeal to the Chinese because of the interesting slippery texture which they acquire after being suitably prepared, and also for their flavor. The method followed in preparing them (often done in the Pacific Islands where they are collected and processed as a cottage industry) is first to boil them in water until they swell; then to slit them open along the underside, wash them, and boil them again, to the point at which they are rubbery but not too hard; next, to remove the guts, and then smoke and dry the creatures over a fire of mangrove wood or coconut husks; and finally, to cure them in the sun for a few days. When the time comes to use them, they are soaked to soften them and make them swell in readiness for being cooked.

The species most prized by the Chinese is *Microthele nobilis*, which comes in two forms, white and black, depending on habitat. It is often called teatfish or mammy fish, the latter name being apparently derived from the native name *mama* in the Gilbert Islands. The white teatfish lives in moderately deep water, on clean sand and in or near turtlegrass; the black version likes shallower water and to be near living coral. Next in order of estimation come two somewhat smaller species, both of the genus *Actinopyga*: the "blackfish" and the "deep-water redfish". The "prickly redfish", *Thelenota ananas*, is of less value. Its "prickles" are large teats which occur in groups of two or three all over the body. There is also the "sandfish", *Metriatyla scabra*, which is still cheaper.

In the 1970s an enterprising restaurateur in Barcelona noticed that fishermen on the Catalan coast had for long had the habit of collecting these creatures, of the species *Stichopus regalis*, and eating them themselves. He went into the matter and put them on his menu, since when they have rocketed up-market to become the most expensive seafood in Barcelona. I tasted them there and found that they deserved this esteem. Oddly, they were quite different from those I had eaten in the Orient, not slippery and gelatinous at all but more like "fingers" of white flesh carved out of, say, fillets of sole.

Apart from Barcelona, Japan seems to be the one place where sea cucumbers are marketed fresh. There, and also in Taiwan, it is *Stichopus japonicus*, a relation of the Barcelona species, which is most favored. Everywhere else, and especially in places where there are ethnic Chinese communities, it is the dried product which is available.

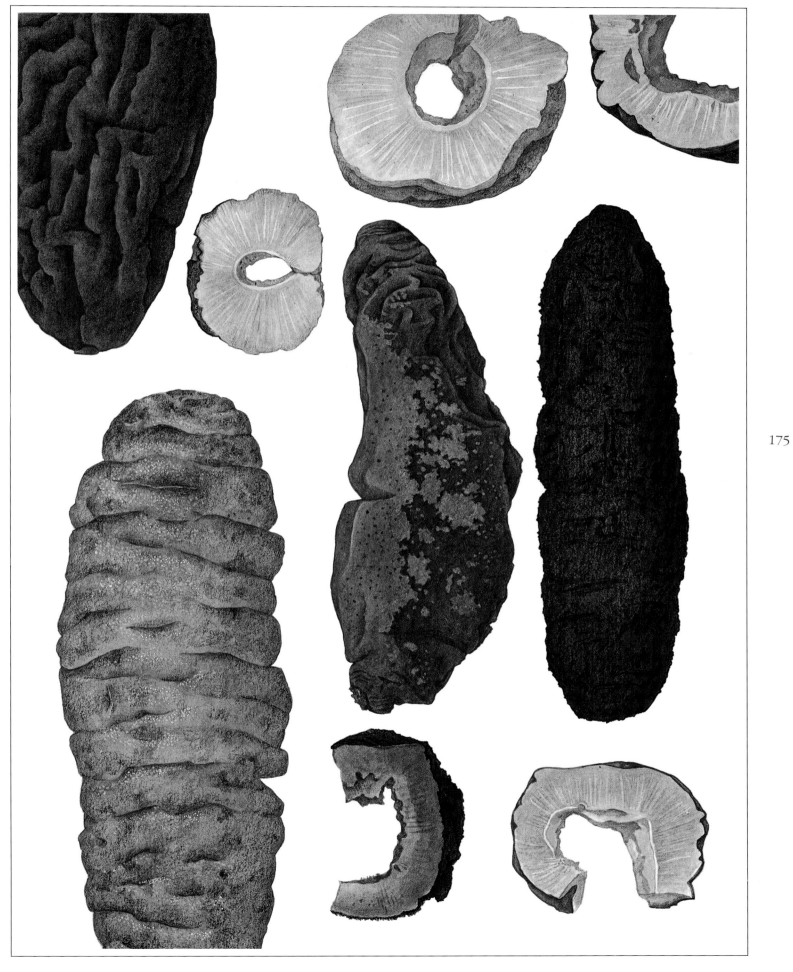

175

Various dried and reconstituted sea cucumbers from China and a fresh specimen (bottom left) from Thailand

Seafood Cookery

To plunge straight into seafood cookery would be to dodge a basic question: why cook seafood?

Part of the answer must be that it isn't always necessary or desirable to cook it. Some seafoods, such as oysters, are best eaten raw. The Japanese have shown the world how delightful raw fish, *sashimi*, can be. So far as that is concerned, my advice is to buy fish from a fishmonger who caters for a Japanese community, and to study the Japanese methods of presenting it. This can sometimes be done by looking in the windows of Japanese restaurants, where remarkable plastic replicas of prepared dishes are displayed.

The next question is whether there are any intermediate stages between "raw" and "cooked"; and indeed there are. Smoked salmon and caviar and a host of other prepared seafood products are not exactly raw, but they are not cooked either, and are eaten without being cooked. For this whole category of "cured" seafoods, the advice is, again, to find a good supplier.

Having dealt with raw and cured seafoods, I address a couple of further basic questions: what do we mean, exactly, by "cooking" a fish, and why do we do it?

When I first began to write about seafood I posed the first question – what happens when we cook a fish? – to the Torry Research Station at Aberdeen, Scotland, where Dr J J Connell (now its Director) kindly provided the answer. To cook a fish is to raise the temperature of its innermost parts to (give or take a degree or two) 145°. The "give or take" factor operates because some circumstances, such as the chemical composition of the liquid in which the fish is being cooked, may slightly affect the temperature reached. But the temperature given is the one to aim at, and care should be taken not to exceed it more than slightly otherwise the fish will be overcooked. This is the most common fault in fish cookery. The consequences of overcooking when you are broiling or poaching can be disastrous, but in some dishes, where the fish is being baked in a sauce, no harm will come from prolonging the cooking. In the Middle East and North Africa cooks may deliberately do this so that the fish flakes apart.

Dr Connell explained the effects of this raising of the temperature. The first is that the protein in the flesh coagulates, resulting in the white, curdy appearance which is a characteristic of cooked fish. This coagulation liberates a substantial proportion of the water present in the flesh, together with flavoring substances in it. Secondly, the thin membranes which hold the flakes of flesh together are broken down so that the flakes separate easily. Thirdly, chemical changes take place; and it is these which produce the odors and flavors which we associate with cooked fish.

As for the purpose of cooking fish, this must surely be considered on two levels. On one, it is a matter of making it palatable and digestible. True, many kinds of fish, if very fresh, do not need to be cooked to achieve this; but, broadly speaking, fish do need to be cooked in order to become food ready to eat. However, there is a second level; many people cook with a more ambitious aim – they want to produce something really delicious, to explore new combinations of flavors, to bring special pleasure to the people they cook for. Most recipe books assume that one is operating on this second level.

There are, incidentally, two fallacies which need to be dispelled here. One is that the more effort that goes into a dish, the better it will be. The other is that a hot dish is intrinsically superior to a cold dish, and more honorific for those invited to partake of it.

The first fallacy arises from a confusion. If a person works hard to cook a dish, the person deserves praise; all hard work directed at worthy ends deserves praise. But the dish is not itself any better just because it is the product of hard work; it may be less good than something more simple and easy.

The second fallacy does have some basis. One important element of taste in a dish, sweetness, seems to be most perceptible if the dish is at a temperature of around 95°. This effect gradually disappears as the temperature of the dish moves downwards or upwards from this point. Also, heating foodstuffs releases appetising aromas, as volatile flavor-compounds are dissipated into the air of the kitchen.

The whole question of flavor compounds in cooked fish is almost unbelievably complex. Scientists have made some progress in identifying the desirable elements (mainly in order to see whether they can be replicated and added to fish products); but these elements interact among each other, so this is very difficult. It is fortunate that cooks do not need to venture into this labyrinth, but can be content with the knowledge that properly cooked fish will be appetising. However, it is perhaps worth mentioning that certain seafoods contain significant amounts of sugars, which account for the desirable sweet taste of, say, canned crabmeat, and that a touch of the opposite primary taste (acid, as when one adds a drop of vinegar) has an enhancing effect on this.

Another principle of great practical importance concerns the transmission of heat. The objective is to raise the temperature of the innermost part of the fish to a certain level. The greater the distance between the source of heat (whatever that is) and the innermost part of the fish, the longer it will take to cook. The weight of the fish is not directly relevant, since an eel, no part of which is more than a short distance from the heat being applied, may weigh the same as a cube-shaped joint of, say, sturgeon, where the distance is much greater. Hence a principle which has become known as the Canadian principle, according to which one measures the maximum thickness of the fish and determines cooking time according to that. This is a step in the right direction, but overlooks an important fact: the length of time which heat takes to penetrate anything does not vary in a direct ratio to its thickness, but in proportion to the square of the thickness. To put it another way, the rate of penetration of heat progressively, and markedly, slows down as it gets further and further into the object being heated. (This applies to all forms of heating except microwave heating.)

Scoring a fish. The cuts are made to match the thickness of the fish. If the greatest distance from skin to backbone is, say, one inch, and the cuts are one inch apart, cooking time will be only a fourth as long.

It follows from this that if a piece of fish whose maximum thickness is X takes Y minutes to be cooked, a piece with a thickness of 2X will take 4Y minutes (not 2Y, as one might think). It also follows that, if effective steps are taken to reduce the distance to the innermost part of the fish, the time required for cooking will also be not just reduced but dramatically reduced. Hence the importance of "scoring" the sides of a fish. Hence, too, the need to do the scoring in a knowledgeable and scientific way, as shown in the diagram.

Before going on to examine specific cookery techniques and to set out further recipes, I should say something about two basic preparations which are often useful preliminaries – *court bouillon* and fish stock (or *fumet*, its concentrated form).

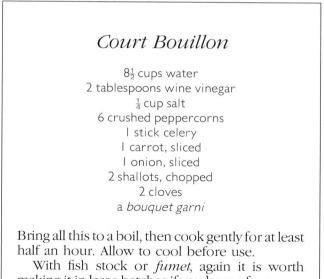

Court Bouillon

8½ cups water
2 tablespoons wine vinegar
¼ cup salt
6 crushed peppercorns
I stick celery
I carrot, sliced
I onion, sliced
2 shallots, chopped
2 cloves
a *bouquet garni*

Bring all this to a boil, then cook gently for at least half an hour. Allow to cool before use.

With fish stock or *fumet*, again it is worth making it in large batches if you have a freezer so that you can freeze it and draw on it as needed. Making it is easy. You just take some wholesome fish trimmings (head, tail, skin, bones) add a few vegetables and herbs if you wish, and simmer them in seasoned water for half an hour. Then strain the result. If you then continue to simmer the *court bouillon* so as to reduce the liquid to about a third of its original volume, you have the more concentrated *fumet*. These preparations are often used in making sauces.

A *court bouillon* is simply flavored liquid used for poaching a fish. The point here is that fish does not take long to cook, so that if one wishes to impart flavors to it from the cooking liquid it is well to get the flavors into the cooking liquid before you start. How you flavor the liquid is up to you – the possibilities are infinite – but a recipe which is representative of usual practice is given in the box below. If you have a freezer, it is worth making more than you need for immediate purposes, since what is not used can be frozen and will be ready for use on another occasion. (Incidentally, *court bouillon* means something different in Louisiana: there it refers to a kind of finished fish dish, not to the preparatory liquid.)

Some Special Flavors

It seems hardly necessary to say that lemon goes well with fish, but it is worth mentioning that lime is equally good, and that it gives a somewhat different and slightly stronger effect. Lemon grass, a herb which is much employed in Asian seafood cookery and which grows like a weed even in warmish temperate climates, is also a really valuable ingredient, and can be had in powdered form (often as "sereh powder").

Many herbs go well with fish. Parsley is an obvious example. The Asian equivalent, coriander, which is also used in Portuguese cookery, has a much stronger flavor and is not liked by everyone; so use coriander sparingly and parsley in abundance. In northern Europe much use is made of dill. In Mediterranean countries thyme and rosemary add their special flavors. In most parts of the world, one or other kind of basil is used, and suitable mints.

Spices used with fish are too numerous to list, but I should like to put in a word for nutmeg (see the recipe on page 122), and also for ginger. Cooks in Burma use ginger to suppress the seafood flavor of seafood, since they prefer freshwater fish. This curious piece of information reminds those of us who like a seafood flavor that we should be discreet in the use of ginger; but it certainly suits some seafoods.

Coconut cream and coconut milk occur in a number of recipes I give. These can conveniently be prepared from commercial products, following the directions on the package. If you prefer to make your own from the grated white meat of a fresh coconut, mixed with water and squeezed through muslin, remember that cream is the first and thicker extraction you obtain, while milk is the second and thinner one which is got by repeating the process with the same lot of grated coconut.

177

Buying Seafood

Like land animals, fish pass through the stage of rigor mortis (rigor for short) shortly after death. There are two main causes of this, both hinged on the using up of the residual energy which is still present in a newly dead fish. One is that the enzymes whose activity was necessary during life to keep the muscles flexible gradually cease to operate. The other is the accumulation of lactic acid as the energy reserve disappears. How quick the onset of rigor is, and how long it lasts, varies considerably. Generally speaking, in small fish or fish which died in a state of exhaustion (for example after struggling in a trawl, or after spawning), it all happens quite quickly. But larger fish, which were in tip-top condition when they died, may take up to 24 hours to enter rigor and may stay in it for several days. There is also a variation between species; for example, rigor acts much faster on plaice and haddock than on redfish. Rigor has usually come and gone before a fish is sold, but people at the seaside who buy freshly caught fish should be aware of it.

Otherwise, the familiar list of points to look out for applies.
* The gills should be moist and red, not gray.
* The eyes should be bright, and stand out; not be dull and sunken.
* The body should be firm to the touch.
* There should be almost no smell, and what there is should be "fresh".
* The fishmonger should have a pleasant open countenance (he or she almost always does) and be ready to discuss (not lecture you about) the fish and prepare it as you wish.

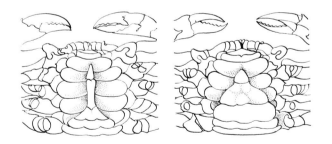

When buying live crabs, choose those that seem lively, and heavy for their size. The same applies to lobsters. In most species of crab, the male crab will have a higher proportion of white meat than the female, because its claws are bigger; so, if white meat is what you prefer, you need to know which is which (or ask the fishmonger). The drawing above shows the undersides, with their differently shaped tails, of an adult male (on the left) and female of *Callinectes sapidus*, the blue crab (page 138).

Clams and the like should be visibly alive. For many of them the rule is that the double shell should be tightly closed, or else opening and closing.

Equipment

Since any fish can be cut up into convenient pieces, it is not really necessary to have a fish-kettle. However, there are many pleasing effects which can be achieved by cooking fish of moderately large size whole, and the cost of a heavy aluminum fish kettle, although considerable, is not great if one reflects that it will last for a generation or more. The drawing shows the three parts of such a kettle, including the grid which enables you to lift out the cooked fish without damage. (If you also wrap the fish in cheesecloth, that will protect it on its subsequent transfer to a platter.) There will be a problem if you wish to cook a large flatfish (or triggerfish, or other thin, deep-bodied fish) whole. What the French call a *turbotière*, which is a lozenge-shaped fish-kettle, provides the answer.

Fish kettle

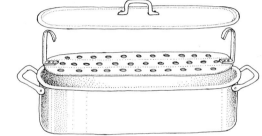

When grilling fish over a charcoal fire, which is a good way of doing it, the fish will either have to rest on an oiled grid above the fire (in which case turning it or them can be awkward) or be encased in a hinged grid of the kinds shown in the drawing (one suitable for several small fish side by side, the other for a single larger fish).

Flat grill

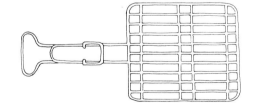

Convex grill

It is convenient if your fishmonger will do whatever gutting, scaling, and other preparation you want; but if you have to do it yourself you need a proper fish scaler, preferably of the kind shown opposite, which has a box to catch the scales as they fly off.

Equipment for a seafood cook should also include an oyster-knife and a clam-knife; and perhaps a *coupe-oursin* (see page 172).

Filleting knife

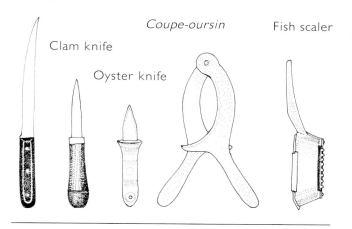

Clam knife

Coupe-oursin

Fish scaler

Oyster knife

Cooking Methods

The primary distinction is between cooking fish by radiant heat, notably broiling, and cooking fish in a medium such as water, steam, or oil. The first way carries with it the risk of having the fish dry out, but this is avoidable by means which I will explain below.

Broiling and Grilling

This is exposing fish, at fairly close range, to heat either above or below it. The term "barbecue" is often used for grilling fish out of doors over a charcoal fire. Inside, for example using an oven grill, the heat will be over rather than under the fish. Having the heat above carries one slight advantage; it is easier to collect, say, on a sheet of aluminum foil placed under the fish, juices escaping from it or surplus basting juices.

If oily fish, such as mackerel, are being broiled or grilled, and care is taken not to overcook them, no added fat or moisture will be needed. But for other fish it is desirable to brush the outside with oil before cooking starts. (Some people also dust the outside thinly with flour.) It is a good idea to baste while the cooking progresses. This can serve the additional purpose of adding appropriate flavors. A basting liquid composed of olive oil with lemon juice and herbs is suitable, and the basting can be done with a sprig of rosemary if you have one handy, or by impaling on a fork, through the skin, a quarter of a lemon (cut lengthways) and using the open side of this as a "brush".

There are other ways of adding flavors. The gut cavity can be filled with herbs, and the choice of wood or charcoal, in the case of a barbecue, can be important. There has been enthusiasm in the States recently for mesquite, which has a less sweet aroma (indeed, harsher, some would say) than more tra-

ditional sources of charcoal, such as hickory. Connoisseurship has reached such a point in California that there is one restaurant in Los Angeles which daily changes the kind of charcoal it uses. In Provence, Aleppo pine or wood from an old olive tree, well dried, are still favored.

If a moderately large fish is being broiled or grilled, the sides must be scored as indicated on page 177 so that the penetration of heat will be speeded up.

If scoring halves the distance from the exposed surface to the innermost points, cooking time will be reduced to a quarter.

If a fish is put in an oven with very little added fat, and simply exposed to the heat for a while, it would be described by some as "baked" and by others as "roast". In any case, the cooking is done by radiant heat, and basting is called for. I use the term "bake" in a more general way, for just about any cooking in the oven.

Completely plain broiled or grilled fish, served with lime or lemon, can be very good indeed. But it is likely to be better still if you are able to grill it over a charcoal fire and baste it while it is cooking – with the marinade, if you have used one.

However, good results can also be achieved by "pan-grilling", a technique used in the recipe for Grilled Norway Lobsters, overleaf.

179

Sole au Glui
(Sole Broiled with Straw)

Glui means ordinary wheat straw; and this is one of those very old, traditional methods of cooking which has survived to the present day in the region of Dieppe, France. The flesh of the sole turns a pale Naples yellow and acquires a subtle taste, reminiscent of lightly smoked fish.

Gut and trim the sole, but do not skin it. Make a cut right along each side, following the line of the backbone, and smear some good fresh butter into each of these incisions. Season the sole lightly.

Have ready a charcoal fire and a folding metal grid suitable for grilling fish. Open the grid and cover one side of it with straw. Put the sole on the straw, then cover it with a second layer of straw before closing the grid over it. Grill the sole, thus prepared, over the fire. The straw will flare up dramatically almost at once. Allow about five minutes for the first side and three minutes for the other.

Meanwhile, prepare a cream sauce by placing equal quantities of butter and fresh cream in a warm *bain-marie*. Whip these together, add salt and pepper and grated nutmeg and, just before the sauce is ready, add two teaspoons of chopped shallot.

When the sole is ready, open the grid and puff away the bits of burned straw, put the fish on a warm serving platter and serve, with the sauce.

Kılıç Balığı Izgara
(Grilled Tuna, Turkish Style)

4 tuna steaks, ½ inch thick
salt
for the marinade
scant ½ cup olive oil
scant ½ cup lemon juice
4 tablespoons onions, finely diced
2 teaspoons paprika
½ teaspoon salt
8 bay leaves
for the lemon sauce
4 tablespoons olive oil
4 tablespoons strained lemon juice
4 tablespoons parsley, chopped
salt to taste

Sprinkle the tuna steaks lightly with salt and let them stand for an hour or so. Meanwhile, mix the marinade ingredients in a non-metal dish. Set the fish steaks to marinate in this for four to five hours.

Have a charcoal fire glowing under a well-greased grid and place the steaks on the grid. Cook for four to five minutes on each side, basting frequently with the marinade.

Serve hot, with a lemon sauce made by mixing the ingredients listed. Serves four.

Samak Kabab
(An Egyptian recipe from Alexandria for grilling pieces of fish on skewers)

2 pounds sea bass
1 pound small tomatoes
a little olive oil
4 tablespoons parsley, chopped
for the marinade
juice of 3 lemons
3 onions, finely diced
4 bay leaves
salt and pepper
2 teaspoons cumin seed

First make up the marinade by combining all the ingredients. Cut the fish into cubes measuring ½ inch or a little more. Leave them in the marinade for half an hour.

Cut the tomatoes into quarters. Impale cubes of fish alternately with the tomato wedges on thin stainless steel skewers. Brush with olive oil and grill over charcoal. Serve on a bed of parsley, accompanied by lemon wedges. Serves four.

Grilled Norway Lobsters

It seems appropriate to have a recipe from a Norwegian chef and author (Bengt Petersen) for Norway Lobsters (see page 130).

16 Norway lobster tails in their shells
½ cup white wine
1 lemon
for the marinade
½ cup olive oil
juice of ½ a lemon
a few drops of Worcestershire sauce
1 drop of tabasco
2 teaspoons paprika
a pinch of salt
freshly ground white pepper

Cut the tails open lengthways, but without cutting the shell on the underside. Open them out butterfly fashion, and place them in the marinade, flesh side down, for 15 minutes. Then pan-grill them in a very hot dry pan for three to four minutes on each side. Sprinkle with wine just before they are ready.

Serve immediately with lemon wedges and horseradish butter (a compound butter of the sort described on page 200); or, if you prefer, with horseradish sauce (page 202). Serves four.

Pan Frying

Here the cooking is done by the partial immersion of the fish in hot oil or fat or butter. It is usual, but not an invariable practice, to coat the fish first with a batter which will prevent it from absorbing the oil or fat.

When seafoods are fried thus, the pan may be kept stationary, in which case whatever is being fried will have to be turned over, or it can be agitated, which is to sauté. This word, highly convenient for the French to whom it belongs, but more awkward for English-speakers, just means to make the things in the pan jump about. It is the right procedure when you are pan-frying small things.

Even when the stationary pan technique is being followed, it is normal to give the food a bit of a shake, but this does not apply when fish are fried according to West Indian recipes. Cooks there are insistent that the pan should not be shaken or moved; all you do is loosen the fish with a jab of the spatula (if they have stuck) and turn them, once.

The choice of the frying medium is important. Butter burns at a comparatively low temperature. If it is clarified, it works better and Indians, for some reason, are much more attentive to this point than most people in the West (the standard Indian ingredient "ghee" being simply clarified butter). When fish is cooked in hot clarified butter, and a little fresh butter is then heated and poured, frothing, over it, that is fish *à la meunière*, as it should be done.

If the butter is mixed with a vegetable oil, it can be taken to a much higher temperature. Or, of course, vegetable oil can be used by itself. There are also dishes where bacon fat is right – I think here of a German recipe for plaice; and pork fat is often used in some South East Asian countries.

Patience Gray's beautifully written recipe (see page 182), is only one member of an extensive tribe of recipes of ancient origin for frying fish and then preserving them in a vinegar mixture as she herself points out. In French the term is *en escabèche*, in Catalan *en escabetx*, in Spanish *en escabeche*, and so on; and similar recipes with similar names pervade Latin America.

Muc Xao Dua
(Squid Sauté with Pineapple, from Vietnam)

1½ pounds fresh squid, cleaned
1 pineapple
2 scallions
¼ cup pork fat
1-2 cloves garlic, crushed
1½ tablespoons fish sauce (*nuoc mam*)
a little flour
for the marinade
2 tablespoons or more fish sauce
salt and pepper
1 piece fresh ginger, pounded

Wash and dry the squid then cut it into small pieces and let these sit in the marinade for at least ten minutes, stirring occasionally. Then remove and drain them, keeping the marinade on one side.

Cut four slices from the pineapple and then cut these into small pieces. Cut the green parts of the scallions into pieces 1 inch long, leaving the bulbs aside.

Put half the pork fat into a pan, heat it, and add the garlic and squid. Cook over a high heat, stirring constantly, until the squid is done; then remove the squid.

Add the rest of the fat to the pan, put in the scallion bulbs and then the pineapple with half a tablespoon of fish sauce and some salt. Once the pineapple has absorbed the fat, add the rest of the fish sauce, this time mixed with a little flour. After a couple of minutes, add the squid, mix all well together, toss in the green parts of the scallions and remove from the heat. Serve hot, with pepper and parsley sprinkled over. Serves four.

Shrimp Badum
(From Sri Lanka)

1½ pounds shrimp
4 tablespoons vegetable oil
1 piece (2 inches) screwpine (pandanus) leaf
a few sprigs of curry leaf
4 ounces small red onions, peeled and chopped
2 cloves garlic, peeled and chopped
¼ teaspoon turmeric
1 teaspoon salt
1 inch stick cinnamon
2 cloves
2 tablespoons chili pepper, coarsely pounded
2 cardamoms
1 teaspoon lime juice

Peel and wash the shrimp. Heat the oil, add the pandanus leaf and curry leaves, followed by the onions, and sauté until the onions are turning gold. Then add all the other ingredients and continue to sauté until the shrimp are cooked through. Garnish and serve. Serves four.

West Indian Fried Tuna Steaks

4 tuna steaks, ¾ inch thick
½ cup flour
1 tablespoon curry powder
salt and pepper
½ cup coconut or vegetable oil
for the marinade
½ teaspoon salt
1 tablespoon ginger root, grated
½ onion, finely chopped
3 scallions, finely chopped
1 clove garlic, chopped
¼ teaspoon tabasco sauce

Mix the marinade ingredients together and smear the steaks with it. Leave overnight.

On a large plate, mix the flour and curry powder together with the salt and pepper and dredge the steaks in it. Shake off the excess. Cover the bottom of a heavy skillet with at least ⅛ inch of oil and heat until it is hot but not smoking. Place the steaks in the skillet but do not then move the skillet or shake it about – this is important when frying fish in the West Indian way: it seals in the flavor and juices and ensures that the outside becomes quite crisp. After three to four minutes, check that they move freely in the skillet and then turn them over and cook for another few minutes.

A good addition to this dish can be made by adding flour to the remaining marinade juices, kneading it into small balls and frying the little dumplings at the same time as the tuna. Serves four.

181

Sardoni in Saor
(Sardines Fried and Conserved)

Fish temporarily conserved in this way are sold from little stalls in winter in Venice, Vicenza, Padua and Treviso with a comforting slab of *polenta*, a pudding made of maize or chestnut flour. The custom probably originated from the ancient Roman discovery that hot vinegar poured over fried fish conserved it. Versions of this process are found in many parts of the Mediterranean.

As the sardines improve with keeping, you can make more than will be eaten at one sitting.

2¼ pounds fresh sardines
flour
4 tablespoons olive oil
2 large onions
2 cups red wine vinegar
a few pine kernels
a few seedless raisins
a piece of candied lemon peel, chopped

Leaving the heads on, clean and scale the sardines, dry them and shake them in flour. Cover the bottom of a heavy pan with the olive oil, heat it, and gently fry the fish so that they turn golden. Then lift them from the pan and put them in an earthenware dish.

Slice the onions in fine rounds and simmer them in the remaining oil. Heat the vinegar to boiling point and add to the onions once they have become transparent. Add the pine kernels, raisins and candied peel.

Pour this hot mixture over the sardines, cover the dish and put it in a cool place. Leave to marinate for two or three days, time for the fish to imbibe the liquor, and turn them over once or twice.

Serve with a salad of red chicory.
(Patience Gray, *Honey from a Weed*)   Serves four.

Deep frying

In my experience, people either deep-fry or don't, and those who do know what they are doing and have their own favored methods and equipment. I limit my comments to suggesting that it is highly desirable to have fine control of the temperature of the frying medium; and that the medium needs to be chosen with care. The choice here, obviously, does not include butter! Cooking oils are what are generally used, and all those sold for the purpose have burning points which are a safe distance above the temperatures at which deep-frying is normally done (around 360°). A batch of oil can be used several times if it is strained after each operation, but must not be retained and used too many times: that would be a false economy.

To achieve good results, be sure to use good fat or oil at the right temperature, and to select a batter which suits what you are going to fry. An egg and breadcrumb batter will be better for fillets of plaice than the flour and milk batter in the first recipe, which is good for cod or haddock.

Although Fish and Chips (french fries) almost counts as the British national dish, very few books give recipes for it, no doubt because most people in Britain buy from a Fish and Chip shop. But it is well worth knowing how to do it at home. The recipe which is given here incorporates directions specially prepared for this book by Carol Merryweather, owner of Harry Ramsden's famous Fish and Chip restaurant at Guiseley in Yorkshire. Note that the quantities given provide four, generous, north-country portions.

Fish and French Fries

Since I lived both in Lancashire (haddock terrain) and Yorkshire (where cod is favored) as a boy, I am torn between the two fish. In fact, either will do admirably.

1½ pounds fillets of cod or haddock
for the coating batter
2 cups flour
2 pinches of salt
2 eggs
1 scant cup milk
scant ½ cup water
for the deep-frying
flour for dusting
pure beef dripping (or vegetable oil)
3 pounds potatoes

Sift the flour and salt together into a mixing bowl. Form a well in the center and drop in the eggs. Working from the inside outward, beat the mixture well until all the lumps disappear. Gradually beat in enough of the milk and water to make a smooth batter, then add the remainder of the liquid. Put aside for at least half an hour in the refrigerator.

Dust the fish fillets in flour and then coat them in the batter. Have your deep-fat fryer half full of dripping or oil and heat this to a temperature of 360°. Immerse the battered fillets in this for six minutes. Remove and drain them and keep them hot.

Meanwhile, cut the peeled potatoes into french fries of about ⅜ inch thick. Wash and dry them well. Heat the deep-fat fryer, which must now be only a quarter full of oil, to 350°, then place the french fries in the hot fat for just three minutes. Remove them and leave to stand for ten minutes. Just before serving, immerse them again in the hot fat for a further two minutes, then drain them on kitchen paper. By this double frying, the french fries emerge properly crisp on the outside and fluffy within. Serves four.

Ukrainian Fish Rolls

Ukrainian authors suggest making these with sturgeon, but the recipe works for any fish from which long thin fillets can be cut.

8 thin fillets of fish, weighing 1¾ pounds
salt and pepper
2 eggs, hard-cooked
2 leeks, finely chopped
3 teaspoons parsley, finely chopped
2 teaspoons dill, finely chopped
2-3 tablespoons sour cream
flour for dusting
wholewheat breadcrumbs
oil for frying

Season the fillets. Grate the eggs and combine them with the leeks, parsley and dill. Mix well, adding the sour cream as you do so, then spread the mixture along the fillets and roll them up. Lightly flour them and roll them in the breadcrumbs. Deep-fry them, drain, and put in a warm oven for a couple of minutes before serving. These rolls are also very good if served cold. Serves four.

Tempura

A full range of *tempura*, the famous Japanese speciality, would include various seafoods (shrimp, squid, neat small fillets of fish, etc) and many vegetables, all encased in *tempura* batter and served with a special dip. The dish is best when prepared professionally at a *tempura* counter, with the succulent morsels handed across to you at intervals, each freshly prepared.

For the frying, you need a *tempura* pan or something similar, in which you maintain a fair depth of oil (2-3 inches) at 350°, frying small quantities at a time and skimming between each operation.

for the tempura batter
1 large egg
½ cup water
1 cup all-purpose flour
for the dip
¾ cup Japanese soy sauce
¼ cup *mirin* (Japanese rice wine)
a good pinch of *hana-katsuo* (dried bonito flakes)
2 teaspoons grated ginger

Prepare the dip by mixing the ingredients listed.

Use chopsticks throughout the operation. Break the egg into a bowl and stir it gently until white and yolk are well mixed. Add the water and mix again. Then sift in the flour, mixing again lightly. The result is what you dip the pieces of seafood in, to be fried only until they are golden (not brown), turning once. This should take about two minutes.

Poaching

Although older cookery books refer quite often to boiled fish, it is only rarely and in special cases that it is appropriate literally to boil fish. One example where boiling cannot be avoided is *Bouillabaisse*. As a general rule, for "boil" read "poach".

This is cooking in barely simmering liquid. I once spent an engrossing evening with a French chef in Melbourne comparing definitions of "poach" in his large library. We were both surprised at some of the ones we found, but I think this formula is the one generally understood. Fish can be poached in a wide variety of liquids, one of which is just plain water, perhaps with a thread of vinegar added. But it is better to go further and use a *court bouillon*, the composition and advantages of which I have already explained. Some fish respond well to being poached in milk; I always use this for smoked haddock. And there are dishes which use beer or cider.

Other liquids, less commonly used in Europe and North America, can produce good results. A spiced coconut milk is one example.

183

Maquereaux à la façon de Quimper

This versatile recipe from the north of France incorporates an excellent mustard sauce.

4 mackerel of 10 ounces each, or 2 larger ones
court bouillon (see page 177)
2 tablespoons Dijon mustard
4 egg yolks
3-4 teaspoons vinegar
salt and pepper
4 tablespoons herbs: parsley, chives, tarragon;
all finely chopped
1 stick butter
sprigs of fresh parsley

The mackerel should be very fresh. Gut them and cook them in a highly-seasoned *court bouillon*, then remove them, drain them, let them cool and lift off the fillets.

In a terrine, combine the mustard with the egg yolks. Add the vinegar, seasoning, and finely chopped herbs. Melt the butter until it is lukewarm, then pour it into the sauce, which should assume a creamy consistency. Tarragon should provide the dominant flavor.

Arrange the fillets of mackerel round a platter, pour the sauce into the middle, and garnish the whole with the sprigs of parsley. Serves four.

Tilliliemessäkeitetytlalakääryleet
(Sole Rolls in Dill)

This Finnish recipe has to be included because of its marvellously long name but also to illustrate Nordic use of fresh dill with fish.

1½ lb fillet of sole or other suitable fish
1¼ tablespoons salt
9 tablespoons of fresh dill
2 teaspoons white wine vinegar
2-3 tablespoons flour

Rinse and pat dry the fillets, then sprinkle over them 1 teaspoon of the salt and a third of the dill. Roll each one up and fasten it with a toothpick.

Choose a large pot, put in it enough water to cover the rolls, add the rest of the salt plus another third of the dill and the vinegar, then bring to a boil. Reduce the heat, put the rolls in and let them barely simmer until done: about ten minutes.

Remove the rolls to a warm serving dish. Strain the cooking broth, and combine a scant ½ cup of it with the flour to make a paste. Heat the broth to boiling point again, and stir in the paste. Continue stirring and cooking until the sauce is smooth and any taste of flour dispelled. Then add the remaining dill and pour the sauce over the rolls. Serves four.

Grønsaltet Kuller
(Green-salted Haddock)

4 fillets of haddock
salt
as accompaniments
potatoes, small carrots, onions; all steamed
2 hard-cooked eggs, chopped or sliced
melted butter

Salt the haddock fillets all over and leave for about 12 hours. Then rinse under the faucet and poach. Serve with the accompaniments indicated.

In this Danish speciality, the carrots are important; their sweetness balances the saltiness of the fish. Serves four.

Anguille au Vert

Belgians can become quite passionate when discussing exactly which greens should go into this famous speciality of theirs (called *Paling in 't Groen* in the Flemish-speaking part of the country). My suggested list can be modified as desired, except that the sorrel is essential since flavor should be dominant.

1 piece of fresh eel, cleaned and skinned, weighing 1¼ pounds
¾ stick butter
1 tablespoon minced onion
a generous handful of sorrel leaves
celery tops from 3 stalks
6 sprigs parsley
a little of any or all of the following: mint, sage, chervil, lemon balm, summer savory
salt and pepper to taste
1 tablespoon vinegar
beurre manié (about 2 tablespoons butter with the same amount of flour worked into it)

Melt the butter in a heavy-based pan. Chop the onion and greens very finely, season, and sweat them in the pan for half an hour.

Cut the piece of eel into four or eight sections. Put enough water in a pan to cover the eel, add the vinegar and bring to the boil. Put the eel in the water and simmer for five to ten minutes, depending on the thickness of the sections. Remove the eel from the water, drain, and add to the stewed greens to finish cooking. When they are almost cooked through, stir the *beurre manié* into the pan to bind the sauce. Continue to simmer for at least five minutes after the *beurre manié* has been absorbed. (If the pieces of eel are cooked for a little longer than strictly necessary, this will not matter). Serve hot, with buttered brown bread. Serves four.

Scallops in Cider (or Muscadet)

12-16 scallops (depending on size) and the corals if available
about 1 cup medium cider (or Muscadet)
beurre manié made with ½ stick butter worked into a little flour
½ cup light cream
salt and pepper
1 teaspoon lemon juice

Place the scallops in a casserole and barely cover them with the cider (or Muscadet). Bring to the boil and then simmer gently for 10 minutes. If you have the corals, add these for the last two minutes only, since they cook very quickly.

Take out the scallops, cut each of them into slices and keep them hot. Reduce the cooking liquid in the casserole and bind it by whisking in the *beurre manié*. Complete the sauce by adding the cream, seasoning and lemon juice, stirring, and heat gently until thoroughly hot but not quite simmering. Place the slices of scallop in the sauce, and serve.

In the Charente-Maritime region in France, where this recipe comes from, they would use Muscadet, but cider works just as well. Serves four.

184

Steaming

Steaming is a very "pure" way of cooking fish, ideal for retaining the subtle flavor of delicate fish without letting it dry out or become crisp. Steamed fish, especially whiting, has been thought of as an especially good dish for invalids. But now there is increased interest in steaming a wide range of fish, and often with added flavors; an interest which stems in part from the Orient.

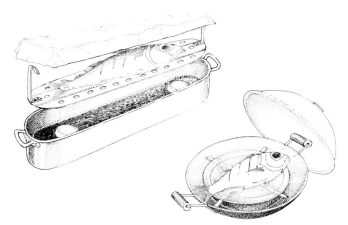

A fish kettle can be adapted for steaming. Two small inverted pots hold the grid higher up than usual, so that there is plenty of room below it for the boiling water. Aluminum foil has to be fastened over the top, since the handles of the grid will stick up and prevent the cover from fitting.
Adapting a wok for steaming. A pair of chopsticks are placed in the wok at right angles to each other, and support a glass plate on which the fish rests. The cover of the wok is fitted on as usual.

No one who has some sort of steaming apparatus ever had a problem steaming fillets or steaks of fish; they fit easily. But a whole fish, even of moderate size, is a different matter and is best dealt with by adapting a fish kettle in the manner shown above. A fish can be stuffed before being steamed; or the ingredients for added flavors, for example ginger, can be strewn over it (or under it, as in the case of crab steamed with lemon grass). It is also possible to add flavoring to the water which produces the steam, and this is a good plan if the water is to be used later as an ingredient of a sauce.

Saké no Oyako-mushi
(Steamed Salmon and Roe)

The Japanese frequently steam things in individual serving bowls; but fairly deep soup bowls will do. Professor Tsuji, whose recipe I follow here, comments that the the name *oyako* in the Japanese title of the dish means "parent and child", and that it is also used for a chicken and egg dish.

I pound fresh salmon, boned and skinned
2-3 tablespoons oil for frying
I cup grated giant oriental radish
½ egg white, lightly beaten
pinch of salt
4 tablespoons salmon roe
I lemon, quartered
and for the sauce
I cup *dashi* (basic Japanese soup stock: you can use "instant *dashi*" from a packet)
2 tablespoons light soy sauce
3 tablespoons *mirin* (sweet *saké* for cooking)
2 tablespoons vinegar
2 teaspoons cornstarch mixed with 2 teaspoons water

Sprinkle salt on a board, place the salmon on the salt and sprinkle more salt over the fish. Leave for one hour. Then cut the salmon into bite-size pieces and fry them briefly in hot oil on both sides. Remove them to a colander and rinse them with boiling water, then distribute them in four bowls suitable for steaming.

Combine the grated radish with the beaten egg white and salt, and then with the salmon roe. Spoon this mixture onto the salmon pieces in their bowls, cover the bowls tightly with aluminum foil, and steam them for five minutes. Meanwhile, make the sauce by combining the first four ingredients and bringing them to a boil. Then add the cornstarch-and-water, stir until thickened, and remove from the heat. The sauce goes on top of the steamed preparations when they are uncovered, and a quarter lemon is squeezed over each portion before it is served. Serves four.

Chinese Shrimp Dumplings

Chinese "*dim sum*" restaurants in Hong Kong often feature this dish. Count it as an appetizer.

I pound peeled shrimp
2 spring onions, the white part only, shredded
4 water chestnuts, peeled and finely minced
I teaspoon soy sauce
I teaspoon salt
pinch of white pepper
3 teaspoons peanut oil
for the wrapping
8 egg roll or *won ton* wrappers (bought ready-made)
I egg, beaten

Chop the shrimp roughly, mix them with the other ingredients, and leave them to stand for 20 minutes.

Cut the *won ton* wrappers into circles about 2½ inches in diameter. Spoon the mixture onto these in equal amounts. Fold each over to form a half circle, sealing with beaten egg, and pinch the edges together. Place the packages on wax paper in a steamer and steam them for ten minutes. Serves four.

185

Moules Nautile

Toulon is famous for its mussels, and this recipe comes from the Hotel Nautilus in that great port.

60 mussels
I cup white wine
2-3 shallots, chopped
I medium onion, chopped
olive oil
2 teaspoons flour
3 tomatoes, peeled and chopped
a *bouquet garni*
black pepper
pinch of saffron
2 sprigs parsley, chopped

Scrub the mussels clean and remove their "beards". Put half the white wine and the chopped shallots in the bottom of a large pot, add the mussels and heat until they all open. Remove them, take off the surplus half shells, and arrange the other halves with the mussels in them on a platter. Strain and reserve the broth.

To make the sauce, first color the onion in hot olive oil, then add the sprinkling of flour, the tomatoes, the *bouquet garni*, the remaining white wine and an equal quantity of the reserved mussel broth. Cook this gently for seven or eight minutes only, and at the last moment remove the *bouquet garni* and add a dash of black pepper (no salt) and the pinch of saffron.

Pour the sauce over the mussels and garnish with chopped parsley. The sauce, which is not thick, is orange, which contrasts well with the blue-black mussel shells. Serves four.

Steamed Clams

The simple procedure is to put the washed, live clams in a large pot with a couple of inches of water in the bottom, bring to a boil, cover and steam the shells open. Strain the whole contents of the pot through a cheesecloth placed over a clean bowl. Transfer the clams to soup bowls to be eaten; providing each person with a small bowl of melted butter and a cup of the hot, strained, clam broth.

Hugh Zachary, in *The Beachcomber's Handbook of Seafood Cookery*, suggests that you use a very large cooking vessel (a steamer or stock pot) and put into it in layers: shucked roasting ears of corn; small sweet potatoes; clams; 4 cups water. Then you close the pot allowing some steam to escape. Start cooking and carry on until steam stops coming out. "As the clams are opened by the steam, their juices run down and permeate the corn and yams, making for a taste that, when enjoyed under a warm, friendly sun or a full, glowing moon on a lonely strand, is purely out of this world." A fine idea.

Oven-baked Dishes

For most people, a typical baked fish dish would be like the first or third of those below, or Spétsai Baked Fish (page 68). The advantage of such dishes is that they can be left to cook in the oven, and a pleasing marriage of flavors occurs in them.

But the word "bake" can also be used in a very general sense for cooking things in an oven; that is why the recipes for Planked Fish and *Fish en Papillotte* appear in this section.

Saur's Fish Dish

Saur's is the most famous fish restaurant in the Hague, a lovely art deco creation at the end of the eighteenth century Lange Voorhout. When we lived in The Hague in the 1950s we went often to have this dish as an economical family lunch. Returning thirty years later, I found the restaurant unchanged, but was disconcerted to be told that the dish was unknown. However, the oldest surviving waiter understood what I meant and produced it – it had simply been rechristened "Poisson au Gratin", an act for which he apologized ("very confusing for our old customers"). It is a really flexible recipe, as you will see, and suited to a shallow oval dish.

a mixture of seafood, enough for four people, including some fish and if possible shrimp
I cup milk
½ cup flour, ½ stick butter for white sauce
slivers of red or green bell pepper for color (optional)
mashed potato, enough to surround the dish

Poach the seafood in milk, then drain it and strain the now fishy milk for use in making a white sauce. Flake the pieces of fish, discarding any bones or skin. Make the white sauce and combine it with the seafood and bell peppers. Pipe the mashed potato around the edge of the dish and put tiny dabs of butter on top of it to help it brown. Spoon the seafood mixture into center.

Place in the oven at 350° for about 10 minutes, until the potato peaks are browned and the sauce gently bubbling. Be carefree and inventive when you make this dish; it is never exactly the same on two successive occasions at Saur's. Serves four.

Planked Fish

Fish can be planked in various ways: nailed to a plank tilted up over an open fire; nailed down to a plank under a broiler; or, as here, in the oven. The plank is important. It must, obviously, fit easily into your oven, but otherwise should be as large as possible, since

186

there has to be room for the fish and for the decorative mashed potato border. It must be of hardwood (oak, hickory, ash, for example) cut across the grain. It will improve with use.

1 round fish such as a striped bass, weighing just over 2¼ pounds uncleaned
salt and pepper
1 tablespoon lemon juice
2 tablespoons parsley, finely chopped
2 tablespoons butter, melted
mashed potato for piping

Have the fish cleaned and the head, tail and fins removed. Open it up down the middle, butterfly-fashion. Season it, sprinkle on the lemon juice and parsley and brush it all over with most of the melted butter.

Brush the remaining melted butter over your plank, put it in a cool oven, then heat it up to 400°. Remove the plank and secure the fish to it, skin side down. Put it back in the oven and bake it for 15 to 30 minutes, depending on thickness of the fish. Five minutes before it is going to be ready, take it out and pipe a border of mashed potato all the way round; this will then have time to brown on top before you serve the dish. (You can also use other pre-cooked vegetables to fill any gaps between fish and border.) Serves four.

Fish Baked with Tahini

A Middle Eastern dish, of which I have worked out my own version, starting with what was probably a Lebanese version. It can be adapted for use with most kinds of fish but is not suitable for those of very delicate flavor; nor for ones with a high oil content. *Tahini* is sesame paste, which is conveniently available in jars.

1½ pounds (cleaned weight) of whole small fish (eg rockfish, gurnards, small members of the sea bream family)
juice of 2½ lemons
3 teaspoons salt
2 medium onions, chopped
scant ½ cup olive oil
¾ cup *tahini*
1-2 tablespoon pine-nut kernals (optional)

Ensure that the fish are scaled as well as cleaned, and remove heads, tails and fins. Rub the fish with the juice of half a lemon, sprinkle on one to two teaspoons of salt, and leave them for 20 minutes. Sauté the onion in two thirds of the olive oil.

Brush the fish with a little more of the oil and bake them briefly in a pre-heated oven at 355°. Then put them (still in their baking dish) under the broiler for a minute or two to crisp the skin, turning them once.

Pour the sautéed onion over the fish. Blend the *tahini* with the rest of the lemon juice and salt and enough water to obtain a creamy consistency. Pour this sauce over the dish and return it to the oven and bake for a further 20-30 minutes, during which time the sauce will thicken.

Serve with rice, mixed if you wish with pine-nut kernels and diced onion which have first been lightly browned in a pan.

Although I have made the pine-nut kernals optional, I highly recommend their inclusion. They always seem to me to enhance fish dishes by their texture – contrasting with the softer flesh of the fish – as well as by their flavor. Serves four.

Fish en Papillote

This recipe, which I learned at the Kimbridge Trout Farm in Hampshire, England has been adapted to become a family favorite. It suits a moderately oily fish; bluefish would be a good candidate, or sea trout.

1 whole fish weighing 3¼ pounds
salt and pepper
2 tablespoons lemon juice
2 tablespoons fresh ginger root, grated
2 tablespoons each parsley and chives, chopped
1 tablespoon each thyme and sage, chopped
½ stick butter
about a dozen sorrel leaves
for the sauce
4 teaspoons creamed horseradish
2 teaspoons dill seeds
½ cup soured cream

Clean the fish but leave the head on. Season inside and out with salt, pepper and lemon juice. Sprinkle the cavity with the grated ginger and stuff it with the chopped herbs (reserving some for garnish) and half of the butter.

Lay half the sorrel leaves on a large square of greased foil. Place the fish on top, cover with the remaining sorrel and dot with the remaining butter. Wrap the parcel securely, put it in a baking dish and cook in the oven for one hour at 350°.

Turn off the heat but leave the trout to cool in the oven for 30 minutes. Then unwrap it and remove the skin. Serve warm, surrounded by the reserved fresh herbs and accompanied by a bowl of sauce made by combining the sour cream, horseradish and dill seeds. Serves six, or four with some left over to eat cold.

187

Braising

This is a hybrid technique. An oven dish is prepared with a bed of lightly sautéed vegetables (carrots, shallots, leeks, for example) and the fish is placed on this. Liquid, usually white wine, perhaps mixed with fish stock, is poured in so that it comes half way up the fish, seasoning added, and the dish brought just to the boil. Then it is transferred to a pre-heated oven to continue cooking slowly, with frequent basting.

Braised Fish Hunan-Szechwan Style

This recipe, adapted slightly from one in Yan-Kit So's admirable book on Chinese cooking, can be used for many different fish.

I cleaned striped bass or mullet, weighing 1½ pounds, with the head left on
½ teaspoon salt
generous ½ cup peanut or corn oil
3 cloves of garlic, peeled and finely chopped
I inch fresh ginger root, peeled and finely chopped
2-4 tablespoons hot soya bean paste
I tablespoon Shaohsing wine or medium-dry sherry
I teaspoon teaspoon sugar
½ cup clear stock or water
I tablespoon hot chili oil
8 scallions, green parts only, cut into small rounds

Wash the fish in cold water and dry. Rub salt all over it, including the cavity, and let it stand for about 15 minutes. Place a wok over a high heat for a minute or so, then pour in the oil. Tip the wok carefully to swirl the oil all around the sloping edges. Pour the surplus oil into a (heatproof) container.

Lower the heat. Add the fish at once and brown for about two minutes. Slip two metal spatulas underneath the fish and turn over carefully. Brown the other side for about two minutes and transfer to a plate.

Turn up the heat. Return another 2 tablespoons of the oil to the wok and heat until the smoke rises. Now add the garlic and ginger and, as they sizzle, add the hot soybean paste, wine or sherry and sugar. Pour in the stock or water and bring to the boil, stirring the mix. Return the fish to the wok, lower the heat, cover and simmer in the sauce for ten to 15 minutes. Turn the fish over carefully, and simmer, covered, for another 12 to 15 minutes, until the fish is cooked and some of the sauce has been absorbed. Remove the cover. Turn up the heat to reduce the sauce, spooning it over the fish continuously. Transfer the fish to a warm serving plate.

Add the hot chili oil to the sauce, then the scallions. Stir for a few seconds, then scoop the sauce over the fish. Serve immediately. Serves four.

Mero en Mac-Cum
(Striped Bass in Sauce)

This dish with annatto, cumin, and Seville orange juice is typical of Mayan cookery in Yucatán. It is adapted from *The Book of Latin American Cooking*, by Elisabeth Lambert Ortiz.

2 pounds striped bass, cut into 4 steaks
6 large cloves garlic, crushed
black pepper
¼ teaspoon ground cumin
½ teaspoon oregano
I teaspoon ground annatto
salt
generous ½ cup Seville (bitter) orange juice, or ⅔ orange juice to ⅓ lime juice
generous ½ cup olive oil
I large onion, thinly sliced
I fresh hot pepper, de-seeded and chopped
2 red bell peppers, de-seeded and sliced, or 2 canned pimientos, cut into strips
4 tomatoes, peeled and chopped
2 tablespoons parsley, chopped

Put the fish steaks on a platter in a single layer. Make a marinade of half the garlic, the black pepper, cumin, oregano, annatto, salt and enough orange juice to make a thin paste. Coat the steaks on both sides with the mixture and let them stand for 30 minutes. Pour into a shallow baking dish enough olive oil to coat the bottom. Arrange the fish steaks, with the remaining marinade, in the dish. Top the steaks with the onion, the remaining garlic, tomatoes, and peppers. Pour the rest of the oil over the fish, cover, and cook over a low heat for about 15 minutes until the fish loses its translucent look. Sprinkle with the parsley and serve with rice (and fresh hot tortillas, if you wish). Serves four.

Atun Asado
(Tuna in Tomato and Garlic Sauce)

a piece of fresh tuna weighing I pound
3 tablespoons olive oil
3 tablespoons rendered pork fat
flour for dusting
I onion, sliced
2 tomatoes, chopped
2 cloves garlic, minced
I bay leaf
generous ½ cup white wine

Choose a deep casserole with a heavy cover. Set the oil and fat to heat in this. Flour and salt the piece of tuna, then put it in the hot fat and turn it several times until it is browned on all sides. Add the remaining ingredients, cover, and leave over a moderate heat for 30-50 minutes until the tuna is thoroughly cooked (the time will depend on the shape and therefore the thickness of the tuna). Lift out the tuna and let it cool somewhat. Rub the sauce through a fine strainer and gently reheat it. Meanwhile slice the tuna and lay the slices out on a serving dish. Pour the sauce over them and serve. Serves four.

Stewing

As I see it, a fish stew (which is a fish soup with a lot of solid matter in it) is not the same as a stewed fish. The latter is fish cooked gently in a liquid, with or without other solids, but always with the intention that everything, fish and cooking liquid, will be consumed together. That is how stewing differs from poaching. It is a method which is especially well suited to seafoods that call for long, slow cooking.

Elizabeth David once said that Eliza Acton's book *Modern Cookery for Private Families*, first published in 1845, was probably "the greatest cookery book in our language". She also put the spotlight on this particular recipe as a model of its kind, so I have not tampered with its text in any way. The title says "Baked", but the text says "stew", so this page is where the recipe belongs. It is interesting to see that Eliza Acton, a pioneer in giving lists of ingredients, puts her list at the end, not the beginning.

Eliza Acton's Baked Fillets of Sole

Prepare some very fresh middling sized soles with exceeding nicety, put them into boiling water slightly salted, and simmer them for two minutes only; lift them out, and let them drain; lay them into a wide stewpan with as much sweet rich cream as will nearly cover them; add a good seasoning of pounded mace, cayenne, and salt; stew the fish softly from six to ten minutes, or until the flesh parts readily from the bones; dish them, stir the juice of half a lemon to the sauce, pour it over the soles, and send them immediately to table. Some lemon-rind may be boiled in the cream, if approved; and a small teaspoonful of arrowroot, very smoothly mixed with a little milk, may be stirred to the sauce (should it require thickening) before the lemon-juice is added. Turbot and brill also may be dressed by this receipt, time proportioned to their size being of course allowed for them.

Soles three or four: boiled in water for two minutes. Cream, half a pint [1 cup]; salt, mace, cayenne; fish stewed, six to ten minutes. Juice of half a lemon.

Pinais na Hipon
(Shrimp with Coconut Milk)

A southern Tagalog dish, from the province of Quezón in the Philippines.

1¼ pounds peeled shrimp
1 teaspoon (at most) salt
generous ½ cup coconut cream (thick coconut milk)
4 cloves garlic, finely chopped
squash or banana leaf, for wrapping
1 cup coconut milk

Combine the peeled shrimp with the salt, coconut cream, and garlic. Make packages with the leaves, each containing one quarter of this mixture. Place these packages in a saucepan and cover them with the coconut milk, then simmer for half an hour. Serves four.

Gulai Ikan
(A Fish and Coconut Stew from East Malaysia)

189

This recipe is often used for freshwater fish, but is fine if made with sea fish of firm flesh, such as Spanish mackerel.

1 fish weighing 1½ pounds or a little less
coconut or peanut oil for frying
cream and milk of 1 coconut
1 teaspoon salt
1 tablespoon tamarind water
pounded ingredients
2 teaspoons onion, chopped
2 teaspoons garlic, chopped
2 teaspoons dried red chili pepper, chopped
2 fresh chili peppers
1 small piece ginger root
1 small piece galingale (optional)
1 teaspoon turmeric
½ teaspoon coriander seeds
½ teaspoon cumin seeds

Clean the fish, soak it in water, then cut it into pieces. Rub into the fish the pounded mixture.

Heat the oil and fry the pieces of fish in it until they are golden. Then pour 1¼ cups water over them, bring back to simmering point and go on cooking until the water has evaporated. As soon as this has happened, add the coconut milk. When the oil separates on top of the coconut milk pour in the coconut cream and bring back to simmering point.

Add the salt and tamarind water about one minute before serving. Serves four.

Moqueca de peixe
(Brazilian Fish Stew)

This is an adaptable recipe, which works for any kind of fish with white flesh. It belongs to a whole family of *moquecas*, typical of the Bahian cuisine. Elisabeth Lambert Ortiz thinks that in their current form they are best called stews, but points out that they are probably descended from what were originally Indian *pokekas*, dishes wrapped in banana leaf and cooked over charcoal.

2 pounds fillets of fish
4 tablespoons palm (*dendê*) oil
for the marinade and sauce
1 large onion, chopped
1 fresh hot chili pepper, de-seeded and chopped
3 tomatoes, peeled and chopped
2 cloves garlic, peeled and chopped
2 tablespoons coriander leaves, chopped
salt
3 tablespoons lime juice

Put the fish fillets, cut into convenient pieces, in a large bowl. Use a blender or food processor to make a purée of the marinade ingredients, pour this over the fish, stir lightly and leave for a couple of hours.

Transfer the fish and the marinade to a large pan, add $\frac{1}{2}$ cup cold water and half the palm oil, then simmer until the fish is cooked: six to 12 minutes, depending on thickness. Now add the remaining palm oil and cook a little longer, just enough to heat the oil thoroughly. Then transfer the *moqueca* to a heated platter and surround it with cooked rice.

As an alternative to the plain cooked rice, you could serve the *moqueca* with what is called a *pirao*. This is a preparation made by combining rice flour with a little salt and a half-and-half mixture of coconut cream and coconut milk, the whole to be cooked, turned into a buttered bowl, allowed to stand and finally unmoulded. Serves four.

Stuffing

What really cry out to be stuffed are squid and the carapaces of crabs. But fish are often stuffed too, and this procedure can range all the way from just putting some herbs into the gut cavity, to filling it with edible stuffing, to emptying the skin of the fish completely and refilling it with the flesh and other ingredients (as in the fourth recipe below).

The term is also used for covering fillets, or fish which have been opened out "butterfly" fashion, with a mixture of other ingredients.

Grondin Gris Farci à la Boulonnaise
(Gray Gurnard Stuffed Boulogne Style)

1 large gray gurnard, weighing $4\frac{1}{2}$ pounds, uncleaned
2 tablespoons butter
2-3 finely chopped shallots
salt and pepper
scant $\frac{1}{2}$ cup white wine (Mâcon if possible)
scant $\frac{1}{2}$ cup fish *fumet* (see page 177)
scant $\frac{1}{2}$ cup fresh cream
parsley for garnishing
for the stuffing
$\frac{1}{2}$ pound pork, minced and blanched
2 eggs
6 tablespoons fresh breadcrumbs
2 tablespoons parsley, chopped
1-2 tablespoons chives, chopped
1 shallot, chopped

Gut the gurnard, cutting it open as little as possible in order to do so. Make the stuffing with the ingredients shown, stuff the fish and sew it up with sturdy thread or fine string.

Cover the bottom of a buttered baking dish with the 3 shallots, and put the fish on this bed. Season it and sprinkle the wine over it, then cook it in the oven at 355° for 45-50 minutes, until cooked through. Remove the fish and keep it hot while you strain the cooking juices and combine them with the *fumet*. Reduce this mixture by a third, check the seasoning and bind it with the cream. Then arrange the fish on a platter, garnish it with parsley and serve it with the sauce in a warmed sauceboat. Serves four.

Txangurro Relleno
(Stuffed Spider Crab, Basque Style)

2 spider crabs weighing $1\frac{1}{2}$ pounds each, plus 2 empty carapaces
salt
2 bay leaves
1 cup olive oil
$\frac{3}{4}$ cup each of onion, carrot and leek, finely chopped
2 tablespoons flour
2 teaspoons paprika
scant $\frac{1}{2}$ cup cognac
$1\frac{3}{4}$ cups white wine
2 scraps of hot chili pepper
1 pound tomatoes
2 teaspoons each of breadcrumbs, chopped parsley, melted butter

In a pot large enough to take the two crabs bring to the boil plenty of water, to which salt and the bay leaves have been added. Put in the crabs, bring back to a boil, boil for 12 minutes, then remove from the heat and

190

leave for at least five minutes. Take out the crabs and extract all the meat from the body and legs. Clean the carapaces so that you have four in all. Put the meat into the four carapaces and reserve all the debris.

Heat the oil in a pan, add the chopped onion, carrot and leek, and cook until tender. Move the pan from the heat and add the flour, paprika and crab debris, mixing it well. Pour the cognac over all and light it. When the flames die down, add the wine, scraps of chili, and tomatoes. Bring all this to a boil, rub through a coarse strainer (or purée in a blender), cook for a further 20 minutes and then pass it through a fine strainer, using a wooden spoon to rub it through. Continue cooking until it is reduced by half, then pour it over the crab meat in the carapaces and mix well. Finally, sprinkle breadcrumbs, parsley and melted butter over the top.

Place the carapaces, thus filled, in the oven at 425° for five minutes. The finished dish will be dark brown, with the consistency of a thick soup. Serves four.

Calamari Ripieni
(Neapolitan Stuffed Squid)

Versions of this dish are found all round the long Italian coastline. This is the one which Assunta Viscardi demonstrated to me in Naples.

I squid (or 2 smaller ones), cleaned weight about I pound
olive oil for frying
4 cloves garlic, peeled and chopped
8 black olives, pitted and halved
I tablespoon capers
4 tomatoes, peeled and chopped
I teaspoon hot chili pepper, finely chopped
I tablespoon breadcrumbs
I teaspoon oregano
salt and pepper

Heat a little olive oil in a pan and fry in it two cloves of garlic, the chopped head and tentacles of the squid, the olives, the capers, two tomatoes, and the chili pepper. When these ingredients have lightly browned, add the breadcrumbs. Stuff this mixture into the squid, taking care to leave room for expansion, and sew the squid up with thread or fine string.

Heat a little more olive oil in a roomy pan, let the remaining garlic take color in it and add the remaining tomatoes with the oregano, salt and pepper. Put the stuffed squid into this sauce, cover, and cook gently for 25-30 minutes. Serves four.

Uskumru Dolmasi
(Stuffed Mackerel)

There are probably more than two places in the world where this sort of thing goes on, but the only two I know of are Indonesia and Turkey. "This sort of thing" is emptying a fish without breaking the skin and then stuffing its flesh, with additions, back in. In Indonesia they use milkfish and the name of the dish is *Bandeng Isi.* In Turkey, the fish are mackerel. In both places the art is regarded as a good test of a young woman's skill in the kitchen, but even a man can learn the technique quite quickly.

I large or 2 smaller mackerel, uncleaned weight 3 pounds
flour for dusting
2-3 eggs, beaten
I cup dry breadcrumbs
olive oil for frying
for the stuffing
scant $\frac{1}{2}$ cup olive oil
4-6 small onions, chopped
2 heaped tablespoons pine-nut kernels
3 heaped tablespoons currants
2 tablespoons ground walnuts
$\frac{1}{2}$ teaspoon cinnamon
$\frac{1}{2}$ teaspoon allspice
3 tablespoons dill, chopped
3 tablespoons parsley, chopped
salt and pepper

Cut off the head of the fish and gut it through the opening thus made at the front end of the belly. Do not slit the belly or otherwise break the skin. Wash the fish and dry them. Still without breaking the skin, break the backbone just short of the tail.

The next task is to loosen the inside of the fish. I recommend rolling it backwards and forwards on a board, but some prefer to do it by manipulation with thumb and forefinger. This is the only difficult part.

When it is done, grip the backbone at the front and waggle it, then draw it carefully out. Remove and reserve any flesh which is adhering to it. Then start squeezing the fish at the tail end, moving gradually forward, so as to force out the remaining flesh. Collect all the flesh, see that it is free of bone, and reserve it.

Now make the stuffing. Heat the olive oil in a pan and cook the onion gently in this until it begins to take color. Add the remaining ingredients (except for the dill, parsley and seasoning) and the flesh of the fish. Continue to cook, stirring, over a medium heat for another five minutes. Stir in the dill and parsley, season, remove from the heat and allow to cool. Then stuff the mixture gently into the fish from the front end.

Dust the stuffed fish with flour, dip it into the beaten egg and then the breadcrumbs, fry it on both sides in hot olive oil, drain it and let it cool. Serve it cold, sliced. Serves four.

191

Soups, Stews and Chowders

Here we look at a very few fish soups, from the Mediterranean and North America, plus a highly versatile Italian recipe for clam soup.

There is so much to be said about the confusing dish called *Bouillabaisse* – its history, etymology, rival recipes for it, and the chemistry of its cooking – and I have said it so fully elsewhere (in *A Kipper with My Tea*) that I omit it here and pass straight to my preferred Mediterranean fish soup, which has the merit of being just a soup and much easier to make at home.

Fish Chowder

Whatever their origin chowders have become a thoroughly American subject, and feelings run high on the eastern seaboard about questions such as whether or not tomatoes should be included. The excellent historical survey given by Richard J Hooker in *The Book of Chowder* is unique in being dispassionate. I play safe by giving one recipe, from Mrs Mary Lincoln, whose majestic and lucid prose exactly suits the classic (northern New England) fish chowder without tomatoes, and by simultaneously proclaiming my liking for the Manhattan (and southern New England) version with tomatoes. Mrs Lincoln uses a fish kettle, but a large pan with a tightly-fitting cover will do.

Mrs Mary Lincoln's Fish Chowder (1884)

4-5 pounds cod, haddock or bass
6 potatoes
a 2 inch cube of salt pork
2 small onions
1 teaspoon salt
$\frac{1}{2}$ teaspoon white pepper
1 tablespoon butter
4 cups hot milk
6 oyster crackers

When buying a fish for a chowder, have the head left on but the skin removed. Begin at the tail and cut the fish from the bone on one side. Then, keeping the knife as close as possible to the bone, remove the bone from near the head. Wipe the fish carefully with a damp cloth, cut it into pieces about 2 inches square, and store in a cool place. Break the bones and head, cover with cold water, and put them on to boil.

Pare and slice the potatoes $\frac{1}{8}$ inch thick (the resulting volume of potato should equal the volume of fish). Cut the pork into cubes of $\frac{1}{4}$ inch, and fry it in an omelet pan. Cut the onions into thin slices and fry them in the pork fat, being careful that they do not burn. Pour the fat through a strainer into the kettle, leaving the pork scraps and onions in the strainer. Put the sliced potatoes into the kettle; hold the strainer over the potatoes, and pour through it enough boiling water to cover them. Bring this to the boil.

When the potatoes have boiled for ten minutes, strain the water in which the bones were boiled, and pour it into the kettle. Add the salt and pepper, and when the chowder is boiling briskly, put in the fish, and set it back where it can simmer for ten minutes. Do not break the fish by stirring it. Add the butter and the hot milk. Split the crackers, put them in a tureen, and pour the chowder over them.

If you wish the broth thicker, stir in 1 cup of fine cracker crumbs, or 1 tablespoon flour cooked in 2 tablespoons butter. More milk and a little more seasoning may be added to this amount of fish and potato, if you wish to make a larger quantity. When wanted richer, beat two eggs, mix them with the hot milk, and put in the tureen before turning in the chowder. If added while the chowder is in the hot kettle, the eggs will curdle.

If a highly seasoned dish be desired, boil an onion, cut into thin slices, with the potatoes; add more pepper, and either cayenne pepper, Worcestershire sauce, or curry powder. Serves four.

Ciorba de Peste cu Smântâna
(Romanian Fish *Ciorba* with Sour Cream)

Ciorba, which has become a well-known term on the western seaboard of the USA, means a sour soup, typical of the Balkans. The sour stock which is its base used to be prepared from the liquor of fermented wheat bran, but sauerkraut juice can be used, or diluted lemon juice.

$2\frac{1}{4}$ pounds of any fish, cleaned weight
5-6 cups sour *ciorba* stock (see below)
2 carrots, halved lengthways
1 large potato, halved
1 leek
1 or 2 stalks celery
1 sprig fennel
4 sprigs parsley
salt and pepper
2 tomatoes, sliced
1 tablespoon lovage, finely chopped
1 tablespoon tarragon (or dill), finely chopped
2 egg yolks
$\frac{1}{2}$ cup sour cream
$\frac{1}{2}$ stick butter
2 tablespoon parsley, chopped

for the ciorba stock
several fresh pork bones
I veal shank bone
2 carrots, halved
2 whole parsley roots (the Hamburg or "turnip-rooted" variety, not ordinary parsley)
the thick end of a bunch of celery, halved
I medium or 2 small tomatoes
5-6 sprigs fresh parsley
1¼ cups sauerkraut juice or diluted lemon juice

First, make the *ciorba* stock. Put the bones in 1½ cups cold water, bring to the boil, add the vegetables and boil until all the vegetables are cooked. Then add the sauerkraut juice or diluted lemon juice, bring back to a boil, remove from the heat, set aside to cool for a while, then strain.

To the strained stock add the carrots, potato, leek, celery, fennel, parsley, and seasoning. Cook until the vegetables are all tender, then add the fish, cut up into pieces, and the tomatoes. Continue cooking until the fish is done. Remove from the heat, replace the parsley with the lovage and tarragon (or dill). Taste to check the sourness. If necessary, add more of the souring liquor.

Meanwhile, beat the egg yolks with the sour cream. Pour this carefully over the *ciorba*, add the butter in dabs, and sprinkle chopped parsley over all. Serve hot. (In Romania there would be an accompaniment of tiny chili peppers which people would nibble as they ate this.) Serves four.

Mediterranean Soup of Rockfish

It is a good idea to make a substantial amount of this soup, which is a fine way of using small rockfish, including small scorpion fish, wrasses and gurnards.

3½ pounds small rockfish
3 tablespoons olive oil
white parts of 2 leeks, finely chopped
I onion, finely chopped
2 large tomatoes
2 cloves of garlic, crushed
I sprig of fennel
2 or 3 sprigs of parsley
a little fresh thyme
I bay leaf
a small piece of orange peel
8 cups water
I pound pasta, such as French *nouilles* or Italian *fettucine*
salt and pepper
a pinch of saffron (optional)

Heat the olive oil in a large soup pot. Add the leeks and onion. When they are saturated, add the tomatoes, peeled and roughly chopped, and as they dissolve, the bouquet of herbs, the orange peel and the water. Lastly put in the fish, bring the water to the boil and keep it bubbling for 15 minutes.

Pass the soup through a fine strainer, rubbing the fish to extract their juices. Return the bouillon to the soup pot and bring it back to the boil. Add the pasta, broken into short strips, seasoning and the pinch of saffron (if used) and cook gently until the pasta is *al dente.*

Serve with *rouille* and croûtons. One way of making *rouille* is this: in a mortar pound two cloves of garlic and one sweet red pepper (or half a large one) adding a tablespoon of soaked breadcrumbs or cooked potato, seasoning, and an egg yolk; when all is well pounded, add up to ½ cup olive oil little by little, stirring, as if you were making aïoli (see page 201). Serves four.

Zuppa di Cannolicchi
(Razor Clam Soup)

4½ pounds razor clams
5 tablespoons olive oil
I medium onion, finely sliced
2 cloves of garlic, sliced
½ stick celery, chopped
fresh basil, chopped (or use thyme)
2 teaspoons ground black pepper
I pound 10 ounces fresh tomatoes, peeled and chopped (or canned tomatoes, drained)
½ cup dry white wine
2-3 tablespoons parsley, chopped
2 teaspoons lemon peel, grated
8 small pieces toast

Heat the olive oil in a large, deep pan. Add the onion and let it take color, then add the garlic, celery, basil (or thyme) and pepper. Let this cook for two minutes, then add the tomatoes and cook for four to five minutes more.

Now add the white wine. Turn up the heat and let it bubble briefly, then lower the heat again, cover, and continue cooking until the tomatoes are turning into a mush. At this stage add about 1 cup of hot liquid; this can be plain hot water, or a mixture of hot water and the liquid drained from the canned tomatoes. Give it all a good stir, and simmer for a few minutes longer, when you should have a fairly thick soup. This can be left and reheated when you are ready for the final operation.

About 15 minutes before the meal, heat the soup. Then add the carefully cleaned razor-shells. Keep the soup over a high heat for a couple of minutes, then sprinkle the chopped parsley and grated lemon peel on top and serve. The pieces of toast should be placed in each person's bowl before the soup is added. Provide a large bowl for empty shells. Serves four.

193

Pies and Puddings

A fish pudding or pie can be designed to fit the traditional meat-and-two-vegetables formula or it can have more than fish in it and be a meal in itself like the Maltese Lampuki Pie on page 67. On a smaller scale, one could take something like Cornish Crab Pasty (page 140) and treat it either way; if vegetables are introduced, a little crab will go a long way.

I have never seen an explanation of the fact that the Portuguese are world leaders in making fish puddings; but they are. The first recipe below is an example. Similar dishes can be found wherever Portuguese influence has extended.

Norwegians are also strong on fish puddings, but it is in the next section that their prowess in everything to do with minced fish is discussed.

There are no indigenous pies in Asia, although some have crept in where American influence has been at work; but Asians do have strong traditions of pastry-wrapped seafood dishes, such as Spring Rolls and the Shrimp Dumplings described on page 185.

Pudim de Peixe com Tres Molhos
(Portuguese Fish Pudding with Three Sauces)

Fish puddings are a speciality of Portugal. This one is an old family recipe of Maria Isabel Raposo of Ribatejo.

3 tablespoons vegetable oil
1 medium onion, chopped
$\frac{3}{4}$ pound cooked fish, flaked
salt and pepper
generous $\frac{1}{2}$ cup white wine
5 ounces white bread
generous $\frac{1}{2}$ cup milk, diluted with scant $\frac{1}{2}$ cup water
2 eggs, separated
a little butter
scant $\frac{1}{2}$ cup white sauce
scant $\frac{1}{2}$ cup tomato sauce
scant $\frac{1}{2}$ cup mayonnaise

Heat the oil and cook the onion in it until golden. Add the fish, salt, pepper, and wine, and cook for ten minutes over a gentle heat, stirring all the time. Meanwhile, soak the bread in the milk-and-water, add the egg yolks and mix well. Then add the fish mixture and beat all together thoroughly (the tradition is to beat for ten minutes by hand). Beat the egg whites until stiff and fold in. Pour the mixture into a buttered oven mould and cook it in the oven at 350° for one hour.

To serve, turn the pudding out onto a suitable dish and pour over it the three sauces, so that they partly run into each other. Serves four.

Impanata di Piscispata
(Sicilian Fish Pie)

The fish usually destined for this pie is the swordfish, which is abundant in waters near Sicily. It is certainly very suitable, but lots of other fish could be used instead, including halibut, pompano and snappers. Note the use of sugar in the pastry. If making a pie containing a rich, oily fish such as tuna, omit this.

$1\frac{1}{2}$ pounds white fish
2 tablespoons olive oil
2 onions
3 medium tomatoes, skinned and chopped
2 celery stalks, finely chopped
4 sprigs of parsley, finely chopped
$\frac{1}{2}$ cup green olives, pitted and chopped
2 tablespoons capers, rinsed
1 egg yolk
for the pastry
$3\frac{1}{2}$ cups flour
$1\frac{3}{4}$ sticks butter
1 cup superfine sugar
4-5 egg yolks
grated peel of 1 lemon
pinch of salt

First prepare the short pastry, working the ingredients to a firm dough, adding only a very little water if it is too crumbly. Shape it into a ball, flour it and leave it to rest for an hour in the refrigerator.

Heat the olive oil in a heavy-based pan, chop the onions finely and fry them in the olive oil until they soften. Add the tomatoes, the celery, the parsley, the olives, and the capers. Cook gently for ten minutes to concentrate the flavors. Add the fish, cut into small pieces and simmer for ten minutes more.

Butter and flour a pie plate 8 inches across and $2\frac{1}{2}$ inches deep, of the kind that can be unclasped and taken apart.

Gently roll out the pastry so that it will make three discs. The first of these should cover the bottom and partly cover the sides of the plate. Put it in place and fill it with half of the fish mixture. Repeat. Top with the third layer of pastry, making sure that it reaches the side of the plate all round. Brush it with egg yolk. Bake the pie in the oven at 350° for about 50-55 minutes. Serves four.

Soho Fish Pie

The Adventurous Fish Cook, George Lassalle's thoughtful and expert contribution to the literature of seafood cookery, has an excellent section on fish pies and original ideas about their topping, which need not be just potato or just pastry. This recipe is essentially his and, as he says, it suits conger eel or other strong-textured or strong-flavored fish such as skate and dogfish; it is also good with squid.

1½ pounds fish
3 shallots
2 cloves of garlic, chopped
3 tablespoons olive oil
1 pound tomatoes, skinned and chopped
3 anchovies, pounded
a *court bouillon* (see page 177)
2 cups *sauce béchamel*
for the covering
3-4 potatoes
1 fennel root
salt and black pepper
1 tablespoon chives, chopped
milk, as required
½ stick butter

Prepare the potato and fennel root covering first. Peel the vegetables and slice them thinly. Seasoning with salt, pepper and chives as you go, put the slices in a small, tightly covered pot so that they are quite densely packed. Pour in milk to cover and dot with the butter. Seal with foil so that the cover fits tightly and cook in the oven at 350° for 35-40 minutes or until soft.

Poach the fish in the *court bouillon*. Skin and fillet the fish and cut it into small pieces of about 2 inches square. These should be kept warm in the pie dish.

In the meantime, sweat the shallots and garlic briefly in the olive oil. Add the tomatoes and anchovies and continue cooking on a lively heat. The mixture should reduce to an aromatic purée. Add it to the béchamel and season, then cook gently for a further ten minutes.

Pour the sauce over the fish, cover with the fennel and potatoes, spreading them as evenly as possible. Bake in the oven at 350° for 10-15 minutes. Serves four.

Rappie Pie with Soft-shelled Clams

Rappie stands for the French word *râpure* (gratings), this being an Acadian dish brought to Canada by French settlers. It can be made with meat or chicken, but there is reason to believe that the earliest version was the one with clams. All versions have the same strange feature; they involve extracting the liquid from potatoes and replacing it with another liquid.

12 or 16 soft-shelled clams
2 pounds potatoes
6 ounces salt pork, finely diced
black pepper

First, peel and grate the potatoes. Working with a large handful at a time, put the grated potato in a cheesecloth and twist it so as to wring out as much liquid as possible. Collect the liquid in a bowl so that it can be

measured. The wrung-out potato, looking like snow, goes into another bowl.

Steam the clams open, reserve the juices and mince the meat. Dry out the diced salt pork in an oven pan until the bottom of the pan is coated with melted fat; then remove and reserve the pieces of pork.

Add to the clam juices enough water to make their volume equal to that of the liquid extracted from the potatoes. Bring this mixture to a boil, then add the wrung-out potato to it, little by little. The potato will swell up as it absorbs its new liquid. Having finished this operation, place a layer of the potato in the bottom of the oven pan, then a layer of minced clam, then more potato and so on, and finishing with potato (the pie may have either three or five layers in all). Season with pepper as you do this, and sprinkle the bits of salt pork onto the top.

Bake in the oven at 400° for 15 minutes, then lower the heat to 350° and continue to bake for another 45 minutes or so. The top of the pie should be brown and crusty. Serves four.

Fish or Crab Soufflé

George Lassalle emphasised the suitability of almost all fish, and above all of crustaceans, for use in soufflés; and drove home his point by declaring that one not only could, but should, have a different seafood soufflé in every week of the year; a robust pronouncement in favor of a very delicate dish. Here is a versatile recipe, which works well with any good fish including salmon, red mullet, smelt smoked haddock; and with any crustacean, but especially crab.

½ pound boned and skinned cooked fish, or crab
generous ½ cup cream sauce (page 203)
2 teaspoons green peppercorns, pounded, or 2 tablespoons chives, finely chopped
3-4 tablespoons fish *fumet* (page 177)
3 egg yolks
4 egg whites

Pound the fish or crustacean flesh to a purée and amalgamate it with the cream sauce, adding either the green peppercorns or the chives. Add the *fumet* and beat in the egg yolks.

Meanwhile heat the oven to 350°, warm a 7-inch soufflé dish, and butter it well.

Beat the egg whites to a stiff froth and fold them lightly into the fish mixture. (Do not beat, do not stir; the aim is to preserve the tiny air pockets intact.) Scoop the whole mixture out of the bowl and into the soufflé dish and set this in the middle of the oven. Cook for 25 minutes. Serves four.

Fischlabskaus

Not exactly a pie or a pudding, this is a seamen's dish, which is found all along the German seaboard and is also known in Denmark and Norway. It is essentially a way of making preserved meat and salted fish, such as ships' crews used to eat on their voyages, tasty. But it lives on in modern times, sustained by its special and hearty flavor. Liverpudlians (from Liverpool, England) may like to know that their meat dish "lobscouse", from which comes the name "scouse" applied to anyone from Liverpool, is derived from *Labskaus*.

14 ounces salted, smoked or fresh fish
14 ounces corned or salted beef, or similar preserved meat
1½ pounds potatoes
3 ounces beef dripping or other fat suitable for frying
3 onions, finely chopped
salt and pepper
1 tablespoon mustard
6 eggs
1 cooked beet, sliced
3 pickles from a jar, halved lengthways

Prepare, cook and flake the fish. Roughly chop the meat. Peel, par-boil, and roughly mash the potatoes. Heat the dripping or other fat in a large pan and fry the onions in it, then stir in the seasoning and mustard. Add the fish, meat and potato and stir some more, enough to mix up the various elements but not to blend them. Cover and cook until everything is piping hot. In the meantime fry the eggs separately.

To serve, transfer everything to a heated platter, decorate it with the sliced beet and halved pickles and place a fried egg for each person on top. Serves six.

Oyster and Sweetbread Pie

If oysters are to be cooked, I think they should be cooked with something, and something which is compatible (rather than strongly contrasting) in texture and flavor. Really tasty mushrooms would do, but Mrs Mary Randolph's suggestion (in *The Virginia House-wife*, 1824) of veal sweetbreads seems even better. I give her instructions in her own pleasant language, from the point where you have ready some poached sweetbreads.

". . . stew the oysters, season them with pepper and salt, and thicken with cream, butter, the yolks of eggs and flour, put a puff paste at the bottom and around the sides of a deep dish, take the oysters up with an egg spoon, lay them in the bottom and cover them with the sweetbreads, fill the dish with the gravy, put a paste on the top and bake it. This is the most delicious pie that can be made."

Quenelles, Balls and Cakes

There are various seafood confections which fall into what I perceive as a group, all being small or fairly small in size, round or partly round in shape, and containing minced or chopped seafood. They all deserve attention. Fish cakes, for example, should not be seen as a way of using up surplus cooked fish (although this is a purpose which they fulfil very well), but as an interesting and tasty dish in their own right. Cooks in the western world have, on the whole, much more to learn from the Orient in this respect than vice versa. The small selection of recipes here, which start off reassuringly with a high-status item, quenelles, is intended to quicken interest in the whole group – which, by the way, also includes some dumplings and fritters.

Crab Quenelles

Quenelles of fish or other seafood often appear on menus but are less frequently made in the home, perhaps because they seem difficult. Lynda Brown, whose *Fresh Thoughts on Food* lays much emphasis on lightness, gives a really clear account of what to do. The seafoods used can be varied.

6 ounces fresh crab meat
2 ounces white fish (plaice, lemon sole or whiting) skinned and boned
1 egg and 1 egg white
generous ¼ cup heavy cream
for the sauce
shell and other debris from the crab
1 medium onion, sliced
1 stick of celery, chopped
butter
2 tomatoes, chopped
¾ cup white wine
bouquet garni, to include a little tarragon and fennel, if possible
to finish
1 large egg yolk
1 scant teaspoon potato flour, slaked in milk
1-2 tablespoons heavy cream
chopped chives or fennel

Put the crab and fish in a blender or food processor, keeping back 2 teaspoon or so of the brown crab meat to enrich the sauce, and process until the mixture resembles a thick, pinkish whipped cream. Transfer to a bowl, season to taste, cover and chill in the refrigerator until required.

Next, make the stock for the sauce. Scrub the crab legs and shell. Sweat them with the vegetables in a little butter, covered, over a low heat. After ten minutes, add the wine, *bouquet garni* and enough water to cover.

Bring to the boil, skim, and simmer for 30-40 minutes. Strain, return to the rinsed pan, and reduce to a scant cup, skimming as necessary. It should now be of a fine flavor. Set aside until needed.

For the final cooking and assembly of the dish, have a large pan full of lightly salted water, barely simmering (if the water more than murmurs, the quenelles will break up). Also have ready: a serving dish in a warm oven; the crab stock heating in a separate pan; and the egg yolk, beaten with the potato flour and a little of the crab stock.

Shape the quenelles, one at a time, between two medium spoons; I use deep, oval dessert spoons which give me nine quenelles from this mixture. As each is formed, lower it gently into the simmering water. Within seconds it should slip off the spoon easily; if not, ease it off gently. It will sink to the bottom only to rise again almost immediately. Poach gently for five to seven minutes. Taste the ninth – cook's perk – to check. It should be slightly creamy inside.

Meanwhile finish the sauce. Pour the hot stock onto the egg mixture, whisking as you do so. Return to the pan and cook gently, stirring all the time until the sauce thickens somewhat. Don't let it boil, though you can safely bring it to boiling point. Finish with the cream and the reserved crab meat. Check consistency and seasonings, and add a little cayenne or tomato purée if appropriate.

Lift the quenelles out of their water-bath with a slotted spoon, drain them briefly on a kitchen towel, then arrange them in a warmed serving dish. Spoon the sauce over, finish with a dusting of herbs and serve immediately. Serves four.

Malaysian Fish Balls

These are very diverse, and not all of them are ball-shaped; some are like little loaves from which small slices can be cut to go into soups. They differ in color also. Some are themselves stuffed into red bell pepper or cucumber rings, or in a thin blanket of beancurd; or they may have strips of red or green bell pepper inside them; or incorporate finely chopped herbs to give a green-speckled effect.

Although the architecture of the balls is a matter for artistry and expertise, their basic preparation is easy. Take any good fish with white flesh; gut, skin, and bone them; flake the flesh finely; and leave it for an hour or two in a large bowl of sea water or fresh salted water. Then drain, pound, and mould into the desired shapes after adding any other ingredients. Typical balls would be just over $\frac{1}{2}$ inch in diameter, and thus suitable for putting in soup, which is often their fate. For one large bowl of fish ball soup for one person, start by putting a handful of thick rice noodles, already cooked, in the bottom of the bowl; then add two ladlefuls of clear fish broth and up to a dozen (preferably assorted) fish balls. Sprinkle a finely chopped scallion and a tablespoonful of dark brown sugar on top. The accompaniment is light soy sauce with tiny slivers of fresh red chili pepper in it.

Fiskeboller
(Norwegian Fish Balls)

Norway has a valuable and unique institution: the *fiskemat* shop or *fiskemat-butikk*. This is a special shop which sells minced fish, not from inferior fish or left-over stock but really fresh and first-class fish minced and made into forcemeat for use at home, or already turned into fish balls or fish puddings. Whether the *fiskemat* shops exist because Norwegians are so keen on fish balls and puddings and so good at making them, or whether it is the other way round, I do not know. But those of us who live elsewhere can profit from Norwegian expertise, as in this recipe, which takes us progressively through the stage of making fish forcemeat to that of making fish balls.

Of the fish available in Norway, haddock and pollack are considered to be highly suitable and to have the whitest flesh. Coley is fine but its flesh is less white. The cleaned and rinsed fish should be hung up by its tail overnight in a cool place, to facilitate scraping off the flesh.

$1\frac{1}{2}$ pounds scraped fish flesh (see above), boned and
skinned
1 teaspoon salt
1 tablespoon potato flour
2 tablespoons cold butter
$\frac{1}{2}$ teaspoon mace
2 cups light cream
1 cold boiled potato, grated (optional)
1 teaspoon white pepper
1 teaspoon salt
enough fish stock to poach the balls

Using (to be traditional) a long pestle and a marble mortar, pound the fish with the salt, potato flour, butter, and mace. (Or use a blender or food processor.) Add the cream (and a little of the fish stock, if you wish) by the spoonful, beating well, to form a smooth mixture. The more you beat (or blend) between spoonfuls, the better and lighter the forcemeat will be.

The mixture should be firm enough to mould. This is where the optional grated potato may come in useful; it will help the fish balls to keep their shape.

Now make the forcemeat into fairly large balls, seasoning them lightly, and poach them in the fish stock. The recipe can be varied, for example by adding a tablespoonful of finely chopped chives to the forcemeat when you form it into balls.

Serve the fish balls with melted butter and boiled potatoes. Serves four.

197

Lithuanian Gefillte Fish

This is the most famous of Jewish fish dishes and appears in many forms. Some reconstitute the shape of a whole fish, either by stuffing the whole skin or by filling individual rounds of skin with the stuffing. There are grounds for thinking that the dish originated in Lithuania, and the recipe given here is from a Lithuanian. Jews in Riga would add beet to the cooking liquid, while Jews in Poland would prefer more sugar in the fish mixture.

Freshwater fish are more traditional than sea fish for this purpose, but sea fish have often been used and are every bit as good.

2 pounds fish, uncleaned
1 soft white roll
milk or water, to soak
2 medium onions
2 eggs, beaten
2 teaspoons olive or other salad oil
1-1½ teaspoons salt
¾ teaspoon sugar
pinch of pepper
2 tablespoons water
1-2 tablespoons *matzos* (Jewish unleavened bread) crumbs, or ordinary toasted breadcrumbs
for the cooking liquid
2 large onions, chopped
3 carrots, chopped
salt and pepper
parsley (optional)

Clean, skin and bone the fish. Mince the flesh in a grinder or processor.

Soak the roll in milk or water and squeeze it free of any excess moisture. Mince it with the onions, and mix these thoroughly with the fish and remaining ingredients. Form the mixture into ten or 12 round but flattened fish cakes, adding a little more breadcrumbs if the mixture is not of the right consistency.

Take a large heavy-bottomed casserole of about 12 inches in diameter. Put in the chopped onions, carrot, seasoning and parsley, add enough water to cover two layers of fish cakes. Bring this liquid to the boil, and then add the fishcakes, flat side down, in two layers. Reduce the heat, cover, and simmer very gently for 1½ to 2 hours.

When the fish is cooked, leave it to cool for a while, but remove it while still warm, and arrange the fish cakes on a dish. Pieces of the chopped cooked carrot can be used as a garnish. Strain the broth and pour over the dish as a sauce. Serve chilled. Serves four.

Cold Dishes

Some fish are exceptionally good when served cold, salmon for example. Others, such as the firm-fleshed goosefish, lend themselves well to incorporation in a mixed seafood salad. Shrimp relentlessly take their bow in shrimp cocktail all round the clock in countless restaurants the world over.

Here I find space for just half a dozen items starting with the famous *ceviche* or *seviche*, which is "cooked" in such a novel way.

Ceviche

Old English cookery books usually contain a recipe "to Caveach fish", sometimes "the West Indian way". This is all mixed up with the old "escabeche", and the two things no doubt have a common ancestry, but they are different. In "escabeche" the fish is conventionally cooked by frying, and then preserved in a vinegar-based marinade, while in *ceviche* the fish is not conventionally cooked at all, but "cooked" by the action of lime or lemon juice.

¾ pound fresh thin and skinless fillets of any good white-fleshed fish (flatfish and John Dory are among those suitable)
scant ½ cup dry white wine
4 tablespoons lemon juice or 3½ tablespoons of lime juice
2 teaspoons orange juice
2 tablespoons virgin olive oil, or a nut oil
½ teaspoon salt
2 bay leaves, crumbled
a few wisps of orange and lemon peel

Divide the fillets into strips and lay these in a shallow dish. Mix all the liquid ingredients, add salt and pour over the fillets. Scatter the pieces of bay leaf and the slivers of citrus fruit peel over all. Cover, and leave in the refrigerator, turning the fillets occasionally. The fillets will have become opaque, which signals that they are ready to eat, in five to six hours, but the flavor improves if they are left for 24 hours. Serves four.

A Filipino Fish and Guava Salad

1 cup of cooked, flaked fish
salt and pepper
24 ripe guavas
1 orange, peeled
2 bananas, peeled
½ cup coconut cream (see page 177)

Season the cooked fish with salt and pepper.

Peel eight of the guavas, open them and remove the seeds, then cut them into small pieces. Separate the orange into sections, removing all the pith, and cut the bananas into small pieces. Mix the fish and pieces of fruit together, then add the coconut cream and chill the mixture.

Cut the tops from the remaining 16 guavas, remove the seeds and fill the cavities with the fish mixture. Replace the tops and serve while the contents are still well chilled.

This is not a recent invention inspired by nouvelle cuisine. It was recommended by Maria Y Orosa, a Filipino heroine of World War II, who was equally interested in flavor and nutrition, and who was inspired both by Filipino traditions and her own lively imagination. Serves four.

Fish Salad Provençal

Begin by poaching your fish, taking care not to overcook it – it should be firm enough to cut up into small cubes.

1½ pounds cooked fish (see above), cubed
2 tablespoons capers
2-3 *cornichons* (pickled baby cucumbers), quartered
12 slices of fresh cucumber, peeled
6 anchovies, roughly chopped
4 small potatoes, cooked, peeled and diced
1 cooked beet, sliced
vinaigrette dressing (page 200)

Combine the ingredients, apply the vinaigrette dressing, then arrange the salad in a becoming way on a platter. Serves four.

A Thai Salad of Spanish Mackerel

1½ pounds Spanish mackerel fillets
vegetable oil for frying
juice of 1 fresh lime
2 shallots, peeled and chopped
1 piece (1 inch) fresh ginger, chopped
1 tablespoon crushed peanuts
1 or 2 small chili peppers, de-seeded
and cut into small rings
2 tablespoons finely cubed green mango flesh

Steam the fish fillets until they are almost cooked through. Complete the cooking by frying them briefly in vegetable oil. Leave to cool, flake the flesh, sprinkle it with the lime juice, and mix in the other ingredients. Serve warm or chilled. Serves four.

Dressed Crab

The first thing to be said is that cooks need to have a small stock of handsome empty crab carapaces, preferably in a variety of sizes (to serve one, two or four – if the small sizes are lacking, use scallop shells). Otherwise there will be trouble over dressing snow or king crab, whose legs only are marketed; and possibly over other crabs too. Besides, even if the crab you are dealing with has a suitable carapace, this may sustain damage in being prepared.

1 large crab, cooked, or sufficient canned or frozen
crabmeat to serve four
2 tablespoons olive oil
pepper
2 teaspoons lemon juice

Extract and chop up all the meat and coral. Dress the meat as Venetians would, very simply with olive oil, pepper and lemon juice. Arrange it in the carapaces (or on scallop shells). It is usual to have the brown meat at the sides and the white meat in the middle. Serves four.

199

Musclos
(A Catalan Dish of Mussels)

This is another recipe which I owe to Patience Gray and that part of her life, so vividly described in *Honey From a Weed*, which she spent in Caralonia.

4½ pounds mussels
3 tablespoons olive oil
2 onions, finely chopped
3 ripe tomatoes, peeled and crushed
¼ teaspoon paprika
salt and black pepper
1 clove of garlic, peeled and finely chopped
2 sprigs parsley, finely chopped

Steam open the cleaned mussels as usual. Discard the upper shells and arrange the mussels in their half-shells on a large flat dish. Strain and reserve the cooking liquid.

Heat the olive oil in the pan and brown the onion slowly. Add the tomatoes and simmer for 25 minutes over a low heat, to reduce.

Now pour a little of the strained cooking liquid into the sauce and add the paprika, seasoning, garlic and parsley.

Pour the sauce over the mussels and serve cold. Serves four.

Sauces

The whole question of sauces for fish is important, since these greatly affect our enjoyment of fish dishes. It is often said that in order to enhance rather than mask the flavor of fish one should base the sauce on a fish stock or *fumet*, or build seafood ingredients such as shrimp into it. This is a good principle to bear in mind, but don't forget the other one: contrasts are often successful. There is nothing fishy about a sweet-and-sour sauce, but it goes very well with fish.

I have a weakness for the kind of sauce where you just mix some ingredients together and that's it. Quick, easy, and often very good. But most people think in terms of sauces which need to be cooked, or anyway more than just mixed; and it is sauces of this kind that are usually recommended in seafood cookery books, and which deserve some comment.

The genealogy of these sauces is a subject which has attracted many an author. It is easy to form most of the sauces into groups, each group resting on one basis; and such grouping gives the reader a pleasant glow of insight and illumination. Two works that are especially recommended for this purpose are the *Sauces* volume in the Time/Life *Good Cook* series (for which Richard Olney was the master-mind) and George Lassalle's *The Adventurous Fish Cook*; the latter, naturally, is focussed on sauces for seafood. However, I find that the technique of classifying sauces in families is really geared to classic French cuisine, which I am neither equipped nor eager to promote, so while saluting and recommending these two lucid expositions, I have not categorized the sauces which follow, but simply divided them into those you (more or less) just mix and those which need cooking.

SAUCES MADE BY MIXING

Vinaigrette

A vinaigrette is several (four, some say, while others suggest three) parts of olive oil to one of wine vinegar, seasoned.

Drawn Butter Sauce

Drawn butter is melted butter, to which you add a little lemon juice (not as much as in the next recipe).

Lime or Lemon Sauce

I prefer lime to lemon here, but either is fine. All you do is melt $\frac{3}{4}$ stick butter and stir it over a very low heat until it foams, then stir into it 2 tablespoons lime or lemon juice, possibly with one grind of black pepper. A point often overlooked here is that the quality of the butter and the delicacy of its flavor are important; use the best you can buy.

Compound Butters

The basic procedure is to amalgamate, by kneading, $\frac{1}{2}$ stick butter with 1 tablespoon finely chopped something-or-other (parsley is the obvious example). Any quantity can be made and frozen, for future enhancement and use. Enhancement, if you feel that this is needed, can be achieved by melting the compound butter and beating into it, over a very low heat, cream (proportions suggested: generous $\frac{1}{2}$ cup to 1 stick butter).

This is the gateway to numerous excellent accompaniments for fish. Many, many herbs work well in this, and so do things like watercress, pounded horseradish, pounded anchovy, and powdered almond.

Chameleon Sauce

George Lassalle gives this attractive title to his mother version of a whole brood of easily prepared sauces.

I teaspoon prepared English mustard
I shallot or small onion, grated
4 tablespoons wine vinegar
juice of $\frac{1}{2}$ lemon
I teaspoon sugar
I heaped teaspoon parsley, finely chopped
$\frac{1}{4}$ teaspoon salt
black pepper to taste

Stir all the ingredients together and leave to stand, so that the flavors mingle. The sauce is served as a kind of relish.

It is suitable for endless variations, achieved for example by substituting for mustard another strongly flavored ingredient: capers, horseradish and watercress are possibilities.

It can be further enhanced by the addition of 2 tablespoons of olive oil. The next recipe, which dates back at least to the thirteenth century and crops up in many countries in different forms, provides an example of this sort of enhancement and also illustrates further the wide variations which our chameleon can exhibit.

Green Sauce

The first ingredient can be just parsley or a mixture in which a dominant amount of parsley is supplemented by small amounts of other green herbs (sweet marjoram, sage, mint, for example).

2 cloves of garlic, peeled
6-12 capers
2 anchovies
1 slice bread, without crust
1 tablespoon red wine vinegar
a handful of fresh parsley, finely chopped
4 grinds of black pepper
2 tablespoon olive oil

Pound together the garlic, capers and anchovies. Soak the bread in the wine vinegar, then pound it and the parsley into the mixture. Add black pepper. Loosen the whole by stirring in the olive oil.

Mayonnaise

3 egg yolks
salt and pepper
1 tablespoon wine vinegar or lemon juice
2 cups olive oil

Break the yolks into a bowl and beat them, seasoning with salt and pepper. Add the vinegar or lemon juice and mix thoroughly. Still beating constantly, start adding the oil, drop by drop at first. When the sauce starts to thicken, the remaining oil can be poured in a thin stream, stirring all the time.

If the mayonnaise is too thick, it can be thinned with a little warm water.

When making mayonnaise, the egg yolks and oil should be at room temperature. A curdled mayonnaise can be rescued by dripping it slowly on to a new yolk in a second bowl, beating thoroughly.

Mayonnaise will keep for several days, covered, in a cool place or refrigerator. Stir before use.

Aïoli

Proceed as in making mayonnaise, but before you start, crush a few cloves of garlic in the mortar with a little sea salt to make a fine paste, and add a few drops of water to this. Then carry on with the egg yolks and the olive oil; but delay adding the wine vinegar or lemon juice until the very end.

Sauce Tartare

Mix the following ingredients thoroughly:

2 cups mayonnaise
2 teaspoon of each of: chives, capers, parsley, pickles, green bell pepper (or green olives), all finely chopped

Salsa Romesco

40 whole almonds, toasted
4 cloves of garlic, toasted
1 hard dry biscuit (*carquinyoli* in Catalonia)
2 teaspoons paprika
1 teaspoon cayenne or other hot chili powder
2 sprigs parsley, chopped
3 broiled tomatoes
1 teaspoon wine vinegar
enough olive oil to bind the sauce

Put all the ingredients except the oil in a large mortar, in sequence, and pound them long and hard. Bind with the olive oil, using a wooden spoon to stir the mixture.

Skorthaliá
(Thick Garlic Sauce)

The Greek version of a sauce which occurs in various forms, for example the Catalan *allioli*, in other parts of the Mediterranean region. This version is from Rena Salaman's *Greek Food*. It is very good with fried fish.

4 medium slices stale bread, crusts removed, soaked in water for ten minutes
4 cloves garlic, peeled and sliced
2 tablespoons wine vinegar
4-5 tablespoons olive oil
salt to taste

Squeeze excess water form the bread. Blend it with the garlic and vinegar in a blender; add the olive oil gradually and blend. Season. If the mixture appears too dry, add up to two tablespoonfuls of water. The sauce should be of a runny consistency. Serve separately.

Sorrel and Mustard Sauce

Remove the midribs from two handfuls of young sorrel leaves, and turn what is left into a purée. Add two teaspoons of a mild, made mustard and five tablespoons sour cream. Use as a relish.

201

SAUCES MADE BY COOKING

Fish Velouté

This is a basic preparation, in which a *fumet* (see page 177) is whisked into a roux (butter and flour blended to a smooth paste over a gentle heat) and cooked gently. It is usual to enhance it by adding, to give just some examples, a compound butter (page 200) or a vegetable purée or finely chopped cooked shrimp.

2 tablespoons butter
2 tablespoons flour
2½ cups fish *fumet*

Melt the butter in a pan until it is just foaming, then shake the flour evenly onto it and use a whisk to blend the two ingredients into a paste. Cook for only a minute or two – until it begins to bubble – then add the fish *fumet*, still whisking. Continue whisking until the mixture comes to a boil, then reduce the heat to very low and simmer, stirring from time to time, for 30-45 minutes (the period which purists think necessary if all taste of flour is to be eliminated; but some cooks think ten minutes enough).

To enrich with cream, strain the sauce into another pan, set it over a low heat, and whisk in a scant cup heavy cream.

Sauce Mornay

Make velouté as described above, enriched with cream, then add ¼ cup grated cheese (ideally a mixture of Gruyère and Parmesan). Stir until the cheese has melted. Then, away from the heat, add 2 tablespoons butter, in small pieces.

Avgolémono Sauce
(Greek Egg and Lemon Sauce)

2 cups fish stock
salt and black pepper
1 tablespoon cornstarch
2-3 egg yolks
juice of 1 lemon, or more

Strain the fish stock into the top of a double saucepan or a thick-bottomed ordinary pan. Season to taste with salt and pepper. Mix the cornstarch with a little cold water and work the paste gradually into the hot stock, mixing vigorously to avoid lumps. Cook gently, stirring, until the sauce thickens: about 15 minutes.

Beat the eggs in a bowl, add the lemon juice and stir.

Add a little of the hot sauce, beating it in, then gradually incorporate this mixture in the sauce, stirring with a wooden spoon and over a low heat, until the sauce thickens to a smooth, custard-like consistency. (Do not let it boil or it will curdle.)

Serve hot or cold, poured over poached, fried or baked fish or as a separate accompaniment.

Horseradish Sauce

5 tablespoons butter
2 tablespoons flour
2 cups fish broth
salt and pepper
2 tablespoons lemon juice
2 tablespoons freshly grated horseradish
2 tablespoons heavy cream

Melt two tablespoons of the butter, add the flour and simmer for five minutes over a very low heat, without browning. Leave to cool, then add the fish broth, return to a low heat, and simmer and stir constantly until thickened and smooth.

Add the seasonings and lemon juice, and beat in the remaining butter a tiny piece at a time, followed by the grated horseradish and the cream.

Sauce Hollandaise

3 egg yolks
1 tablespoon cold water
½ teaspoon rice flour or arrowroot
a little salt and pepper
2 sticks butter, cut into small cubes
1 tablespoon strained lemon juice
1 teaspoon white pepper

In a *bain-marie*, beat the egg yolks, cold water, rice flour or arrowroot, and seasoning with a small amount of the butter until smooth.

Now heat the *bain-marie* gently, while you continue whisking. As each lot of butter is absorbed, whisk in another lot, and so on, until all the butter is used.

Beat the sauce until it is creamy and quite thick. Finally, whisk in the lemon juice and white pepper.

Mousseline Sauce

Make a Sauce Hollandaise as explained above, but with slightly more seasoning. Then mix into it a scant ½ cup of whipped heavy cream.

Sweet and Sour Sauce

There are many recipes for this in currency, including European ones with a medieval ancestry; and many of them are sauces which cook with the main ingredient, not separately. But it seems appropriate here to choose what might be called a "free-standing" sauce, and to give an authentic Chinese recipe (from Dr Yan-Kit So's book), since the Chinese are currently the greatest users of these sauces.

$\frac{1}{4}$ cup water
4 tablespoons sugar
3 tablespoons rice or wine vinegar
1 scant teaspoon salt
2 tablespoons tomato catsup
$2\frac{1}{2}$ tablespoons potato flour, dissolved in 2 tablespoons water

Put the water, sugar, vinegar, salt and catsup in a saucepan and bring to simmering point. Gradually add the dissolved potato flour, stirring as the sauce thickens. Pour into a bowl and leave to cool.

Gooseberry Sauce

1 pound gooseberries
1 good pinch nutmeg
sugar
3 tablespoons butter

Stem the gooseberries and put them over a slow heat with two tablespoons water, increasing the heat after the juice begins to collect in the bottom of the pan. Cook them until soft, then mash them, add the nutmeg, and just enough sugar to take the edge off the acid (add one teaspoon, and taste before adding more). Beat in the butter a small piece at a time.

Especially good with mackerel and with boiled eel.

Gin-an
(Japanese Silver Sauce)

generous $1\frac{1}{2}$ cups *dashi* (see below)
$\frac{1}{2}$ teaspoon salt
1 teaspoon light Japanese soy sauce
$1\frac{1}{2}$ tablespoons cornstarch mixed with $1\frac{1}{2}$ tablespoons water

Dashi is the basic Japanese soup stock, made with water, kelp (*konbu*) and dried bonito flakes (*hana-katsuo*); but you can buy "instant dashi". Put the *dashi*, salt, and soy sauce in a saucepan and place over moderate heat. When it reaches simmering point, drizzle the cornstarch mixture into the pan and stir until thickened.

Môlho de Camarao para Peixe
(Shrimp Cream Sauce for Fish)

2 tablespoons olive oil
1 onion, thinly sliced
1 small hot chili pepper, finely chopped
5 ounces fresh shrimp, peeled and chopped
$\frac{1}{2}$ teaspoon nutmeg
2 cups milk
2 tablespoons cornstarch mixed with 2 tablespoons water
salt and pepper

Heat the oil and sauté the onion, pepper and shrimp in it until softened. Add the nutmeg and milk. Thicken with the cornstarch-and-water and season to taste.

Sauce Béchamel

$\frac{1}{2}$ stick butter
$\frac{1}{2}$ cup flour
scant 4 cups milk
a *bouquet garni*
salt and pepper
pinch of nutmeg

Melt the butter in a saucepan and add the flour. Stir well for about three minutes. Pour on the milk little by little, still stirring, and add the *bouquet garni*, the seasoning and nutmeg. Bring the sauce to simmering point, then cook it gently for 20 minutes (some would advise 40-45 minutes), stirring occasionally to prevent it from sticking.

To make cream sauce, enrich the béchamel with a generous $\frac{1}{2}$ cup of heavy cream, bring to a simmer, and stir over a gentle heat for a minute or two. This further step leads to many others, of which I give one example.

Parsley sauce can be made by adding 3 tablespoons of finely chopped parsley and 2 teaspoons of lemon juice to the cream sauce.

Bibliography

Abbott, R Tucker: *Seashells of North America*: New York, Golden Press, 1968.

Albuquerque, Rolanda Maria: *Peixes de Portugal e Ilhas Adjacentes*: Lisbon, 1954-56.

Algar, Ayla: *The Complete Book of Turkish Cooking*: London, Kegan Paul International, 1985.

Allen, G R: *Snappers of the World*: Rome, FAO, 1985.

Allyn, Rube: Dictionary of Fishes: St Petersburg, Florida, Great Outdoors Publishing Co, 1952.

American Fisheries Society: *A List of Common and Scientific Names of Fishes from the United States and Canada*, 2nd edn: Ann Arbor, Michigan, 1960.

Andrews, Jean: *Shells and Shores of Texas*: Austin, University of Texas, 1977.

Arnold, Augusta Foote: *The Sea-Beach at Ebb-tide*: New York, Dover, 1968 (reprint of first edn of 1901).

Ayling, Tony & Cox, Geoffrey J: *Guide to the Sea Fishes of New Zealand*: Auckland, Collins, 1982.

Badham, Rev C David: *Ancient and Modern Fish Tattle*: London, 1854.

Bagnis, Raymond and others: *Poissons de Polynésie*: Paris, Albin Michel, 1972.

Barrow, Errol W & Lee, Kendal A: *Privilege – Cooking in the Caribbean*: London, Macmillan Caribbean, 1988.

Bauchot, M L, Bianchi, G & Rey, J C: *Guide des Poissons Commerciaux de Madagascar*: Rome, FAO, 1984.

Beebe, William & Tee-Van, John: *Field Book of the Shore Fishes of Bermuda and the West Indies*: London, Constable, 1933.

Bell, Thomas: *A History of the British Stalk-eyed Crustacea*: London, John Van Voorst, 1853.

Bianchi, Gabriella: *Commercial Marine & Brackish-Water Species of Pakistan*: Rome, FAO, 1985.
  Commercial Marine & Brackish-Water Species of Tanzania: Rome, FAO, 1985.
  Guide Des Ressources Halieutiques de l'Atlantique Marocain: Rome, FAO, 1984.
  Espécies Comerciais Marinhas e de Aguas Salobras de Angola: Rome, FAO, 1986.

Bigelow, H B & Schroeder, W C: *Fishes of the Gulf of Maine*: Washington, DC, US Government Printing Office, 1953.

Bini, Giorgio: *Atlante Dei Pesci Delle Coste Italiane*, vols I-VIII: Rome, Mondo Sommerso Editrice, 1967.

Blackman, Grant: *Australian Fish Cooking*: Melbourne, Hill of Content Publishing, 1978.

Breder, Charles M, Jr: *Field Book of Marine Fishes of the Atlantic Coast*: New York, 1929.

Brown, Cora, Rose & Bob: *The Fish and Seafood Cook Book*: New York, Grosset & Dunlap, 1940.

Buckland, Frank: *The Natural History of British Fishes*: London, SPCK, 1883.

Burgess, Warren & Axelrod, Herbert R: *Pacific Marine Fish*, vols 1-2: New Jersey, TFH, 1971.

Böhlke, James E & Chaplin, Charles C G: *Fishes of the Bahamas and Adjacent Tropical Waters*: Philadelphia, Academy of Natural Sciences, 1968.

Brown, Lynda: *Fresh Thoughts on Food*: London, Chatto and Windus, 1986.

Çakiroglu, Said Bilâl: *Karadeniz'de Balıkçıkığımız*: Ankara, 1969.

Capel, José Carlos: *Manual del Pescado*: Madrid, Penthalon Ediciones, 1982.

Carl, G C: *Guide to Marine Life of British Columbia*: Victoria, British Columbia Provincial Museum, 1971.

Castro, Jeronimó de Melo Osório de Castro: *Nomenclatura Portuguesa do Pescado*: Lisbon, Gabinete de Estudos das Pescas, 1967.

Cavanna, G: *Doni di Nettuno*: Florence, nd (c 1905).

Centelles, J: *De la Méditerranée aux Etangs et Marécages*: Banyuls-sur-Mer, published by the author, 1981.
  Les Dedans de la Mer: Banyuls-sur-Mer, published by the author, 1979.

Cervigón, F & Fischer, W: *Catalogo de especies Marinas de interes Economico Actual o Potencial Para America Latina*, vols 1-2: Rome, FAO, 1979.

Chace, Fenner A, Jr & Hobbs, Horton H, Jr: *Freshwater and Terrestrial Decapod Crustaceans of the West Indies*: Washington DC, Smithsonian Institution, 1969.

Chandy, M: *Fishes* [of India]: New Delhi, National Book Trust, 1970.

Clark, Eleanor: *The Oysters of Locmariaquer*: London, Secker and Warburg, 1959.

Cole, John N: *Striper, a Story of Fish and Man*: Boston, Little, Brown, 1978.

Collette, Bruce B, & Nauen, Cornelia E: *Scombrids of the World*: Rome, FAO, 1983.

Compagno, Leonard J V: *Sharks of The World*, parts 1-2: Rome, FAO, 1984.

Conand, C: *Les Resources Halieutiques des pays insulaires de Pacifique*, pt 2: Rome, FAO, 1986.

Couch, Jonathan: *A History of the Fishes of the British Islands*, vols 1-4: London, 1877.

Cousteau, Jacques-Yves: *Octopus and Squid*: London, Cassell, 1973.

Cronin, Isaac, Harlow, Jay & Johnson, Paul: *The California Seafood Cookbook*: Berkeley, Aris Books, 1983.

Cutting, C L: *Fish Saving – A History of Fish Processing from Ancient to Modern Times*: London, L Hill, 1955.

D'Angelo, Giulia, & Gargiullo, Stefano: *Guida Alle Conchiglie Mediterranee*: Milan, Fabbri Editori, 1978.

Dahlberg, Michael D: *Coastal Fishes of Georgia and Nearby States*: Athens, University of Georgia, 1975.

Davidson, Alan: *A Kipper with My Tea*: London, Macmillan, 1988.
  Mediterranean Seafood, revised edn: London, Penguin, 1987.
  North Atlantic Seafood, revised edn: London, Penguin, 1988, New York, Harper & Row, 1989.
  Seafood of South-East Asia: Federal Publications, Singapore, 1977.

Day, Bunny: *Catch'em and Cook'em*: New York, Gramercy, 1961.
  Hook'em and Cook'em: New York, Gramercy, 1962.

Day, Francis: *The Fishes of Great Britain and Ireland*, vols I & II: London, 1880-1884.
  The Fishes of India, vols I and II: London, Bernard Quaritch, 1876.

De Andrade, Margarette: *Brazilian Cookery*: Rutland, Vermont, & Tokyo, Chas E Tuttle, 1965.

De Haas, Werner & Knorr, Fredy: *Was lebt im Meer an Europas Küsten?*: Stuttgart, Kosmos Bücher, 1971.

Dell, R K: *Seashore Life of New Zealand*: Wellington, A H & A W Reed, 1971.

Dissanayake, Chandra: *Ceylon Cookery*, 2nd edn: Colombo, published by the author, 1976.

Doborgel, Michel: *La Pêche en Mer et au bord de la mer*: Paris, Le Livre de Poche, 1967.

Doerper, John: *Eating Well – A Guide to Foods of the Pacific Northwest*: Seattle, Pacific Search Press, 1984.

Egerton, John: *Southern Food*: New York, Knopf, 1987.

Emerson, William K, & Jacobson, Morris K: *Guide to Shells – Land, Freshwater, and Marine from Nova Scotia to Florida*: New York, Knopf, 1976.

Eschmeyer, William N & Herald, Earl S: *A Field Guide to Pacific Coast Fishes of North America*: Boston, Houghton Mifflin, 1983.

Euzière, Jean: *Les Pêches d'Amateurs en Méditerranée*: Cannes, Robaudy, 1961.

Faber, George L: *The Fisheries of the Adriatic*: London, 1883.

FAO: Species Identification Sheets, *The Eastern Indian Ocean and Western Central Pacific*, vols I-IV: Rome, FAO, 1974.
  The Mediterranean and Black Sea, vols I-II: Rome, FAO, 1987.
  The Western Central Atlantic, vols I-VII: Rome, FAO, 1978.

Fishing Industry Board: *New Zealand Seafoods – Buyer's Guide*: Wellington, Fishing Industry Board, nd (c 1960s).

Fitch, John E: *Common Marine Bivalves of California*: California, Resource Agency, 1953.
  & Lavenberg, Robert J: *Marine Food and Game Fishes of California*: Berkeley, University of California Press, 1971.
  Tidepool and Nearshore Fishes of California: Berkeley, University of California Press, 1975.

Fontana, André: *Milieu Marin et Ressources Halieutiques de la République Populaire du Congo*: Paris, ORSTOM, 1981.

Frederick, J George and Joyce, Jean: *Long Island Seafood Cook Book*: New York, The Business Bourse, 1939.

George, C J and others: *The Fishes of the Coastal Waters of Lebanon*: Beirut, American University of Beirut, 1964.

George, R W & Holthuis, L B: *A Revision of the Indo-West Pacific Spiny Lobsters of the Panulirus Japonicus Group*: Leiden, E J Brill, 1965.

Gibbons, Euell: *Beachcomber's Handbook*: New York, David McKay, 1967.
  Stalking the Blue-eyed Scallop: New York, David McKay, 1964.

Gloerfelt-Tarp, Thomas, Kailola, Patricia J: *Trawled Fishes of Southern Indonesia and Northwestern Australia*: Australia, Development Assistance Bureau & others, nd (c 1980).

Goode, G Brown & associates: *The Fisheries and Fishery Industries of*

204

the United States: Section 1, *The Natural History of Useful Aquatic Animals*: Washington, Government Printing Office, 1884.

Gosline, William A & Brock, Vernon E: *Handbook of Hawaiian Fishes*: Honolulu, University of Hawaii, 1960.

Gousset, J, & Tixerant, G: *Les Produits de la Pêche* (plus supplement): Issy-Les-Moulineaux, Services Vétérinaires, nd.

Gray, Patience: *Honey from a Weed*: London, Prospect Books, 1987.

Gregg, William H: *Where, When, and How to Catch Fish on the East Coast of Florida*: Buffalo and New York, 1902.

Grey D L: Dall, W: Baker, A: *A Guide to the Australian Penaeid Prawns*: Darwin, Northern Territories Printing Office, 1983.

Grigson, Jane: *Fish Cookery*: London, International Wine and Food Society, 1973, and subsequently in a Penguin edn.

Gyllensköld, H: *Att Koka Fisk*: Stockholm, Wahlström & Widstrand, 1963.

Hall, D N F: *Observations on the Taxonomy and Biology of some Indo-West-Pacific Penaeidae*: London, HMSO, 1962.

Hall, H Franklyn: *300 Ways to Cook & Serve Shell Fish*: Philadelphia, 1901.

Hart, J L: *Pacific Fishes of Canada*: Ottawa, Fisheries Research Board, 1973.

Herklots, G A C & Lin, S Y: *Common Marine Food-fishes of Hong Kong*: Hong Kong, published by G A C Herklots, c 1950.

Heron-Allen, Edward: *Barnacles in Nature and Myth*: London, Oxford University Press, 1928.

Herre, Albert W & Umali, Augustin F: *English & Local Common Names of Philippine Fishes*: Washington, DC, Department of the Interior, 1948.

Herrick, Francis H: *The American Lobster – A Study of its Habits and Development*: Washington, DC, Gvmt Printing Office, 1895.

Hersey, John: *Blues*: New York, Knopf, 1987.

Hildebrand, Samuel F, & Schroeder William C: *Fishes of Chesapeake Bay*: New Jersey, T F H, 1972.

Hinton, Sam: *Sea Shore Life of Southern California*: Berkeley, University of California Press, 1969.

Hodgson, W C: *The Herring and its Fishery*: London, Routledge & Kegan Paul, 1957.

Holthuis, L B: *Shrimps and Prawns of the World*, FAO Species Catalogue, vol 1: Rome, FAO, 1980.

Hong Kong Fish Marketing Organization: *Sea Life Around Hong Kong*, 5 vols: Hong Kong, Government of Hong Kong, 1970.

Hooker, Richard J: *The Book of Chowder*: Harvard, Harvard Common Press, 1978.

Hornell, James: *Fishing in Many Waters*: Cambridge University Press, 1950.

Hosaka, Edward Y: *Shore Fishing in Hawaii*: Hawaii, Petroglyph Press, 1973.

Howorth, Peter C: *The Abalone Book*: Happy Camp, Ca, Naturegraph Publishers, 1978.

Humfrey, Michael: *Sea Shells of the West Indies*: London, Collins, 1975.

Hureau, J C, & Monod, Th (ed): *Check-list of the Fishes of the North-Eastern Atlantic and of the Mediterranean*, vols I & II: Paris, UNESCO, 1973.

Ingle, Ray: *A Guide to The Seashore*: London, Hamlyn, 1969.

Irvine, F R: *The Fishes and Fisheries of the Gold Coast*: London, Gvmt of the Gold Coast, 1947.

Jaine, Tom: *Cooking in the Country*: London, Chatto & Windus, 1986.
Fish Times Thirty – Recipes from a Dartmouth Restaurant: Allaleigh, Devon, published by the author, 1980.

Jenkins, J Travis: *The Fishes of the British Isles both Fresh Water and Salt*: London, Warne, 1936.

Jensen, Albert C: *The Cod*: New York, Thomas Y Crowell, 1972.

Jordan, David Starr & Everymann, Barton Warren: *American Food and Game Fishes*: New York, Doubleday, 1902.
The Fishes of North and Middle America, vols I-IV: Washington, DC, Government Printing Office, 1896.

Joseph, James & Klawwe, Witold, & Murphy, Pat: *Tuna and Billfish Fish without a country*: La Jolla, Inter-American Tropical Tuna Commission, 1980.

Joubin, Louis, & Le Danois, E: *Catalogue illustré des animaux marins comestibles des côtes de France et des mers limitrophes*: Paris, 1925.

Kamohara, Dr Toshiji: *Fishes of Japan in Colour*: Osaka, Hoikusha, 1967.

Karol, Sevinç: *Zooloji Terimleri Sözlüğü*: Ankara, 1963.

Karsenty, Irène & Lucienne: *Le Livre de la Cuisine Pied-noir*: Paris, Editions Planéte, 1969.

Khin, U: *Fisheries in Burma*: Rangoon, Gvmt Printing and Stationery, 1948.

Kornhall, David: *Sydsvenska Fisknamn*: Lund, C W K Gleerup, 1968.

Kozloff, Eugene N: *Seashore Life of the Northern Pacific Coast*: Seattle, University of Washington, 1973.

Kreuzer, R: *Fishery Products*: West Byfleet, Fishery News & FAO, 1974.

Kuronuma, Katsuzo & Abe, Yoshitaka: *Fishes of Kuwait*: Kuwait, Institute of Scientific Research, 1972.

Lane, Frank W: *Kingdom of the Octopus*: London, Jarrolds, 1957.

Lanfranco, Guido G: *A Complete Guide to the Fishes of Malta*: Malta, Dept of Information and Tourist Services, 1958.

Lassalle, G: *The Adventurous Fish Cook*: London, Macmillan, 1976.

Leim, A H, & Scott, W B: *Fishes of the Atlantic Coast of Canada*: Ottawa, Fisheries Research Board of Canada, 1966.

Lemery, L: *A Treatise of All Sorts of Foods* (translated from the French by D Hay), London, 1745.

Leonardo, Lydia R & Cowan, Marti Ellen: *Shallow-Water Holothurians of Calatagan, Batangas, Philippines*: Manila, University of the Philippines, 1984.

Linberg, G U: Heard, A S: Rass, T C: *Multilingual Dictionary of Names of Marine Food-Fishes of World Fauna*: Moscow, Ministry of Fisheries, 1980.

Lord, W B: *Crab, Shrimp and Lobster Lore*: London, 1867.

Lovell, M S: *The Edible Mollusca of Great Britain and Ireland*: London, nd (c 1882).

Lovett, Donald L: *A Guide to the Shrimps, Prawns, Lobsters, and Crabs of Malaysia and Singapore*: Selangor, Malaysia, Universiti Pertanian, 1981.

Lozano, Fernando: *Nomenclatura Ictiológica, Nombres científicos y vulgares de los peces españoles*: Madrid, Instituto Español de Oceanografia, 1963.

Luther, W, & Fiedler, K: *Guide de la Faune sous-Marine des Côtes Méditerranéennes*: Neuchâtel, Delachaux et Niestlé, 1965.

Lyon, Ninette: *Le Guide Marabout du Poisson*: Verviers, Belgium, Marabout, 1967.

MacKellar, Jean Scott: *Hawaii Goes Fishing – Techniques of Yesterday and Today*: Rutland, Vermont, Charles E Tuttle, 1968.

MacKie, Cristine: *Trade Winds*: Bath, Absolute Press, 1987.

Mackie, I M, Hardy, R, & Hobbs, G: *Fermented Fish Products*: Rome, FAO, 1971.

Maigret, J et Ly, B: *Les Poissons de Mer de Mauritanie*: Venette, Sciences Nat, 1986.

Manooch III, Charles S: *Fishes of the Southeastern United States*: Raleigh, NC, State Museum of Natural History, 1984.

Maxwell, C N: *Malayan Fishes*: Singapore, 1921.

McClane, A J: *Saltwater Fishes of North America*: New York, Henry Holt, 1978.

McCormick, H W & others: *Shadows in the Sea – The Sharks, Skates and Rays*: Philadelphia and New York, Chilton, 1963.

McMillan, Nora F: *British Shells*: London, Frederick Warne, 1968.

Miller, Daniel J & Lea, Robert N: *Guide to the Coastal Marine Fishes of California*: California, Resource Agency, 1972.

Miloradovich, Milo: *The Art of Fish Cookery*: New York, Garden City Books, 1949.

Ministry of Agriculture, Fisheries and Food: *Torry Research Station Advisory Notes*, 1-69: Edinburgh, HMSO, 1950-70.

Mitcham, Howard: *Creole Gumbo and All That Jazz*: Reading, Mass, Addison-Wesley, 1978.
Provincetown Seafood Cookbook: Reading, Mass, Addison-Wesley, 1975.

Moriarty, Christopher: *Eels – A natural and unnatural history*: Newton Abbot, David and Charles, 1978.

Morris, Percy A: *Pacific Coast Shells including shells of Hawaii & Gulf of California*: Boston, Houghton Mifflin, 1952.
Shells of the Atlantic and Gulf Coasts and the West Indies: Boston, Houghton Mifflin, 1973.

Morrissy, Lesley: *Australian Crustacean Cookery*: Scarborough, W Australia, Claire Dane, 1979.
Western Australian Crayfish Cookery: Scarborough, W Australia, Claire Dane, 1978.

Morton, J E: *Molluscs*: London, Hutchinson, 1958.

Morton, John & Miller, Michael: *The New Zealand Sea Shore*: Auckland, Collins, 1968.

Munro, Ian S R: *The Marine and Fresh Water Fishes of Ceylon*: Canberra, Department of External Affairs, 1955.

Muus, Bent J, & Dahlstrøm, Preben: *Sea Fishes of Britain and North-Western Europe*: London, Collins, 1974.

Netboy, Anthony: *The Atlantic Salmon – A Vanishing Species?*: London, Faber & Faber, 1968.

Nunes, Adao de Abreu: *Peixes de Madeira*: Funchal, Junta Geral do Distrito Autónomo do Funchal, 1974.

Oberthür, J: *Poissons et Fruits de Mer de Notre Pays*: Paris, 1944.

OECD: *Multilingual Dictionary of Fish and Fish Products*: Paris, 1968.

Ogburn, Charlton, Jnr: *The Winter Beach*: New York, Simon and Schuster, 1971.

Okada, Yaichiro: *Fishes of Japan*: Tokyo, Uno Shoten, 1966.

Olney Richard (chief consultant): *Fish*, in *The Good Cook* series: Amsterdam, Time/Life Books, 1979.
Sauces: (ditto) Amsterdam, Time/Life Books, 1982.

205

BIBLIOGRAPHY

Ommanney, F D: *A Draught of Fishes*: London, Longman, 1965.

Ortiz, Elisabeth Lambert: *The Book of Latin American Cooking*: New York, Knopf, 1979, and London, Penguin, 1985.

The Complete Book of Caribbean Cooking: New York, Evans, 1973.

Owen, Sri: *Indonesian and Thai Cookery*: London, Piatkus, 1988.

Indonesian Food and Cookery, revised edn: London, Prospect Books, 1986.

Palombi, Arturo, & Santarelli, Mario: *Gli Animali Commestibili dei Mari d'Italia*: Milan, Hoepli, 1969.

Parrott, Arthur W: *Sea Anglers' Fishes of New Zealand*: London, Hodder & Stoughton, 1957.

The Queer and the Rare Fishes of New Zealand: London, Hodder & Stoughton, 1960.

Pasqui, Nicoletta: *Conchiglie del Mediterraneo*: Milan, Görlich, 1974.

Penso, Giuseppe: *Les Produits de la Pêche*: Paris, Vigot Frères, 1953.

Perlmutter, Alfred: *Guide to Marine Fish*: New York, Bramhall House, 1961.

Piscator: *Fish & Its Cookery*: London, Longman, 1854.

Poll, Max: *Poissons Marins*: Brussels, Natural History Museum, 1947.

Radcliffe, William: *Fishing From the Earliest Times*: London, 1921.

Randall, J E, Allen G R & Smith-Vaniz, W F: *Illustrated Identification Guide to Commercial Fishes – Bahrain Iran, Iraq, Kuwait, Oman, Qatar, Saudi Arabia, United Arab Emirates*: Rome, FAO, 1978.

Randolph, Mary (ed Karen Hess): *The Virginia House-wife*: (originally published 1824), Columbia, SC, University of South Carolina Press, 1984.

Rey, Luis Lozano Y: *Los Principales Peces Marinos y Fluviales de España*, 3rd edn: Madrid, Subsecretaria de la Marina Mercante, 1964.

Ricker, W E: *Russian-English Dictionary for Students of Fisheries and Aquatic Biology*: Ottawa, Fisheries Research Board of Canada, 1973.

Robins, C Richard: *Florida Game and Commercial Marine Fishes*: Miami, University of Miami, 1958.

Roden, Claudia: *A New Book of Middle Eastern Food*: London and New York, Viking Penguin, 1985.

Roper, Clyde F E, Sweeney, Michael J: *Cephalopods of the World*, FAO Species Catalogue, vol 3: Rome, FAO, 1984.

Roth, Alex: *Molluscan Melange – How to Prepare your Molluscs for Eating*: Guam, Aljemasu Enterprises, nd (c 1970).

Roth, Captain Alexander, Jnr: *Mollusks of the Southern Marianas Islands*: Tamuning, Guam, Aljemasu Enterprises, 1980.

Roughley, T C: *Fish and Fisheries of Australia*: Sydney, Angus & Robertson, 1951.

Sahni, Julie: *Classic Indian Cooking*: New York, Wm Morrow, 1980.

Sainsbury, Keith J: Kailola, Patricia J & Leyland, Guy G: *Continental Shelf Fishes of Northern and North-Western Australia*: Canberra, CSIRO Division of Fisheries Research, 1985.

Saint-Ange, Mme E: *Le Livre de Cuisine de Madame Saint-Ange*: Paris, 1927.

Salaman, Rena: *Greek Food*: London, Fontana, 1983.

Samuel, Arthur Michael: *The Herring*: London, 1918.

Saul, Mary: *Shells*: London, Hamlyn & Country Life, 1974.

Schroeder, Robert E: *Philippine Shore Fishes of the Western Sulu Sea*: Manila, National Media Production Center, 1980.

Scott, J S: *Sea Fishes of Malaya*: Kuala Lumpur, Gvmt Press, 1959.

Scott, Trevor D & Glover, C J M & Southcott, R V: *The Marine and Freshwater Fishes of South Australia*: South Australia, Govt Printer, 1974.

Seret, Bernard: *Poissons de Mer de l'Ouest Africain Tropical*: Paris, OSTROM, 1981.

Shen, Shih-Chieh: *Coastal Fishes of Taiwan*: Taipei, National University of Taiwan, 1984.

Sinha, V R P, & Jones, J W: *The European Freshwater Eel*: Liverpool, University Press, 1975.

Smaldon, G: *British Coastal Shrimps and Prawns*: London & New York, Academic Press, 1979.

Smith, J L B: *The Sea Fishes of Southern Africa*: South Africa, Central News Agency, 1950.

& Margaret Mary Smith: *The Fishes of the Seychelles*: Grahamstown, Rhodes University, 1969.

So, Yan-Kit: *Yan Kit's Classic Chinese Cookbook*: London, Kindersley, 1984; also published as *Chinese Cooking – Step by Step Techniques* by Yan-Kit Martin: New York, Random House, 1984.

Soljan, T: *Fishes of the Adriatic* (vol I of *Fauna and Flora of the Adriatic*): Washington DC, US Dept of the Interior and NSF, 1963.

Spencer, Evelene & Cobb, John N: *Fish Cookery*: Boston, Little, Brown, 1921.

Step, Edward: *Shell Life – An Introduction to the British Mollusca*: London, 1901.

Street, Phillip: *The Crab and its Relatives*: London, Faber & Faber, 1966.

Sueiro, Jorge-Victor: *Manual del Marisco*: Madrid, Penthalon, 1981.

Tebble, Norman: *British Bivalve Seashells*: London, British Museum (Natural History), 1966.

Thomson, J M: *Common Sea & Estuary Fishes of Non-tropical Australia*: Sydney, Collins, 1977.

Tinker, Spencer Wilkie: *Fishes of Hawaii*: Honolulu, Hawaiian Service, 1978.

Titcomb, Margaret: *Native Use of Marine Invertebrates in Old Hawaii*: Honolulu, University Press of Hawaii, 1979.

Tortonese, Enrico: *Osteichthyes (Pesci Ossei)*, vols I & II: Bologna, Edizioni Calderini, 1970.

Tsuji, Prof Shizuo: *Japanese Cooking – Simple Art*: Kodansha International, Tokyo & New York, 1980.

Umali, Agustin F: *Key to the Families of Common Commercial Fishes in the Philippines*: Washington DC, Dept of the Interior, 1950.

Üner, Sıtkı: *Balık*: Istanbul, Milliyet Kültür Klübü, 1968.

UNESCO: *Check-list of the fishes of the North-Eastern Atlantic and of the Mediterranean*, vol I: Paris, UNESCO, 1973.

US Fish & Wildlife Service: *Western Atlantic Shrimps of the Genus Penaeus* – Fishery Bulletin, vol 67, no 3: Washington DC, Department of the Interior, 1969.

Valle, K J: *Suomen Kalat*: Helsinginssä, 1934.

Van Immerseel, Frans: *Garnalenvissers te paard*: Utrecht, Lannoo, 1973.

Various: *Animal Life and Nature in Singapore*: Singapore, University Press, 1973.

Various: *Edible Seafood of Thailand*: Bangkok, Committee of Fisheries, nd.

Various: *The Commercial Fishes of Burmese Coastal Waters*: Rangoon, 1972.

Voss, Gilbert L: *Cephalopod Resources of the World*: Rome, FAO, 1973.

Seashore Life of Florida and the Caribbean, enlarged edn: Miami, Banyan Books, 1980.

& Williamson, Gordon R: *Cephalopods of Hong Kong*: Hong Kong, Government Press, 1971.

Walford, Lionel A: *Marine Game Fishes of the Pacific Coast from Alaska to Ecuador*: Berkeley, University of California, 1937.

Walls, Jerry G: *Fishes of the Northern Gulf of Mexico*: Neptune City, NJ, T F H, 1975.

Ward, Rowland: *The English Angler in Florida*: London, 1898.

Warmke, Germaine L & Abbott, R Tucker: *Caribbean Sea Shells*: London, Constable, 1961.

Warner, G F: *The Biology of Crabs*: London, Elek Science, 1977.

Warner, William W: *Beautiful Swimmers – Watermen, Crabs and the Chesapeake Bay*: Boston, Little, Brown, 1983.

Distant Water – The Fate of the North Atlantic Fisherman: Boston, Little, Brown, 1977.

Went, A E J & Kennedy, M: *List of Irish Fishes*: Dublin, Stationery Office, 1969.

Weymouth, Frank W: *The Edible Clams, Mussels and Scallops of California*: Sacramento, State Fish & Game Commission, 1920.

Wheeler, Alwyne: *The Fishes of the British Isles and North-West Europe*: London, Macmillan, 1969.

Fishes of the World: London, Ferndale, 1975.

Whitehead, Peter: *Clupeoid Fishes of the World*, parts 1 and 2, FAO Fisheries Synopsis, vol 7: Rome, FAO, 1985.

Williams, Austin B: *Marine Decapod Crustaceans of the Carolinas* – Fishery Bulletin, vol 65, no 1: Washington DC, Department of the Interior, 1965.

The Swimming Crabs of the Genus Callinectes (*Decapoda: Portunidae*): Washington, National Marine Fisheries Service, 1973.

Yang, Hung-Chia & Chen, Tung-Pai: *Common Food Fishes of Taiwan*, parts 1-2: Taipei, JCRR, 1971.

Yonge, C M: *The Sea Shore*: London, Collins (Fontana reprint of 1963), 1949.

& Thompson, T E: *Living Marine Molluscs*: London, Collins, 1976.

Zachary, Hugh: *The Beachcomber's Handbook of Seafood Cookery*: Winston-Salem, N C, John F Blair, 1969.

Zaitsev, V et al: *Fish Curing and Processing*: Moscow, MIR, 1969.

Zinn, Donald J: *The Handbook for Beach Strollers from Maine to Cape Hatteras*: Chester, Connecticut, Pequot Press, 1975.

Index

207

208